## About the author

Helen Sanderson helps people create beautifully organised, clutter-free homes and live more mindful and meaningful lives. One of the UK's most experienced and well-respected clutter experts, Helen has appeared on TV and radio, spoken at events such as Grand Designs, Mind Body Spirit and 100% Design, and her work has been covered in many newspapers and magazines, including the *Telegraph, Financial Times* and *Good Housekeeping.* She founded interior design studio Ministry of Calm and describes working on the sacred space for a Marie Curie hospice as one of her peak experiences.

Helen uses her insight as a practising psychotherapist, and voice dialogue and Enneagram coach to understand how our homes reflect our psyches and how to transform both. She also draws on her extensive studies of spirituality, Jungian ideas, and personal development. This gives her an intuitive ability to sense what needs to shift in the person and their space. She continues to study today and is researching the relationship between clutter and depth psychology on the psychotherapy doctoral programme at the University of Exeter.

Helen works with her clients in a holistic and integrated way. She helps them uncover the wisdom of their unconscious and then, with compassion, take positive action to clear blocks that stand in their way. This leads to life-changing shifts, which leave people with a new-found clarity and homes that work better on a practical, emotional and spiritual level. The powerful truths she has uncovered through this work and reveals in this book can inform and inspire anyone who wants to build a better relationship with the place they live.

# THE SECRET
# LIFE OF CLUTTER

HELEN SANDERSON

PIATKUS

PIATKUS

First published in Great Britain in 2022 by Piatkus

1 3 5 7 9 10 8 6 4 2

A CIP catalogue record for this book
is available from the British Library.

ISBN 978-0-349-42786-7

Typeset in Sabon by M Rules
Printed and bound in Great Britain by
Clays Ltd, Elcograf S.p.A

Papers used by Piatkus are from well-managed forests
and other responsible sources.

Piatkus
An imprint of
Little, Brown Book Group
Carmelite House
50 Victoria Embankment
London EC4Y 0DZ

An Hachette UK Company
www.hachette.co.uk

www.littlebrown.co.uk

For my mother, who encouraged me
to always think outside the box and
dream big; and Alexander, who helped
make this huge dream a reality.

# Acknowledgements

Firstly, I'd like to thank the brave souls who worked with me on their clutter and gave me permission to write about their stories and our experiences. My thanks also to the hundreds of people who have reached out over the last 15 years, asked for help and shared their struggles with their homes: I've learned something from each phone call and every visit.

This book was a profound journey of discovery, with many key milestones I want to acknowledge. Thanks to my first book coach Jackee Holder: you had a vision, saw my potential and encouraged me to keep going. Kathy Gale: as a fellow psychotherapist I felt you totally got me and my book, and as a writing coach your endless patience and constant focus on excellence was invaluable. To Shelia Crowley at Curtis Brown, who fell in love with this book: your wisdom and opinion I deeply value. And to Zoe Bohm at Piatkus, always calm and supportive, who took a punt on me with my first book. What an amazing team you have been.

I am also deeply grateful for the support and love of the many friends, therapists and coaches who have supported me along the way.

Finally, my heartfelt thanks to Alexander, who lived and breathed the manuscript with me for these past few years.

Your work to make this book its best has been invaluable, and I am deeply moved, not just by your brilliance, but also your generosity. I simply couldn't have done it without you.

# Contents

Author's note     xi

Introduction: Understanding the
psychology of our homes     1

Making room for love     19

A penny saved?     39

Keepage     67

Walls that talk     83

Grounded by Mum at fifty-three     111

In his father's house     139

Nothing on the floor that doesn't have feet     171

Holding back the years     195

The art of letting go     223

The lost key     253

Closing thoughts: Making room for
your future     275

Resources     281

Bonus materials     287

The stories in this book are based on true experiences. However, I have taken great care to protect client confidentiality. I have changed names and altered many identifying details in order to preserve individual anonymity without changing the essence of our work together. All stories were shown to clients in draft form and they were invited to comment. Full consent has been given and all were willing to share their experience with the hope that their story would help others.

# Author's note

What I find most touching when I work with clients to deal with their clutter and organise their homes are the stories that emerge. I am there to support them in working through the practicalities and the emotions that inevitably surface, so that, at the end of the process, we have created a home that truly nurtures and supports them. But this is rarely a simple, one-way transaction. There are often personal lessons and inspiration for me that come from each of these journeys. And the more I worked with people in this way, the more I became aware that there were valuable insights that could benefit others. That's where the idea for this book formed: to bring together some of the most powerful stories to inspire the reader who may have their own challenges around clutter, and to identify some truths that can further our understanding of how we relate to and inhabit those most intimate of spaces, our homes.

Each of the chapters that follows tells the story of a client I have worked with. I've modified the accounts to ensure their ongoing privacy while retaining the essential narrative truth. As you read the stories, you will start to understand more about how aspects of our psyche, our pasts, and issues that remain very present in our lives can become manifest in how we use, organise and relate to our homes. At the end of each chapter, I have included some thoughts and suggestions on how you might work with some of the issues or themes raised if they resonate with you. You might also find it helpful to talk to a professional therapist if you are upset or disturbed by any of the themes or stories that follow. See page 285 for the contact details of organisations that can help you find support from a reputable and trained person.

Every client I have worked with has taught me more about life and our homes, and I hope that, as you read the book, you are led on a similar journey of discovery. Each chapter usually describes a significant and often life-changing shift in the person's understanding. One that enables them to redefine their relationship with their home and their possessions into one that is more empowering. And this, in turn, allows them to move forward in their life beyond the impasse that their clutter represented. This is very much the essence of my work, and I hope that what you read can, in some small way, help you make a similar shift. The intention of this book is that you begin to look at your home in a different way, start to comprehend why you might be holding on to certain things, and come to a place of understanding and compassion for yourself.

If you see aspects of yourself or someone you know in these tales, I ask you to meet this with compassion and care. And please extend it also to the people who generously allowed me to share their stories with you in the hope they might inspire you to make changes in your own life.

# Introduction: Understanding the psychology of our homes

As I write, decluttering and minimalist living appear to be at something of a crossroads. Hit Netflix shows and best-selling books are pushing them into the mainstream, but at the same time, there is something of a backlash. Some – rightly, in my opinion – are questioning the trends of, for example, encouraging people to only have a limited number of books, or to pare down their possessions to a bare minimum overnight. It just doesn't sit well with many. I can understand this. I'm no minimalist, and I certainly don't encourage the people I work with to live in pristine, ascetic white spaces. I believe there's a balance to be struck in our homes between chaos and order, allowing us clear, harmonious spaces that give us room to think, while still having a healthy amount of stuff that we love, find useful or simply don't want to lose. Things are rarely black and white, and in my work I'm much more focused on helping people establish a practical and psychological balance in their homes than on foisting a lifestyle on them. There's a degree of truth in the claim that you'll be happier if you live in a well-ordered, tidy space, but real life is messy and chaotic, and no amount of neatly folded socks is going to resolve that.

Here's the key matter as I see it: things are never just things. We attach meaning to the objects in our lives – or, perhaps more accurately, meanings attach themselves to these objects, seemingly of their own accord. These meanings can be mundane or practical, but they can also be profound and emotionally charged. As a result, the objects themselves can feel intimately connected to deeply significant moments or periods in our lives, binding us to them. We may also feel they help us hold on to memories of people we love or have loved and lost. Other objects can become entangled with events that we are unwilling or unable to move on from because they feel unresolved. In the case of objects associated with painful or even traumatic events, we may struggle to truly see them or what they may represent. That battered hat on top of the wardrobe is rarely *just* a battered hat. 'It's the hat that Sarah gave me when we visited Bath. And just what *did* happen with Sarah? We were so close. I really must try to reconnect with her again.' So, we keep the hat, consciously or unconsciously, as an aide-memoire or because it connects us with someone, and back it goes on top of the wardrobe.

In this book, you'll discover some of the complex inter-connections between the physical and psychological aspects of our homes. Through my work, I've discovered many fascinating ways in which our homes can reflect our internal worlds. When someone is chaotic, or troubled in some way, this is invariably mirrored in their home. So, by reorganising the spaces we inhabit and the objects within them, we are, in a real sense, reordering our psyches. We construct our mental and physical worlds in parallel. For example, if a beloved grandparent gives me a teacup that I feel has significant value or meaning, I am likely to pay more attention to it. Perhaps I'll place it reverently on the 'best china' shelf, a place of prominence or safety. As I put other cups in the same location, they are, by association, likely to also take on greater value in my perception. Years later, if I sort through the best china shelf and move things into a box to go to charity, the place they hold in my inner world of meaning and value shifts.

Unlike some, I don't think of accumulating clutter as simply a fault that needs to be corrected. Rather, it is often a very human response to psychologically significant forces that are at play in someone's life. People rarely struggle to let go of certain things simply due to weak will or a lack of organisational skills. More often it is because of pain that is connected with those objects; pain that they don't want to face. Specific individual elements of the clutter, I believe, can be more usefully seen as symbols that give insight into underlying issues that need to be addressed. The physical manifestation of the psychological, which the clutter represents, and the psychology itself are interlinked. And I find it is through tackling both aspects together that people are best able to make progress.

In dream analysis, client and therapist can access meaning and insight from the unconscious expressed via symbol and metaphor. It's a useful way in, and one of several techniques – including art, word association and drama – that therapists use to access this insight and to support their clients in seeing their psychology more clearly. These images and symbols may reflect what is going on in the subconscious. Similarly, our homes have insightful stories to tell that can be revealed in the way we set up and interact with our spaces and the objects within them. These can provide a valuable window into the psyche. As John Hill describes in his book *At Home in the World*, the home 'as a symbol mediates between outer reality and inner truth'. I find that encouraging people to see their home as a mirror regularly unlocks powerful insights that help them understand what is blocking them from moving on with their lives. When I start to work with people, they may see 'through that glass darkly'. But by looking with care at their relationship with their home and becoming open to the story they can read in that reflection, they often come to see themselves with a new and deeper insight. And from that insight, they can begin to create a home and live a life in which there is more room for what matters most to them.

In this book, I explore some specific ways that this mirroring manifests. Clutter, for example, can be a shield from the world used to create a place of safety. This place can be a sanctuary, but also sometimes a prison. Clutter can also be a kind of ceremonial burial mound to a trauma, dream or creative project that has been neglected or abandoned. Sometimes, our homes and the objects we unconsciously accumulate in them can become a kind of museum of our losses: a way of remembering and staying connected to a loved one, perhaps, or a disappeared part of ourselves. That's not to say that we should simply discard the artefacts of our pasts along with the associated memories. At best, our memories are joyful and empowering, but at worst, they can become traps and bullies. I like to think of objects as vessels of memory, both in terms of them being containers for our reminiscences, and also in the sense of them acting as a symbolic 'personality' into which some valued quality is infused. And, as in the other meaning of 'vessel', objects can also carry us on a journey back to significant points in our past; places we may simply like to revisit, or perhaps where there are things still to be discovered.

It might be apt at this point to consider a word that we use to refer to the objects in our lives: 'possessions'. We tend to think that we possess these objects but, in many senses, they also possess us. And they can be quite demanding owners, sometimes requiring a lot of our time, energy and attention. We may have to carry them around from place to place. To clean, repair and maintain them. Take my smartphone, for example. I have to spend time remembering to charge it, updating apps and software, and responding to endless notifications. In a way, our possessions can sometimes take on a life of their own, almost appearing to propagate their own survival interests rather than serving ours. This can be particularly acute when it comes to objects that come complete with a set of expectations or even obligations, tacit or otherwise, about what we should do with them. For example, family heirlooms or gifts from a loved one.

A word, too, on how objects can also be 'possessed' in the way we talk of a house or person being possessed by a demon or spirit. I'm not talking about some malign entity that animates the object. But in a psychologically very real sense, our objects can speak to us, admonishing us with the injunctions of parents, authority figures or our own inner directives. The toothbrush nags 'Don't forget to brush' in the tone your mother might have used. Your child's old school report says, 'If you really love her, you can't throw me away.' The unwanted family heirloom may simply sit there on its high shelf, pronouncing silent judgement: 'You never quite lived up to my expectations.' It's not all negative talk, of course: when we are able to establish healthier relationships with our objects, they can speak to us in nurturing and supporting ways.

## How we attach to our homes

Although each individual possession may reveal its own unique metaphors, I have found that, overall, people tend to relate to their homes in one of four different attachment styles. These reflect different states of balance – or imbalance – between order and chaos. As in many areas of life, our relationship with our homes and possessions is a constantly shifting dance between these two forces: order and chaos, yin and yang. Order is what creates structure and boundaries, enabling us to navigate life and to function effectively. Chaos is the open and unstructured space we all need for spontaneity, creativity and play. Here are the four attachment styles that I believe characterise the way people relate to their homes and the objects within them. If you are able to identify which of these, or what combination of them, applies to you, it might help you make a psychological shift and understand how to establish a better relationship with your home.

### Secure connection

This is when you have a healthy relationship with your home. It is neither neglected nor obsessively tidy, reflecting a good balance between order and chaos. We understand the importance of secure relationships with parents when it comes to healthy development in childhood. I argue that, similarly, it's vital that people have a secure connection to their home and that this can bring many psychological benefits. The grounding effect of a nurturing and integrated home can provide both a haven from the stresses and demands of life, and a secure base from which to venture forth into the world with confidence. This is very much what I aim to help people to establish.

## Fastidious/Perfectionist

People with this attachment style find they can't relax unless they feel absolutely everything in the home is perfectly ordered and under their control. An excessive desire for order has taken over. As the critics of hardcore decluttering rightly identify, the healthy maxim: 'a place for everything and everything in its place' can be carried to an unhealthy extreme. Instead of bringing peace and ease, the impulse to create order becomes an unhelpful and stressful control system orchestrated by a critical inner voice. In this situation, people may experience a part of themselves continually telling them that they are not okay unless their environment is perfect. A particularly unhealthy aspect of this is that it leaves little room for relaxation, spontaneity and play.

## Hoarding

Hoarding behaviour is characterised by collecting so many things that the home becomes unsafe or seriously detrimental to a person's quality of life. There are many factors behind hoarding. These can vary from underlying mental health issues to strongly held beliefs developed in childhood about acquiring and discarding things. Hoarding is often an attempt to find a way of coping with stressful life events or burying serious trauma. There is also often serious imbalance in how much psychological value is attached to the hoarded objects. Paradoxically, although hoarding leads to very cluttered homes, it is actually an attempt to create more security, albeit one that has been distorted.

Hoarding sits somewhat outside the domain of this book and my work. In the same way that a psychotherapist recognises that a psychotic patient may need different or secondary care, I don't work with severe hoarders as they require a different type of support. Having said that, you may feel that some of the people whose stories I tell in this book are perhaps approaching the hoarding end of the spectrum.

## Cluttered and disorderly

The impact of this situation may not be as obvious or severe as hoarding, but it still has serious consequences for many, which may be significant enough for them to seek out help from people like me. Many people I work with are highly creative, and are often very successful in their careers, yet they feel completely overwhelmed and stuck when it comes to creating sufficient order in their homes. Not being able to establish a secure base can have an impact on many areas of their lives, from mental health problems to difficulty building intimate relationships. They are often chaotic, may sometimes show signs of ADHD, and almost always crave a greater sense of wellbeing at home and a calmer quality of life.

> I have created an online assessment that will help you better understand your relationship with your home and identify the best strategies to improve this. You can take the assessment at helensanderson.com/clutter-score.

By combining practical changes with helping people explore and understand the underlying psychological dynamics, I support them in moving into more secure and healthy relationships with their homes. The insights we uncover along the way can sometimes be profound and the personal shifts are often significant.

Secure attachment to our homes not only connects us to the

past, but also provides a psychologically safe base from which to explore new territory. We talk of 'feeling at home' with some person, experience or thing as a way to denote safety and security. At its best, a home is a container of what we value, a place that preserves a sense of continuity with the past, and connects us to what lies beyond its walls. This containment or holding provides vital boundaries that allow us to gain perspective on the world outside.

In encouraging the move towards a secure connection to the home, I'm not saying let go of everything from your past. But don't hang on so tightly to the objects and what they represent that they hold you back. If you try to carry too much of the past forward with you, it can end up crowding the present out of your life. Rather than setting rigid rules, I encourage people to reconnect to what they have and establish a conscious, mindful relationship with it. When you more fully understand what particular objects represent, both practically and emotionally, you will become empowered to choose whether to keep or discard them.

Our childhood homes were, ideally, places that we trusted and felt secure in, places that, in memory, provide a sense of security and permanence as we move into the future. Many of the people I work with did not have such a positive connection to their homes growing up. For them, the process of enquiry, exploration and change that I encourage is aimed at better understanding the nature of that relationship, gaining a stronger sense of agency and coming to feel more secure in themselves. I have deep respect for my clients, who have shared their stories, their pain and their dreams with me. It's not easy to allow someone in to see your disorganisation and clutter, especially when it's not only the intimate space of your home that's exposed to potential judgement, but also perhaps some deeply personal distress that may lie beneath the surface. No surprise, then, that the attraction of getting some help can often be outweighed by feelings of shame or embarrassment. At some point, though, the fundamental human need for growth reasserts itself, overriding the psychological barriers that are preventing someone from reaching out for support. This is often at a moment of significant upheaval or transition in people's lives. For some, this might be a major change of circumstances, such as pregnancy, grown-up children leaving home, a career change, the end of a relationship, or a bereavement. For others, it can be a time when they are questioning fundamental aspects of their lives or themselves, perhaps as a consequence of personal-development work or psychotherapy.

Deep connections exist between our psyches and our home environments, so simply removing clutter and reorganising is often just a short-term fix. If the underlying issues that have been concretised in the home are not addressed, invariably the clutter will begin to accumulate again, and disorder will return. It's much like how an alcoholic might take the pledge, throw out all their bottles and change their associates and the places they hang out, but if they don't investigate and tackle the psychological factors that led them to drink in the first place, they will often end up drunk again. In the same way, a simple spring clean – although invigorating – rarely brings about a lasting change.

## My decluttering method: Getting Clear™

I don't want to give the impression that my work with clients is all about introspection. It is fundamentally about action and change. People rarely come to me because they want to clear their clutter simply for its own sake. They are almost always driven as much by a desire to move towards something as they are by a wish to move away from the clutter. This thing they want to move towards might be an unrealised dream or a creative project that is dying to be brought into the light of day but remains buried and dormant, like a seed waiting for the right conditions to grow. They may want to kickstart a business, write a book, move on from a bereavement or separation, find a new relationship, or grow their family. Whatever it is, the accumulation of unmade decisions that clutter represents is holding them stuck and preventing them from entering a new phase of their lives. Creating space opens a door into that new future.

Every project with a client begins with an intensive conversation about the journey we are embarking on together. We take stock of where we are starting from, get clear about our destination, and create a map of how best to get there. This means walking through the house and, in each room, looking inside all wardrobes and cupboards to get a full picture of what is there. Equally important is starting to identify what some of the underlying issues are, and setting specific goals. Establishing a clear agreement helps us avoid a lot of pitfalls and ensures the best chance that we'll achieve their objectives. Throughout the practical side of the work, which I'll set out next, I regularly incorporate more exploratory personal-development work to address some of the underlying psychological issues.

There is a huge overlap between my work as a therapist and as a professional organiser. A key aspect of what I do is supporting people in working through difficult thoughts and emotions that are deeply buried within their homes, alongside helping them take action to reconnect to dreams that emerge from beneath the clutter. I do this using any one of the wide variety of techniques I've learned over the years, or maybe a combination, although it can be as simple as just listening with empathy. Sometimes people just need to be heard, their stories witnessed.

I believe our homes are living things and I use the metaphor of gardening to help my clients understand this. My method is based on there being three key stages to unblocking your clutter and unlocking the nurturing power of your home, and these stages reflect what a garden needs in order to flourish: weeding, planting and maintenance.

## Weeding

A cluttered home is like an overgrown garden. It is filled with weeds, vines and brambles. They have taken over and are choking what has been carefully planted, restricting its growth or even killing it. So, on a very practical level, the first stage is about clearing these weeds away, cutting them back and pulling up the roots so they are less likely to grow back. We go through everything carefully, but quickly, identifying the weeds and taking them out of the garden, and choosing the plants that we want to keep. Clutter is made up of decisions that haven't been made, so this process of going through everything and deciding what to do with it is key. There may be things you choose to recycle, to throw out or to give away; an item might require a certain action, such as read, repair or return to its rightful home; or you may choose simply to keep it. For this process, I ask people to divide everything into piles, using a customised selection of illustrated decision cards from my Home Declutter Kit (see Bonus Materials). This provides structure and a clearly identifiable location for each pile of objects, which is vital in what can be a somewhat chaotic part of the project.

By listening to the stories your home has to tell as you go through this process, you may discover what certain things stand for on a symbolic or emotional level. Removing the clutter may also reveal some deeper issues, challenges or even traumas that need to be looked at. So, this work always has to been done with deep compassion, insight and care.

## Planting

As the weeds are taken out, we begin to see what's underneath, which has often been starved of space and light. Green shoots may start to appear. Through the process of discovery and prioritisation that are core to the weeding stage, long-forgotten dreams and aspirations re-emerge. My clients often reconnect to these, and in seeing what they have chosen to keep, begin to recognise how these reflect their deepest values. With these insights, the planting phase can begin. This is where I utilise my skills as an interior designer and work with people to create a beautiful home that truly supports them, and reflects who they want to be. A home where there is a place for everything, and everything is in its place.

After the weeding process, what is left are possessions that have been *consciously* chosen. These may be primarily functional, but they can also be objects that bring meaning and beauty to our lives. And having made all those decisions during the weeding process, the choice becomes what to focus on, and what to give space and light to grow. On a practical level, this is simply about deciding what goes where, and designing systems that support people in pursuing what matters most to them. Beyond that, most people also crave the sense of calm and peace that comes from having a clear space and a clear mind. So, when they walk in through the front door, rather than draining their energy, their home lifts their spirits.

## Maintenance

Like a garden, every home needs to be regularly maintained or it will return to weeds. Creating supportive and empowering homes helps us to care for ourselves. In the absence of a magic wand, this is where discipline comes in. For any dream that has been brought into the light of day, once that initial wave of inspiration has subsided, we need to employ perspiration. Rather than seeing maintaining their home in a tidy, organised state as a chore, I encourage people to consider it as a mindful practice. It can be a way to nurture and heal ourselves and what we have discovered or planted in our lives. Just as a cluttered home is a manifestation of choices that have been postponed or avoided, a well-maintained space echoes a commitment to our highest values and to ourselves. It can become a place that continues to remind us of what matters most to us and where we have chosen to focus our energy and attention.

I've given this outline of my process to provide some context for the rest of the book. If you are inspired to take on a decluttering project of your own, my full methodology is set out in my Home Declutter Kit. You'll read some more detail of how I work in the following chapters, but although the process is vital in giving structure to what I do, it's only the start of the story. The real magic is what happens in the home, in the moment, as we do the work. This emerges from the context of each individual person I work with, their unique environment, and their own personal story.

## It's about more than the clutter

The way we are in our homes is often quite different from how we are out in the world, at work, with our friends or in public life. Our homes are our most private places. When we retire to them at the end of the day and close the door behind us, shutting out the outside world, neglected or repressed feelings and aspects of ourselves may more safely come out to play. Over time, this can begin to materialise in the objects around us and how we use and organise our spaces. As I have said, clutter is decisions that haven't been made. This means that those things we leave unaddressed can start to accumulate, physically and psychologically, and eventually may take on a life of their own – like that dreaded pile in the loft, perhaps, which, despite being out of sight, is never quite out of mind. 'Deal with me,' it says, but you put it off for another day.

On one level, mindful decluttering is a very practical process. On another, it can be a fascinating, mysterious and transformational journey deep into our minds and our pasts. This journey allows people to redefine themselves and reshape their future lives. Marie Kondo famously encourages people to ask: 'Does this spark joy?' A fair question, but I believe it is important to go deeper. There are some far more interesting and revealing things it is worth asking of our possessions. Questions that I encourage people to ask include: 'Why are you still here?' 'What do you need from me?' 'What do you have to tell me?' and 'How can I let you go?'

The answers we receive from our unconscious to questions such as these can be enlightening, liberating and, at times, truly life-changing. As I've worked with people and their homes over the last fifteen years, I've found it deeply moving to discover the roots of their pain and to support them in uncovering liberating truths that have helped unblock aspects of their lives. From healed family relationships to the grieving of long-unmourned losses or making fresh starts, the therapeutic power of this process never ceases to surprise and delight me.

In this book, I describe some fascinating and remarkable shifts that have happened in people's lives during their work with me. These aren't added for dramatic effect; they are true accounts (disguised to respect people's privacy). Am I claiming that simply moving things around in the home can have supernatural effects on people and events? Of course not. But there can be a kind of alchemical reaction, a transformation that takes place in the inner world of a person, alongside the physical changes in the spaces around them. And this can, inevitably, have effects that ripple out into their lives and the lives of those around them.

As I end this introduction, I'm reminded of Socrates' famous dictum, 'The unexamined life is not worth living.' While I cannot exactly say that 'the unexamined home is not worth living in', I do suggest that if we don't carefully consider our homes and our relationships with them, we lose an opportunity for a deeper and more meaningful life. For this reason, I'd encourage anyone to thoughtfully examine their psychological relationship with their home. Carl Jung famously reported a dream that was seminal in his discovery of the collective unconscious. In his dream, he awoke in the upper storey of a strange yet somehow recognisable house. As he explored it, passing down through the various floors, he encountered objects that related to different periods of human history: medieval furnishings, Roman brickwork and, eventually, broken pottery from a primitive culture. Analysing the dream, he read the many-storeyed house as a metaphor for the layers of his psyche. This strikes me as pointing to a powerful universal truth that is borne out in the work described in the chapters that follow. While we consciously inhabit the first floor of our psyche, buried beneath are layers of historical meaning, both personal and universal. By exploring and understanding more deeply what our homes reveal about us, we can process and clear the psychic clutter of trauma, pain and loss that accumulate over our lives, enabling us to return home to our essential selves.

Our homes have stories to tell. Like our dreams, the spaces we inhabit and the objects within them reflect many aspects of our lives and our inner selves. As you become more able to really see your home and your possessions, and to listen to what they are telling you, you will gain some profound insights. I hope this will become clear as you read the stories about my work that I'm privileged to share here. Each will illustrate some of the many different forms this can take. You'll discover, for example, how a lost key allowed a grieving man to reconnect to his recently departed wife; how reconfiguring her bedroom furniture helped a woman find love; and how getting rid of a reclining chair brought a family closer together.

By the end of this book, I hope you will be inspired to take action in your home and finally understand some of the psychological factors that may have been sabotaging your efforts to create more space. With that insight in place, you'll be ready to create a home that truly reflects who you are and what matters most to you, and that empowers you to live your best life. A home that is clear, calm, beautifully organised, and easy to maintain. A home you love, that loves you back.

# Making room for love

Natalie was a self-confessed 'messy person'. Her flat and possessions were spread over three floors of a large, converted five-storey Victorian townhouse in a somewhat well-heeled area of north London. It was a typical London street, lined with elegant plane trees, and my heart rose with every step as I walked the short distance from the tube station on my way to our first meeting. I was familiar with the general area, having rented a small studio nearby when I first moved to London. As I walked, I prepared for the conversation to come, and spent some time reflecting on our initial phone call. Natalie had told me she was a junior doctor, and from our short, business-like conversation, I could tell she was highly intelligent and pretty self-aware. I had also noticed a youthful energy in her turn of phrase. I was looking forward to meeting her.

I felt a real sense of excitement at the prospect of getting to work on this latest puzzle. Because that's how I see it: there's always something going on beneath the clutter, and the process of working with someone often reveals powerful emotional reasons for their sense of being stuck. There can be real 'ah ha!' moments when we both realise the historical and personal reasons behind the problem, and this can be like unlocking a door to greater understanding and awareness. This, in turn, can create real change in the person's home. It is hard to know sometimes which is most important or comes first: the journey to improve the space, or the journey towards personal illumination. Entering the home of each new client is more than just going into their physical space; it also feels like I'm entering through a kind of portal into their inner world. That's a privilege I'm always grateful for.

I turned the corner and arrived at Natalie's home, divided from the street by an ornate cast-iron gate that stood partially ajar. Beyond this, a tiled path led past a ramshackle collection of recycling containers to a wide and somewhat imposing deep-blue door. I was struck by the sophisticated glazed panels and the beautiful sunburst design of the semicircular stained-glass window above it. On the wall to the side of the door were a pair of incongruous and battered-looking aluminium doorbells. The label on the lower one was tatty, handwritten and illegible; the upper bore a crisp, neatly typed label with Natalie's name in capital letters, but stuck on slightly skew-whiff. I rang the bell and waited. After a few moments, I heard footsteps coming down the stairs and the unlatching of two locks on the door. It was opened by a tall, smartly dressed young woman with blonde hair tied up a little unevenly. She greeted me with a confident smile and clearly much-practised handshake, then led me along a slightly dingy and anonymous shared hallway and up a steep flight of walled-in stairs, all typical of a house that's been divided into flats.

Natalie showed me into the first-floor living room and we sat down together at her dining table, its polished surface dappled with the spring sunshine that streamed in through the branches of trees outside that were just coming into bud. It was a beautiful room, spacious and open. Generally, it was pretty organised, although I spotted the tell-tale signs of a somewhat hurried tidy-up. In one corner of the room stood a tall bookcase, full of books and ornaments. Some of the shelves were neatly ordered, but others were crammed with paperbacks, some of which were upside down or back-to-front with the spine facing inwards. Still more were piled haphazardly on top. My attention was also drawn to a large, elegant Victorian sideboard, where a three-tiered modern in-tray stood, crammed with letters and disowned papers. Beside the sideboard, a slightly battered wastepaper bin was overflowing with a large number of torn envelopes that I imagined she'd recently opened. I noted that dealing with her paperwork was probably going to be a big task.

We chatted for a while about her space, her life and what she wanted to get from our work together. But as we began to talk in more depth about the areas we might tackle, I noticed Natalie's posture became more closed and her movements less relaxed, and she spoke without the confidence I had noticed earlier. The buoyant demeanour she'd exhibited when greeting me at the door had dissolved now, and she was struggling to make eye contact. I was reminded of something she'd said to me in our initial phone conversation about being highly professional at work, and I started to really feel for her. She was a functional personality type – it was part of her identity to be together and help people – and here she was, having to accept that she was in a real muddle. However, when we began to talk about actual change, I found myself wondering if there was a part of Natalie that wasn't sure about starting this process.

Natalie had been shifting restlessly in her seat, and now she stood up abruptly. 'After we spoke last week, I read something about this that really made sense – let me read it to you.' She walked confidently to the somewhat overloaded bookshelf, but after a few moments it became apparent that she wasn't going to easily find what she was looking for. She began to rummage through the shelves, becoming increasingly agitated, and then started to pull out books and hurriedly pile them on top of each other.

'God!' she said, with considerable feeling, 'I am *so* useless!' And with that, she gave up searching and returned to her seat, where she slumped angrily. 'I can never seem to find what I'm looking for. It's driving me nuts.' Her eyes had filled with tears.

'Don't worry,' I said. 'That's what I'm here to help you with. I'm sure it will turn up.'

Natalie was struggling to hold back her emotions, and I noticed that, as our conversation continued, even the language she used and the way she spoke seemed to be shifting.

'If I'm really honest,' she said, 'there's a big part of me that doesn't really care about the mess. I just chuck things in drawers: that "out of sight, out of mind" kind of thing. Maybe I should just forget the whole decluttering idea and leave things as they are.'

I noticed that she was speaking more loudly, and the entirely Southern accent I had assumed was her natural voice had taken on something of a Northern burr. Natalie paused and looked out at the flat across the street. A man was standing precariously on a chair to change a lightbulb. I noticed this and smiled inwardly. There was something precarious about Natalie right now, something she was about to start that might prove more dangerous to her than perhaps it would to other people. Maybe the man on the chair, and Natalie's focus on him, was a kind of symbol that we were about to illuminate something of Natalie's psychological shadow.

'Can I be honest with you, Natalie?' I said. 'You've made quite an effort to invite me here, and yet you've just said

you're not sure you want to do this. You seem very ambiv-
alent. My guess is that this *is* bothering you on some level,
more than you care to admit to yourself.'

Natalie sat up in her seat. 'You're right,' she said. 'I *do* care,
and I *do* want this to change. I'd like to be as organised and
efficient at home as I am at work.'

'You've mentioned how different you are at work a couple
of times,' I ventured. 'Why don't you tell me a bit more
about that?'

Natalie frowned in concentration. 'It's as if I'm two different people,' she said. 'The person I am at work wants to
do well, get approval, keep my job and pay the mortgage,
but when I get home, I just want to kick back and relax.'
As Natalie said this, I noticed a kind of sulkiness – she
crossed her arms and screwed up her face, a bit like a rebellious teenager.

'I can really understand that need for ease and order,' I
said. 'I'm sure we can find a way to meet them both. Shall
we take a look around the rest of the flat?'

Natalie showed me around the other rooms with a certain degree of nonchalance. There was still something of a
'Yeah it's messy – so what?' attitude going on. I was hugely
intrigued.

The flat had three bedrooms, one of which was occupied
by a lodger who also shared the kitchen and bathroom.
The lodger's room was out of bounds, but as we walked
around the communal areas, I saw that, like Natalie's living
room, the kitchen and bathroom were all relatively clear.
This isn't unusual. Some people are more motivated to
keep tidy the spaces they share with another, especially an
outsider. They are what I would call externally referenced,
valuing the approval they get from others more highly than
their own judgement. This can be a sign of low self-esteem.

I was reminded of the time I first left my job and became self-employed. Suddenly there was no boss to work for, no externalised parent figure to praise or scold me if I came in late. So, at first, I found it hard to get up and get on with the work of building a business. This is quite common; many of us use other people to be our 'boundary barometer'. The first step in building healthier self-esteem can be to start being more internally referenced: to ask ourselves what *we* think when we find ourselves thinking about others' judgements, and to start taking responsibility for our own opinions and boundaries.

We moved on to the little box room at the end of the corridor. The door was kept closed and the room behind was somewhat in disrepair, with partially stripped wallpaper on one wall. It was illuminated by a bare light bulb hanging from the ceiling. This was clearly a repository for many of Natalie's possessions that didn't have a home. There were clothes scattered across the bare single bed, and boxes and plastic bags full of miscellaneous items piled everywhere on the floor. It all looked quite unloved and uncared for.

Natalie hesitated at the threshold of the room, a somewhat sheepish and embarrassed expression on her face. 'This is the room I mentioned on the phone,' she said. 'It just seems to collect things and I really want to make better use of it.'

'Since we spoke, have you thought any more about what you want to do with it?' I asked.

'I don't know. Maybe rent it, maybe create a meditation room or an office. I've really not decided.'

And there, I had an answer already. A room with no job often becomes a junk room. It's the same as time that is not allocated: we tend to whittle it away, and then wonder why we were not productive. This is why Buddhist monks live to a tightly defined schedule with timings for their whole day.

They say that unscheduled time is when the mind grabs your attention and takes you off for a merry walk. Having a structure allows the mind to focus. Well, it's the same for a room without a job: the lack of clarity means it becomes a space for anything, everything and nothing. I find it helpful to think of space and time as sacred, and to aim for a purposeful use of time, a purposeful use of space.

There would certainly be plenty to do in the box room, but as we moved on through the flat it was Natalie's bedroom that struck me most: her most personal space. My first impression was that this looked like a room in student digs. It certainly didn't seem to reflect the professional I had been talking to in the living room.

It was an awkwardly shaped room. Two of the walls were at an odd angle, possibly another legacy of the house being converted into flats, and this made it hard to configure. Natalie had the bed shoved awkwardly up against the window, and there were shoes everywhere, along with books, clothes and CDs – complete disarray. The word 'discombobulated' came to mind, not only in terms of the clutter, but also in the way the furniture was placed. Dominating one side of the room was a rather stern-looking wardrobe that stood with its back to the angled wall. This placement turned it into an imposing presence in the room, like a tall tree in a small garden. All you could see when you came in was this overbearing wardrobe, which seemed to loom forward into the room.

'I can see what you meant about this room, Natalie; there's certainly scope to make better use of the space. And don't worry, I can definitely help you get on top of the clutter.'

Natalie looked sheepish again. 'I'm really embarrassed.' She cast her eyes around the room. 'And you know what, Helen? Mum's bedroom was just the same.'

Natalie was far from alone among my clients in growing

up without being modelled order and containment in the family home. Again, I was intrigued. I was sure this would come up again.

Before I left, we sat down at the living-room table once more and established a clear set of goals and plan of action, booking in a day we would start work. I was pleased, as I was sure Natalie would feel so much better about herself if we could get things in order. It can't be easy sitting in front of people every day, playing the role of the together professional, while knowing that at home, your personal space is total chaos and you feel ashamed of it. It is a bit like having a dirty little secret. I have a huge amount of respect for my clients. I mean, it's one thing to go to therapy and talk about your messy life and how you don't feel 'together', but it's quite another to actually invite someone in and say, 'Look. Here it is. Here I am, in all my nakedness. Here is my mess – my internal and external mess. Please help!' That takes considerable courage.

Our first session took place a few weeks later, as Natalie had been working the night shift. When I arrived back at her place, the trees on the street were now in full leaf and winter had fully given way to spring, bringing with it a sense of growth and optimism that spilled over into our work that day.

We'd decided to tackle her bedroom first. Now that I was prepared for the huge, overbearing wardrobe, I was able to see other things in the room more clearly. And the position of her bed really was awkward. It was pressed against the window on the far wall and was only accessible from one side, beside it a lone bedside table. This is something I see over and over again with single women clients: a bed that is out of balance and energetically closed on one side. In my experience, this kind of arrangement can often reflect a psychological resistance to finding a partner.

Along with the very large bed and the dominating wardrobe, the bedroom also contained two big chests of drawers and a black upholstered chair, covered in clothes. In one corner – which I suspected had once been to the side of a chimney breast – was a set of built-in shelves, full of loose clutter and storage containers of all shapes and sizes.

As we surveyed the shelves and talked about some practicalities, I sensed that Natalie was getting a little overwhelmed. She'd slumped down on the edge of the bed. 'I don't know why I can't deal with this stuff on my own, Helen. Whenever I make progress, it seems to come creeping back.'

Beneath someone's clutter, there is usually a story waiting to be told, and in telling it, the person can often take a big step towards making a shift in both their clutter habit and their life. Now seemed the time to explore more deeply what might be going on for Natalie.

'Would you like to take a look at some possible reasons for your attraction to clutter?'

Natalie nodded, perhaps slightly warily. 'What do you mean, *attraction*? I hate it.'

'Most people discover that their clutter meets some sort of need that they've not been fully aware of. Once they've identified what's at the root of the problem, it often becomes much easier to move forward. That's what we can start to explore as we work. How does that sound?'

'Interesting, I guess.'

I grabbed a pile of books from one of the overloaded shelves. 'If you like, you could tell me a bit about your family while we work,' I said. 'What was your childhood home like?'

Natalie perked up a little and leaned forward. I guessed the sense of overwhelm she had been feeling had shifted a little, and it was helping her to talk. 'My parents lived in a small terraced house in the north of England. We never went without, but there wasn't a lot of space, and I shared a bedroom with one of my sisters; I'm the middle of three. Dad wasn't around a lot – always out at work or down at the pub – and Mum was constantly busy and a bit chaotic at times. She was a bargain hunter, always on the lookout for a deal, and when she found one, she'd fill the place with stuff. She'd come home with a trolley full of those huge packs of toilet roll because they were selling them two for the price of one. Or I'd come home from school to find her proudly examining things she'd bought at a local jumble sale, saying, "This will come in handy one of these days."' She laughed. 'Mum could probably do with your support more than me, but she'd never ask for help.'

I'd had an intuition that we'd come back to lack of order in the family home. And now a picture was beginning to form. Natalie had evidently grown up in a thoroughly chaotic environment and this could have impacted her in several ways. She was unlikely to have really learned the skill of creating order at home, and may even have felt that domestic chaos was completely normal, perhaps coming to feel familiar and safe with it. Maybe when she had completed her professional training and moved into a responsible role, she had started to recognise that order could be helpful and part of being a conscientious adult. Now, perhaps, there was one aspect of her that wanted the familiar chaos, and another that wanted something new. This could certainly be contributing to her internal conflict. It felt like there might be a battle going on between a childlike part of Natalie and a more adult, responsible part.

I recalled the glimpse I'd had earlier of a slightly sulky teen and decided to follow that thread. 'What was your life like as you grew older?' I asked. 'At thirteen? Fourteen?'

Natalie scowled. 'I was a bit of a cow,' she said. 'I did a lot of yelling and screaming.'

I had imagined something like that; second children are often more rebellious and likely to challenge their parents' values, and there was definitely something of the rebel teen in Natalie, as if her young adult needs had never been met and she was still crying out for her parents' attention. In a complex, contradictory way, Natalie was both conforming by being like her mother and holding on to clutter, as she'd effectively been taught to do, and also rebelling by refusing to grow up into the competent doctor who had everything under control.

Once we'd cleared the shelves, which took a good chunk of the morning, we started on the first chest of drawers. To Natalie and many people who struggle with clutter, a drawer was a place to shove things, be that a sock, hat or book. A quick way to get things out of view when people visit. The drawers were deep and jammed full, so working through them was a slow process. I set Natalie up with the declutter cards I use and started to unpack everything from the top drawer.

In a way, the drawer was a microcosm of Natalie's flat – and perhaps her psyche as well. On the top layer were two or three crumpled T-shirts that had clearly been hastily stuffed in. As I took these out and handed them to Natalie, I saw that in the back-left corner was a neat line of another eight or ten T-shirts, all beautifully folded and arranged by colour. To the right of these was a collection of mismatched and scrunched-up socks, while just behind them was a small, rose-coloured drawer divider partially filled with more socks – these ones neatly paired and rolled. I emptied out half of the drawer and we began to sort through, with Natalie deciding what she wanted to keep and what she no longer needed. When this was complete, we started work on the other side of the drawer, which was filled with tights, stockings and underwear; again, a mixture, some crumpled and shoved in and others neatly folded.

It struck me just how much this demonstrated the two warring aspects of Natalie's psyche. Perhaps this was a good moment to broach this with her.

'I wonder if this issue with clutter may partially reflect a split between your competent "grown-up" role and an inner child or teenager that likes to create a bit of chaos. Perhaps this is your teenage part that still wants something heard and acknowledged. Perhaps it is saying, "Hey! Remember me? I'm still here, and there's something I need."'

This obviously struck a powerful chord with Natalie, because I saw tears welling up, and she grabbed a tissue from the box on the chest of drawers to wipe her eyes. She seemed to be processing what I'd said, and after a while she collected herself a little and replied, 'You know what, I always did feel there wasn't enough attention at home.' She gave a little sniff. 'It's such a relief to talk about it.'

As I'd expected, Natalie's bedroom took quite a few sessions. We did it in combination with the pesky little box room, that often held the other shoe or the missing sock we'd been searching for in the bedroom. And so it went on. Like many people, Natalie was resistant to letting things go. After all, we hold on to things for a reason – even if it's not a reason that we are immediately aware of. But we were making progress, and after each session there were always at least three bags to go to charity, as well as one of recycling and two of rubbish. So, something was shifting. As Natalie was starting to acknowledge and process some of her unconscious reasons for holding on to clutter, maybe she was becoming more willing to let things go. Or perhaps clearing the clutter was affirming her adult self and increasing her sense of security and power. Who knew which? Or perhaps both were true.

At any rate, things were starting to take shape, and Natalie was doing a grand job of embracing her challenges. I could sense her discipline and application growing. With each batch of items, she was really looking at things and either deciding to keep them because they would be useful to her or enhance her life, or choosing to release them and move on. As William Morris said: 'Have nothing in your house that you do not know to be useful, or believe to be beautiful.' When particular objects triggered strong emotions around unprocessed or unresolved matters, we focused on acknowledging her feelings – as we had with her teenage desire for attention – while not allowing them to make the decisions for her. Letting go of the old and creating space for the new is so liberating. At the same time, we were building up her 'organisation muscle'. It seemed that each session represented another layer of the 'old Natalie' being let go of in order to make room for the grown-up Natalie, who was increasingly taking responsibility for creating the home environment she wanted.

Finally, with the rest of the room cleared and organised, we moved on to the imposing wardrobe. A wardrobe can be the most intimate of spaces, and I wondered what we might find inside. Psychologically, the inner space of a wardrobe is deep. The philosopher Gaston Bachelard describes them as 'an unfathomable store of daydreams and intimacy'. For me, they always bring to mind the tales of the secret world of Narnia in *The Lion, the Witch and the Wardrobe,* a book my mother read to me when I was small, and which beautifully evokes the imaginary places that a child can dream of.

Stepping back and sizing it up I said, 'Okay, let's take a look, shall we?' I took hold of the ornate brass handle and opened the heavy, panelled door to reveal a mirror on the reverse. I noticed the musty odour of old linen and camphor. Natalie immediately explained. 'I don't open it much,' she said.

Surprisingly, the wardrobe wasn't that full, and the contents were pretty orderly. It seemed that Natalie preferred to store her clothes draped over a chair, on the bed or even the floor.

On the right side were shelves of neatly folded, old-fashioned-looking sheets and pillowcases.

'I never use them. There's no way I'm putting my mother's sheets on my bed,' Natalie said.

I piled them respectfully on a chair. 'Shall we donate them to charity, then?'

'Hmm, I don't know. Are you sure? Mum would go nuts if she found out.' Natalie was speaking falteringly and seemed almost to be shrinking before my eyes.

'It's your home, Natalie. Your life. Do *you* want to keep them?' I asked, trying to speak to the adult Natalie, not the child part, which was stuck in either conforming or rebelling.

After a short time, I was pleased to see Natalie pull herself up to her full size and say confidently: 'Okay, you're right. Let's go for it. I'm sick of that stuff sitting there.'

As we emptied out the wardrobe, some ideas I'd had about how to redesign the layout of the room began to crystallise. I definitely wanted to address the position of that bed, pressed uninvitingly against the far wall. I wasn't surprised that Natalie was not yet ready to develop an intimate relationship. In many ways, she had still been trying to process childhood and teenage hurts. When we feel childlike, it can feel inappropriate to enter into adult, sexual relationships. Now Natalie was dealing with things, I was hoping this might change. And moving the bed, I was pretty sure, was going to help the process along.

'Why do you have your bed in that position?' I asked.

'Well, there's not really anywhere else for it to go,' Natalie replied in a rather convinced tone of voice.

'I'm sure there is. We'll find another, better place for it. Are you up for moving things around?'

'Yeah ... but we won't be able to move that bed – it's too heavy. And the wardrobe is too tall.'

Again, I could sense Natalie's resistance, but knowing her better now, I understood more of what was behind it.

'Can we just play and see what we can do? It's amazing how moving things around can help you get a new perspective on life. You can always put things back as they were if you don't like it.'

Of course, it was entirely up to her, but I was again hoping to gently encourage the emergence of the adult, responsible part of her she'd asked me to come and support.

'I've had an idea,' I said. 'It may be a bit radical, but hear me out. I think we should move the wardrobe into the spare bedroom. You could do with some storage in there, and it's really taking up a lot of space in here. I suggest we get an open clothes rail for day-to-day wear, and you can use the wardrobe to store clothes that are out of season or that you only wear on special occasions.'

I waited to see what choice Natalie would make. As it happened, she didn't need to give it much thought. After working together for some time, we had built up a fair degree of trust between us. She agreed to give it a go, and we began shifting the furniture around.

Divested of its baggage, the wardrobe wasn't as substantial as it had appeared. And, while awkward, it wasn't too much of a struggle for the two of us to shift it to the adjacent room.

With the wardrobe out of the picture, there was much more room to play with, and we repositioned her bed so it was accessible from both sides, leaving room for a second bedside table. We also rearranged the two sets of drawers, her chair and the laundry basket, creating a space for when the clothes rail arrived. Not only was the room clear of clutter and tidy, it was completely reorganised – almost turned on its head!

When we had a chance to step back and admire our handiwork, Natalie gasped. 'Wow! I love it!'

As she spoke, I felt an amazing surge of energy. This was not pride at pleasing my client, it was a release of energy in the room. I had a real sense that we had set something free.

It's not easy to explain what this was like. The best analogy I can think of is when you are having a massage, shiatsu or some other body treatment. There's that moment when the therapist intuitively finds the exact point in your body where there's a blockage in the nerve or muscle; they apply some pressure, and the tension or pain is released as the energy is freed to flow correctly. In Chinese medicine, they call these meridian points. They are where acupuncture needles are placed to activate or free the flow of chi (energy) around the body. It is also believed that our homes are affected by the flow of this same chi or life energy. This philosophy, known as feng shui, suggests arranging the home in order to create balance with the natural world, with the aim of harnessing energy forces and establishing harmony between us and our environment. I'm not a feng shui practitioner, but when shifting things around in my clients' homes I have often experienced this release of energy, which heralds real change.

Natalie seemed to be revelling in the new energy as well. 'I'm feeling much more open to the thought of inviting people round now,' she said as she looked around the room with pride. 'Maybe I'll have some friends from work over for coffee the weekend after next.'

With the decluttering and reorganisation of Natalie's bedroom and spare room completed, for our next session, we moved on to her living room to tackle the disorderly bookshelves and years of paperwork she'd accumulated in her sideboard. As we worked on whittling down her prodigious collection of paperbacks, I noticed a marked change in Natalie. Her demeanour was more relaxed, and she seemed to be moving around the space with far greater freedom and energy. We worked with great vigour and had finished the bulk of the work by mid-afternoon, so we had a little more time to talk as we took a well-deserved tea break.

As I'd been working, I had looked around the rest of the flat and was pleased to see that it was in pretty good order. No clutter had reappeared between sessions, as had tended to happen earlier in the process.

'How are you feeling about keeping on top of things now?' I asked as I tucked into a chocolate-chip cookie.

'Great! It just feels so much more manageable now we've created some structure. I'm just a bit worried that I'll slip back into my old ways once you're not around to keep me on track.'

'You know you're more than capable, Natalie. You just need a little more help to build up your organisation muscle. A good mantra for you might be, "a place for everything and everything in its place".'

Although the main business of sorting out the space was now done, there was clearly still some work to do in how Natalie related to her home in order to prevent the clutter taking hold again. To support her with this, I explicitly allocated each drawer, piece of furniture and area of the house as a home for specific categories of possessions. For someone as disorientated as Natalie, creating this kind of clear mind map for her space was crucial. I knew that she wouldn't be able to magically maintain the organisation without really clear instructions. Whether she listened and followed them was another thing! But the tough part of my job was pretty much done now. With so much of the clutter gone, now it was about creating a home for an adult professional who was ready to meet someone and move on to the next phase of her life.

To reinforce that she needed to build a habit of putting things away, I carefully labelled all the drawers, and together we went through where everything would live. I see this as a kind of re-parenting, which is often particularly helpful for clients still dealing with childhood pain. I was simply being a kind, helpful adult in her life, supporting her with something she was struggling with and, perhaps crucially for Natalie, giving her attention. This alone can be very healing and support people as they make the changes they want in their lives.

As part of the system, we agreed she'd have one drawer that we called 'Don't Know'. This was for the times when she felt unable to keep to the new process. None of us transform permanently overnight, and I didn't want to set her up to fail. I knew from experience that giving herself some leeway and permission to not be perfect would take the pressure off.

At the end of that day, I took Natalie on a final walk around the flat, reminding her of where we had put everything in order to reinforce her new mind map.

'Are you feeling confident about sticking to the system now our work together is coming to an end?'

'Absolutely,' she said. 'It's so much easier knowing that everything has its proper place. But I have to confess, I think my favourite drawer is going to be that one.' She pointed at the 'Don't Know' drawer and we both laughed together. While Natalie had made great changes, there would always still be a part of her that felt comfortable and safe with clutter. We had found a way that she could satisfy that need without having to live in chaos.

'It will need decluttering every so often, of course,' I said, and she smiled and nodded.

I heard from Natalie again a few months later. I was sitting in my garden, enjoying some late-summer sun, when she rang to ask about the title of a book that I'd suggested she might want to read. I immediately recognised the together and professional person that she had often presented over the phone, but this time her manner was more laid-back, less rigid and had a sense of playfulness I hadn't heard before. Perhaps this reflected that the rebellious teenager part of her personality was becoming more integrated with her adult self. We chatted for a while, and she told me she was feeling much happier and more settled at home.

'I'm finding it so much easier to stay on top of things now, Helen. It's as if creating more physical space has given me more mental and emotional space, too. I was expecting the practical benefits, but I'd not anticipated such a change in the feeling of the house. The entire energy of it has changed, and I just feel so much more peaceful and energised. It's a bit like having a new home!'

I was really pleased to hear the difference our work had made to Natalie and was even more delighted to hear what she shared with me next.

'My big news is that I've met a lovely man. I know it is still early days and don't want to curse it, but I just want to tell everyone right now. I'm so excited and it seems to be going really well.'

'That's amazing, Natalie. I'm so pleased for you. Just enjoy this starting part of the relationship and don't worry too much about the long term for now.'

After our call ended, I sat a little longer in the garden and reflected on my work with Natalie, and how I'd hoped the changes to her bedroom might help shift something. I can't pretend that I can bring a partner into my single clients' lives by simply moving their beds. Natalie had gone through a much more complex process than this, and even then, there was no guarantee that love would follow. However, allowing me in to gently deconstruct, one brick at a time, the wall she had built, in a safe and supportive way that acknowledged why it was there, was a precursor to letting others into her life. By freeing herself of the stuff she had assembled around her and much of what it represented, she had made space for change and opened herself up to new possibilities.

*

There is something very powerful and transforming about combining doing and thinking. Practical action *and* introspection. Of course, there is a vital place for psychotherapy, sitting and talking, finding a way to more deeply understand the subtleties and complexities of your inner world. And getting into action and making physical changes in your environment has a power and energy that is equally valuable. It's about seeing the connection between what's in your head and the way this has materialised in your surroundings, and then taking concrete steps towards a new vision of how you want things to be. Again and again, I've seen how this combination can achieve what the inner work alone cannot. And when something carries such an emotional weight that you feel it's almost impossible to tackle it, but you are able to find a way to just do it anyway, this may have the most profound impact of all.

# A penny saved?

Elizabeth rented a small flat in a beautiful and highly desirable area that I knew well from walks in the nearby park. I admired the elegant houses and well-manicured front gardens as I made my way along her street. But as I walked into the entrance hall of the large mansion block where her flat was located, I was taken aback. I had rarely felt such an immediate sense of melancholy. It wasn't just the gloomy lighting; it felt as if the dark mood was in the very fabric of the building. In marked contrast to the affluence on the street, the interior was pretty decrepit, with ancient peeling wallpaper and yellowed paint blistering on the woodwork. I felt as if I was walking back in time – and not in a pleasant, nostalgic way. The place had clearly seen better days, and had evidently been neglected and left to decline. *Gosh*, I thought, *living here it must be like passing through the valley of death each time you approach your front door.*

I made my way upstairs to the top floor of the building. It was quite a trek up. There were matching doors on every floor, distinguished from each other only by their brass numbers. When I arrived at Elizabeth's flat, though, I was greeted by a cluster of brightly coloured balloons pinned to the front door. I knocked, and moments later the door was opened by an attractive lady in her early fifties with a broad smile and curly blonde hair. She was dressed in a pair of vibrant orange dungarees and moved with a powerful sense of positive energy and purpose.

'Hello! Do come in, please.'

The door opened directly into the main living area. I followed Elizabeth inside.

She spread her arms theatrically. 'Welcome to my humble abode! While you contemplate what you've let yourself in for, I'll stick the kettle on.'

I immediately had a sense we would get on well. I was also struck by the incongruence between this colourful lady and the sense of neglect I'd felt on entering the building.

The first thing I noticed in the flat itself was a strong sense of being boxed in. There were numerous piles of plastic containers, and stacked shelves that seemed to encroach on the space from all directions. But this was countered, in part at least, by the bright light that streamed in from the far side of the room. I was drawn over to the living-room window and, standing in front of it, could see exactly why she chose to live there. There was a fabulous outlook on to London's famous Hampstead Heath.

'Wow! What a fantastic view.' I took a moment to breathe and admire the rolling hills, lush woodland and people out walking their dogs and taking the air. In the distance, a brightly coloured kite danced on the wind, which felt a bit like a symbol of hope.

'It's a lovely flat, but doesn't going into that big depressing hallway affect you?' I asked Elizabeth.

She handed me a cup of herbal tea. 'No. I don't really notice it, to be honest.'

Another look at the cluttered condition of the room we were in told me that Elizabeth probably had a lot more on her mind than the state of the entrance way. Every surface and piece of furniture was loaded to capacity. In addition to the numerous containers and crowded shelves I'd seen when I entered, there were cardboard boxes and carrier bags piled up everywhere.

Elizabeth noticed me sizing up the room. 'I know you've only seen this one part of the flat, but you can understand why I called you.'

'You've certainly been very resourceful with how you utilise every last bit of storage space.'

She laughed. 'That's a very polite way of putting it. I bet you wished you'd said you were too busy, now you've seen the scale of the task.'

'Not at all. I've seen many places that needed a lot more work,' I said.

We continued to talk as we walked through into the kitchen, which was similarly full.

'Right! I bet you say that to everyone,' Elizabeth teased. 'Perhaps you should interview me to see if I'm a suitable candidate.'

Her sense of humour and positive energy was endearing, and I decided to play along with her. 'So, Elizabeth. Thank you for coming along this morning. I've seen your CV, but why don't you tell me a bit about yourself in your own words.'

She laughed and pulled a mock serious face, sitting up straight at the kitchen table where we'd convened, resting her arms on the surface and interlocking her fingers.

'Well, I worked for years as an art teacher. I don't have children of my own, but I'm passionate about helping them thrive. Especially the different kids, the ones who don't quite fit into the boxes expected of them.'

'But you don't do that anymore, what caused you to change?'

Elizabeth's playful tone was waning, and she continued in a more serious vein.

'Eventually, I just got ground down by the bureaucracy of the education system. There was so much focus on targets and box-ticking that it took the joy out of it. Don't get me wrong, my kids always did well at exams, but that was never the most important thing to me. I'm definitely not a box-ticker, as you can probably tell.'

'Yes, I get that impression.' I smiled.

'When the education authorities changed the curriculum for the umpteenth time, and yet again, surprise, surprise, the arts were downgraded in the order of priority, I cracked. I'd finally had enough.'

'What did you do?'

'Oh, nothing dramatic. On previous occasions I'd marched into the head teacher's office and fought my corner, for the kids that I knew needed an outlet. But I think this time was just the straw that broke the camel's back. I simply handed in my cards, kept my head down for the rest of term and then moved on.'

I could sense that, despite Elizabeth's breezy attitude, this was a painful episode.

'Anyway, that was two years ago. I want to focus on the future now. The whole experience gave me the motivation I needed to branch out on my own. I took a little time to take stock of what really mattered to me, and then last year I set up a social enterprise business.'

'Fantastic. What do you do?'

'I run arts and craft workshops for kids who don't fit into the mainstream education system.'

'That sounds wonderful; so, you are helping those same children you loved working with at school. How is it going as a business?'

'Well ... not great, if I'm honest. Yes, I'm doing something that I love, but it's tough going. I'm fine on the day with the kids. But when it comes to the marketing and admin, I find it really hard to focus. I just get lost and overwhelmed.' Elizabeth had slumped back in the chair, and I sensed her mood and energy dropping further.

'I hope you're okay with me asking you about this. I always say, it's not about the clutter, it's about the person. If you choose to work with me, I ask you to give me permission to challenge and support you as a whole person, to make changes on all levels.'

Elizabeth nodded. 'It's all right. I know this isn't just about all the piles of stuff, it's about what's buried underneath.'

I didn't want to shut her feelings down, but I intuited that at this point it would be more helpful to focus on what she wanted to achieve from our work rather than exploring her emotions.

'So,' I said. 'Tell me about your flat and the aspirations you have for the space. How can I help you reconfigure things so it supports you better?'

The shift in focus seemed to re-energise Elizabeth: she sat upright again and leaned forward. 'Ooh, I like that: "reconfigure things". Sounds a lot better than "clear out your crap"! Why don't I take you on a little tour?'

We stood up and walked through the spaces, discussing in detail what was needed and planning how we'd tackle it. It was soon apparent that this was going to be a substantial job. Not only was there a massive amount to declutter, but the flat also needed some radical reorganisation. The kitchen was also functioning as both an office and a storage room for a host of work supplies and equipment. One end was taken up with an adhoc combination of a desk, two chests of drawers and a set of open wooden shelves. All the surfaces were stacked high with a variety of cardboard boxes and open-topped storage containers of different shapes and sizes. Out of these were spilling art materials for her classes: tattered rolls of coloured paper, pencils and crayons, tubes of glue, scissors. Along with this, there were dozens of files of paper-work, again of all shapes and sizes, squeezed in wherever there was a bit of room. Some were neatly arranged, while others were falling over and crammed on top of each other in no discernible order. As with many of my clients, the issue for Elizabeth was not only the quantity of possessions she'd accumulated, but also the lack of structure and containment in how she stored them. She was definitely losing the fight with entropy, and her home was rapidly descending into chaos.

'The main thing for me is to have space to focus on the *business* side of the business. You know what I mean. Marketing, invoicing, paperwork and all that stuff.'

We moved on to Elizabeth's bedroom, which was located in the smallest room in the flat. She had somehow managed to squeeze in a single bed, a wardrobe and a small chest of drawers, along with three large suitcases and numerous bags and piles of clothes. Again, pretty much every available sur-face, including the floor, was covered. Many of the drawers were open, I guessed either because they were too full, or because stuff had fallen down the back, making them impos-sible to close.

The bathroom was similarly chaotic and crammed full of sample soaps, shampoos, conditioner and shower gels from travel packs. From there, we returned to the living room, the largest room in the flat, where Elizabeth had a friend staying.

'I'm helping Fiona out temporarily,' Elizabeth told me in what sounded like a slightly defensive tone. 'She can't afford to rent anywhere, so I said she could live here for free while she sorts herself out.'

'That's very generous of you. How long has she been here?'

'Ooh, blimey. It must be six or seven months now.'

I noted a contradiction; Elizabeth was this bubbly, larger-than-life character, whose whole essence seemed to be about expansiveness and generosity, yet in her home she was constricted by all this stuff, her lodger and the resulting lack of space.

Her challenge wasn't exactly unique, of course. Nowadays, especially for city dwellers, we find ourselves living in ever smaller and smaller spaces. At the same time, we expect our homes to support many different needs. We want somewhere to sleep, to cook and entertain, and to have guests. We might want a dressing room, and perhaps a place to work or study. More and more of us are now working from home at least some of the time, and this trend was amplified, of course, by the COVID-19 pandemic. The fact of the matter is, space is at a premium and how we manage it really matters: not only in practical terms, but also for our psychological wellbeing. Success or failure in this area can make the difference between a home that supports you and one that drains your energy. Asking your home to multitask can be as ineffective as mental multitasking.

'I can certainly help clear a lot of the clutter, but my concern is that decluttering is not going to be enough. It seems to me we also need to find some other ways to create more space.'

'Yes, I agree,' Elizabeth said. 'I did think of moving to a bigger place, but the rent is a very reasonable and my father lives down the road. It's really important that I can visit him regularly.'

'Moving isn't necessarily going to solve the problem. It's often just a temporary fix. In my experience, most people find if they haven't identified the underlying issues, they end up rapidly filling the extra space.'

We sat down on the sofa and I continued. 'The way I see it, energetically, you have made yourself smaller and smaller. Despite now running a business from home, you are asking yourself to take up increasingly less space, so you inhabit only part of this room and the smallest bedroom. Meanwhile, most of the largest room is taken up by your house guest. I'm not surprised you are struggling.'

Elizabeth gave a deep sigh and didn't say anything.

'How is the business going?' I asked.

There was another pregnant pause.

Sometimes the questions I ask may sound blunt, but I find it's important to cut to the chase. And I always try to deliver my words with compassion and never to attribute blame or shame. I saw Elizabeth's ability to cram so much into her home as a reflection of her creativity and resourcefulness – but knew that this resourcefulness could be better directed. My intention is always to support people to get to where they want to be, and one key aspect of getting to where you want to be, is becoming really clear about exactly where you are starting from. So, in many ways, central to the way I work is helping my clients confront some facts of their situation. Nevertheless, sometimes the truth hurts.

'I'll be honest with you, there is a lot to do here. But I know we can create more space and make this flat work better for you. How are you feeling about it? Are you ready to get going and make that change?'

'Absolutely. I know that I definitely need to sort things out, that's why I called you,' she said. 'I'm really stuck, and I just can't stand that feeling. I will have to borrow some money to work with you, but I have a good feeling about it. I know how much the state of the flat is holding me back, and I'm at a point in my life when I really want to deal with this stuff and make a shift.'

This was great to hear, and I decided to ride on the wave of positive energy with a challenge. I find it often helps to start by tackling the elephant in the room. 'Fantastic. I know we can find a way to make this space work for you. Now, I realise this might be difficult to hear, but can I suggest that the first thing you may need to think about addressing is your guest?'

'Oh yes, but I can't . . .'

I could see that Elizabeth was conflicted by the situation, and I acknowledged this. 'Please understand that, although I want to help you make the changes you want, of course this has to be with the consent of everyone involved. Naturally, we don't want to create a situation where your friend might be made homeless, but I wonder if you have a bit of a habit of sacrificing your own needs and putting others first in order to please them. I'm guessing it isn't going to feel easy me suggesting you change that.'

I wanted to help Elizabeth see more clearly what, on some level, she probably already knew. People sometimes make an unconscious choice not to fully recognise things that may be uncomfortable. I know this can be a way to keep themselves feeling safe, and I'm always careful to respect that protection while supporting them to see what is really going on. When I come in with an external perspective, it's as if I'm saying: 'Why not try these lenses, and see how things look different?' By shining that light on what was apparent to me but psychologically hidden from Elizabeth, I hoped it would give her permission to acknowledge something to herself that I suspected she hadn't admitted before.

She took a deep breath. 'I do wonder if I'm actually serving Fiona's best interests by letting her stay here and not encouraging her to move on in her life. It was only supposed to be a temporary arrangement for a few weeks, and that was last July.'

'Are you open to hearing what I think might be going on?'

Elizabeth leaned forward. 'Absolutely. I'd really value your insight.'

'We all have these beliefs about how we should be. Ideas that we often pick up very early in life. As a young child, it can feel really important to follow these, in order to feel safe or loved. They can end up embedded in our thinking, like little scripts that we continue following as adults, often without realising they're there. I'm wondering if perhaps you have one that says, "You must please others, you always have to put them first"?'

Elizabeth nodded. 'Maybe. It does sound quite familiar.'

'Now, of course, it's important to live your values of being a good, charitable, caring person. Those are wonderful qualities, and I'm not suggesting you change them. But that doesn't mean you have to take care of everybody else to such an extent that your own needs aren't properly met.'

Elizabeth nodded again. 'I do have a tendency to do that, it's true. Thank you, I'll give it some thought. Maybe I'll try to talk to Fiona about the situation – but she isn't in a good place, and I don't want to put her in a worse predicament than she was in when she arrived.'

'Of course not. That's absolutely not what I'm suggesting. I'm confident that other options will emerge. I work on the premise that it's almost always possible to find a win-win situation, where both people are better served by allowing energy to move and shift in a new way.'

For Elizabeth, I could tell that setting boundaries was going to be key. I wanted to support her and let her know that it's okay to set limits, make a stand or say: 'Actually, this isn't working for me anymore.' That doesn't always have to mean making a big change; sometimes it may be that a person simply needs to acknowledge what they are feeling and know that that is okay.

We left the discussion about her guest at that. In situations such as this, I aim to become the advocate for a nurturing inner voice in my clients. One that says, 'You're important, too.' I think it's vital to reinforce this quiet, still voice within that is saying, 'Something's not right here. I'm not in balance,' especially as this message is often being drowned out by critical or unhelpful beliefs. When I echo what is being communicated by that nurturing self, people I work with become better able to hear it. In that sense, the work I do is often as much about supporting people in realigning different aspects of their selves as it is about lining up things on their shelves.

Having identified and started to address some of the underlying issues, we ended our meeting by establishing a clear vision for what Elizabeth wanted, agreeing priorities and setting out a schedule of work. As her budget was limited, we decided to focus on the spaces where we would have the biggest impact. I hoped she would learn enough from the process to be able to tackle the bathroom and other areas under her own steam.

A few days later, I arrived back at Elizabeth's and we set to work clearing her space. We had agreed to start with the shelves of art materials and paperwork in the kitchen, so I began by taking down some of the large open boxes. I'd arrived with a good selection of semi-opaque storage containers. I generally suggest these, as they allow you see a little of what's inside. The ones I'd brought were all the same width and depth, or multiples of each other, meaning they stacked easily. Vitally, they also all came with lids that you could click securely closed. A box without a lid is asking to be overfilled, and it becomes easy to simply stuff more things in without thinking. Closable boxes help create containment and structure. And when you have to take a box down off a shelf and remove the lid in order to store something in it, it helps establish a little mindfulness. As I already mentioned, I had a strong sense that Elizabeth really needed to create boundaries: not only regarding her home, her business and how she stored her possessions, but also within herself.

'Okay, let's get started.' I carried a large red plastic box over to the kitchen table where I'd set up Elizabeth with my cards to go through the decision-making process.

'Think of your flat as like an overgrown garden. Right now, it is filled with weeds and brambles, and they are blocking out the light and restricting your growth. So, first we are going to do the weeding: clearing away the unwanted and overgrown things, and pulling up the roots so they are less likely to grow back.'

'Got it, I'm ready,' said Elizabeth. From the way she was shifting around in her seat, though, I could tell she wasn't comfortable about staying put.

'I know you want to get in there with me and move things around, but at this point it's better if you focus your energy on the decision-making process and leave the rest to me.'

I turned my attention to the box I'd carried over. Balanced precariously on top was a large orange file. Inside was a collection of catalogues from art exhibitions dating back many years. Handing this to Elizabeth to sort through, I peered into the depths of the large box. I was confronted with what I'd describe as organised chaos. The first things I pulled out were bundles of pens and pencils. Some were carefully grouped into sets and held neatly together with rubber bands; others seemed just scattered at random. In among them was a huge mixture of other items, including a large desktop pencil sharpener of the type I remember my teacher having at school, a balloon pump and a neat stack of five or six CDs, along with several loose discs minus their cases. It was a pattern I frequently encounter. I wasn't sure if the container had, at one point, been highly organised and had deteriorated over time, or if Elizabeth had sporadically made efforts to tidy it up. Whichever it was, this first box, along with the overall situation in the flat, suggested to me that she had some conflicting tendencies.

'Some of these things are very organised,' I commented as I continued to empty the box and hand the contents to Elizabeth to make decisions.

'Yes, I love to categorise things,' she replied, scribbling with a marker on the sheet of paper I'd given her to check which pens were dried up and which still usable. 'Finished!' she called, and threw the pen with a satisfying clunk into the steel bin we were using for rubbish.

As I finally reached the bottom of the box, I came across a scattering of small coins. Not thinking anything of it, I collected them up and put them in a small pen holder I'd emptied earlier. I took down another box from the shelf and started to work through it. This one was filled with tubes of paint, brushes and more coloured pencils, along with several pairs of socks. Again, there was a real mixture. Some of the paint tubes were shoved in, while others were neatly collected into sets. And the ones that were in sets were organised perfectly according to the colour spectrum. As before, at the bottom of the box I came across another handful of coins, which I added to the pot with the others. By the time I'd emptied the entire container, the small pot was almost full of pennies, tuppences and other 'shrapnel', as my grandfather used to call it.

Throughout the day, we worked steadily and methodically through each old box, weeding out the recycling, charity donations and rubbish. Elizabeth really embraced the process, although at times it clearly wasn't easy for her. As the day progressed, we filled more and more bin bags and recycling bags, and packed the sturdiest of the old boxes with things for charity. There was a huge amount to tackle, and while it was hard work, it was energising, too. People can think of decluttering as an onerous task, but in reality, once you get into the flow, it can be quite invigorating. Elizabeth clearly had a playful nature, so as we worked, in the spirit of fun, I said things such as, 'Let's go, faster, faster! Come on, let it go, give it away!' This seemed to be energising for her, and with some of the heaviness dispelled, she did. We had a great time, laughing and joking and gently teasing each other. Sometimes laughter is the best medicine when it comes to clearing clutter.

As a creative person myself, I really admired Elizabeth for being willing to embrace a new order in her home. To be able to let go of all the richly overflowing boxes that I knew must have felt, in a way, as if they were the source of her creativity – although, of course, they weren't. That inspiration sprung from something deep within her, from a place that was in fact being stifled by the stresses of having to face that chaotic space every day.

I heaved a large stack of coloured paper out of the latest box, revealing a further scattering of coins. And as we worked through this one, filled with a huge variety of paper and card, the coins continued to come. By the time we had finished all the boxes on the shelf, I'd given up on the pen holder and decanted the coins into a large glass vase.

'You're doing a great job, Elizabeth. But what *is* it with all these pennies?' I asked.

Elizabeth gave a nervous half-laugh. 'Oh, I don't know. I'm such a scatterbrain, aren't I?' She turned away to pick up a wooden picture frame from the charity-shop pile. 'I'm having second thoughts about this one. Maybe it is worth keeping – what do you think?'

I noted the quick change of subject and held the question about the coins in my mind. 'It's your call, of course, but I'd encourage you to trust your initial choices and not keep revisiting decisions.'

Ideally, I suggest to people that we complete all the weeding before starting the planting phase, where we categorise and put things away. But because Elizabeth had so much stuff and such limited space, I did some of the categorising as we went along, provisionally allocating the things she was keeping to the new boxes in what seemed like logical sets. It wasn't always a smooth process, though. Despite the boxes and their contents seeming quite chaotic, when I began to rearrange them, Elizabeth clearly had some strong sense of where things should go, meaning there initially were a few disagreements about what should be where. As we worked, though, she was also happy to learn from my categorisation systems.

Elizabeth and I had a couple of further sessions together the following week, during which we finished clearing the kitchen/office before moving on to tackle her bedroom. These sessions were as full-on as that first day. After the third session, although I was tired, I had a restless night. This often happens when I'm fully immersed in an intensive decluttering project. I couldn't quite put my finger on it, but something just wasn't right about the entire configuration of the flat. When I woke in the morning, my unconscious had solved the puzzle overnight. It was clear to me that the organisation of the flat was back-to-front: it needed to be flipped, and some of the rooms changed around.

I was really excited when I got to Elizabeth's the following week. I had sketched out a small plan to show her how

I thought we could rearrange the space. My proposal was to move her bedroom into the main room. Then the small room would become her office, and the kitchen would become an open-plan kitchen-diner and social space.

Although I was inspired, I expected that this would be an 'in theory' conversation, as I knew Elizabeth still had a guest living with her. But the funny thing was that when I arrived, her first words were: 'Guess what? My friend has found somewhere and is moving out!'

'Really, what happened?' I asked. 'Did you speak to her?'

'No! I was gearing myself up for a difficult conversation over the weekend, but then she announced that a friend of hers is going travelling for six months and needs someone to house-sit and look after her cats. I'm a bit jealous, actually; it's a lovely cottage out in the Essex countryside. Anyway, it will be perfect for her; somewhere she can take time for herself and reflect on what she wants to do next.'

'Well, what do you know! It could be perfect timing, because I had a bit of a brainwave the other night about your flat. Let me tell you about it.'

I showed Elizabeth my sketch and explained how things could work.

'I love it,' she said. 'But do I need a whole room for an office?'

'It's your decision, of course, but I believe it would be really helpful for you.'

Elizabeth looked a little uncertain, so I explained my thinking.

'Do you remember when you told me about giving up working in the school? The main issue you described was the admin and red tape, and that is something that running a business requires a lot of. I wonder if you have created all this confusion with the paperwork, making it so difficult to deal with, because something inside you really doesn't want to do it?'

'Hmm, maybe.'

'At the same time, I've seen that there is actually a part of you that really loves to categorise and organise, to focus on those little details. My suggestion is that you create a dedicated space for your lover of routine and detail, and establish a little separation between that aspect of your personality and your more creative side. Sometimes we need to find ways to accommodate different parts of ourselves independently, rather than trying to force them to reconcile in a "one size fits all" way.'

Elizabeth looked around the room. Although we had made a lot of progress, in places there were still random piles of letters and files scattered around. Then she moved over to the shelf where, during our previous session, we had consolidated all of her utility bills and bank statements. She thought for a moment.

'You know what, that makes a lot of sense. I'm sick of trying to process invoices on the kitchen table. Let's do it!'

I was pleased that Elizabeth was back on board, and we were off again – full steam ahead.

It is amazing what happens to me sometimes when I walk into a space: I have this huge surge of energy. I feel as if I'm a horse in the starting gates, raring for the off. I can't wait to roll up my sleeves and get things rejigged. I'm not always able to do this, of course; if the process is slow, I have to pull on the reins and slow my galloping horse down. Sometimes the horse never even gets let out of the gate because people are just not ready for change, and I accept that. But when I have a restless night, I know things are shifting. And when a client makes a shift, I feel it too. Working intensively together in that space of transformation, it often feels as if we are connected in some way.

'Project Elizabeth', as we jokingly called it, was going really well. When I arrived for the next session, she had already moved her bed out of the smallest room and started to create her new office. It was great. She had fallen into a trap many people do when they don't know how to maximise space, though: placing all the furniture up against the walls.

'Can we try something different?' I asked.

Together we moved the desk, repositioning the chair so Elizabeth could sit facing the door. Then we spent quite a bit of time arranging business books and the greatly slimmed-down collection of stationery in an accessible way. By the end of the day, we had made a really cute, compact office without any extra spend, simply utilising all the things she already had.

'You know what could really work here? One of these lockable filing cabinets. It would fit perfectly under the desk.' I pulled out my phone and showed Elizabeth the piece of furniture I was referring to.

'Hmm. That would be great, but I don't have any budget for that right now, I'm afraid.'

'Maybe if you took all the coins that we've collected to the bank, you could afford it,' I joked, but again, for some reason, this seemed to be a taboo subject for Elizabeth, and she didn't respond. What did the coins represent? My intuition was still engaged, but I couldn't get to the bottom of it.

The issue of the coins aside, Elizabeth was bouncing around with excitement. By dedicating a specific space to it, we had made physical and psychological room for her business. I knew managing her work–life balance was going to be easier for her now she had somewhere she could focus exclusively on work. The other spaces in the flat worked better now, too.

The bedroom had more flow and, as I'd pictured, the kitchen became a really nice kitchen-diner. There had been one sacrifice: moving the office meant that she no longer had that lovely view on to the heath when working, but she still had it in the kitchen, and surely a great view is a better thing to share with your friends than with your paperwork.

You may be wondering if Elizabeth did cash in her coin collection. I don't know the answer, but it was left on her to-do list and we did a little piece of work around it during our last session, where we gained a bit more understanding. It had been another successful day: her flat was close to completion and we had bagged up several more bags of clothes to go to the charity shop, as well as shredding two large bin bags of old paperwork. And, once again, I'd uncovered further little collections of coins in various places, this time in her chest of drawers.

'I have to ask you again, Elizabeth, what is it with all these coins? How come you end up with so many of them?'

Elizabeth shrugged and turned away. 'I'm not sure, I just empty my pockets and my purse every few days.'

'Okay. Do you have an idea of why they might build up so much?'

'Coins are just heavy and ... well, I never pay for things with change. I always use a note or a pound coin.'

'What, you pay for a bar of chocolate with a note?' I checked myself, worrying my reaction might have sounded judgemental. But by this time, we had established quite a culture of playful banter between us, and Elizabeth was fine with my comment.

'Well, yes. I know it's silly, but I just don't like rummaging around for the right money, and a note means I can do the transaction quickly.'

'Oh, okay,' I said. 'So, you don't like having to find the right money, and you have a need for speed and efficiency.'

'Yes.'

'I'm curious about that. I wonder why. Are you always in a hurry?'

'No, I just don't like to keep people waiting.'

'Why is that do you think?'

Elizabeth shrugged. 'I really don't know. I am curious, though; there's definitely something going on.'

'May I suggest we do a mini role play? To try and find out what's going on for you?'

By now, Elizabeth was used to my slightly unconventional ideas. I think she had come to enjoy them, in fact.

'Go on, then,' she said.

'Okay, so if you're open to acting the scenario out here, why don't you get your handbag so it's more realistic?'

We took our places opposite each other in the living room.

'Take a couple of deep breaths and picture yourself standing in a queue,' I said.

'Right. I'm at the corner shop, there's always a queue there.'

'Okay, now imagine you have reached the counter. I'm the shopkeeper and you want to get out some change. Have a go.'

'Good morning, just these bananas please.' Elizabeth handed me the imaginary bunch and I pretended to weigh them.

'That'll be sixty-seven pence, please,' I said, putting out my hand.

Elizabeth stood and rummaged in her purse.

'Can you describe how you are feeling right now?' I asked.

Elizabeth grimaced. 'I feel anxious and silly,' she said. 'I just want to get out of here. I hate that feeling of keeping everyone waiting. And I'm also worried about not finding exactly the right money.'

'That's really interesting. What do you think would happen if you keep them all waiting?'

'I don't know. They might get angry with me?'

'Can you stay with the anxiety just for a minute longer?' I asked.

I was quite sure her inner critic was telling Elizabeth she should hurry up, so I offered her some lines: 'Try telling yourself this: "It is okay to take my time, to take as long as I need. It is okay to take the time I need to find the right money to pay for this. I choose how long I take."'

She repeated my words.

'How does it feel when you say that?'

Elizabeth looked at me in surprise. 'It feels quite a bit better, actually. I didn't expect it to make much difference, but I feel more relaxed.'

'Maybe you can try it next time you're at the shop? Have a go at breaking this cycle of anxiety with some reassuring self-talk. A little bit of internal parenting. You can use it as a mindfulness practice or a bit of loving self-care.'

Elizabeth looked pensive. My sense was that, while the role play and suggestion had been helpful, it might also help her to explore what could be at the root of this habit.

'Do you have any sense of where this belief or message that you have to be quick might come from?'

Elizabeth gave a little grin and her pupils turned upwards as she accessed some memories.

'When I was growing up, I remember always wanting to please my dad. When I came home from school with a good mark, I'd get praised and told what a good girl I was. It was nice.'

'You don't need me to tell you this, but I'm sure your dad would have loved you whatever marks you got. But as a child, perhaps you began to associate love with getting things right?'

'Maybe, yes. At school, I also remember feeling that I had

to complete any work set by the teacher before any of the other kids. It was almost as if finishing first and getting a hundred per cent was the only acceptable result.'

'Wow. That sounds like a lot of pressure. Not only do you have to get everything right, but also you have to do it fast.'

Elizabeth sat very still and didn't say anything. She seemed caught up in some difficult feelings, and appeared to be lost in thought again.

'Oh my God!' she said. 'I'm just remembering this time we were on holiday and I was writing a postcard to my grandparents. I was being really careful to have neat handwriting and say the right words, but I kept making mistakes. So, I'd tear up the card and start again. I must have gone through about seven or eight postcards. I got so angry with myself, I felt like I was going nuts. Somehow the idea of sending a card with a word crossed out or a spelling mistake was just intolerable. I can see I'm still repeating that pattern. What am I like?'

'Try to have some compassion for yourself. When you become obsessed with organising things perfectly, imagine it is that little girl wanting to please her father. That's a natural thing, so don't give yourself a hard time. Simply having awareness can be all you need sometimes; then it becomes a choice rather than an unconscious reflex.'

This seemed quite a key insight for Elizabeth, and I wanted to allow it time to marinate. At the same time, there was a related thought that had come to me, and I decided to share it now, not knowing if a better occasion would present itself.

'As we discussed when we talked about the office, I'm also wondering if when you just stuff things away, there's a part of you rebelling against that inner perfectionist. It sounds like a hard taskmaster. I think the key is to find some balance. To recognise when these drives serve you, and when they just get in the way and cause pain.'

I left Elizabeth to ponder what we'd discussed and went back into the kitchen to finish organising the crockery cupboard, which was one of the last jobs on my list.

As I organised the precarious piles of assorted plates, cups and saucers, I found myself thinking about entropy. I'm not a big science buff, but as I work a lot with energy, it is one of the ideas that really resonates with me. It is something that feels very relevant to my work, and so I like to talk to my clients about it. In case you're not familiar with the idea, entropy is a measure of the degree of disorder in a system. In physics, the theory is that everything in the universe, right down to a subatomic level, tends towards disorder and decay, and that it takes energy to keep matter organised. And, as I tell my clients, entropy isn't just confined to theoretical physics. Our homes and the things in them are also moving towards mess and decay, which means we have to apply effort and take regular action to keep them in equilibrium. Picture a person on a unicycle: in order to stay upright, they have to stay in constant motion. This is how I see our homes. If we don't keep tending to them, the order will break down of its own accord, in much the same way as an unkempt garden grows into a jungle of weeds. Unsurprisingly, I am never very popular when I tell clients this. People generally have a longing for their home to be organised as in the proverb: 'A place for everything and everything in its place.' And they want it to stay that way. Although, of course, they realise this is a fantasy, there's a degree to which they want me to come in, wave a magic wand and miraculously provide storage solutions and systems that don't require maintenance. It's like they want to be able to just click their heels and say 'Tidy!' I certainly wish I was Mary Poppins and could render a room perfect with just a snap of my fingers, but we all know that's a children's story. Life is a somewhat more challenging experience. Of course, there are systems and structures that I help people put in place that make maintaining order easier, but even the best systems still require effort and discipline to enact.

It was our final session and, before I left, we sat down at the kitchen table looking out over the heath together. I went through some next actions for Elizabeth to take and made suggestions about ways in which she could build on what we had already achieved in the flat.

'Following the metaphor of your home being like a garden, we have completed the first two phases, the weeding and the planting. What is important now is to build a habit of ongoing maintenance to keep things in order. It will be much easier now. As you know, if you don't do this in a garden, the weeds and brambles will eventually grow back. We've dug quite deep and uncovered and pulled up a lot of the roots, but, inevitably, a few will remain. And as life and time unfold, they will always blow in a few seeds, some of which will take root and begin to sprout. The key thing is to build a routine, and keep an eye out for those unwanted shoots and pluck them out before they get established, while also caring for the positive new growth that comes. Having a good sense of your personality style, and especially in the context of what we talked about earlier, I think it is going to be most helpful if you do this in a consistent, relaxed way.'

'You're right. As you've seen, I certainly have a tendency to get hyper-focused on organising, then burn myself out, at which point things can slip badly.'

'Exactly. If you can establish a more gentle, easeful approach, I think this will serve you much better than putting too much pressure on yourself to get it perfect every time.

What I suggest is you start by setting aside half an hour a week to keep organised. Set yourself a timer, and when it goes off, stop. That will take some pressure off and prevent you from getting too caught up or obsessed. If you want to come back and do more another time, you can, of course, but make sure you leave a decent gap – and use the timer again.'

I took a few photos of the space on my phone. I like to send my clients some before-and-after shots to remind them of what we have achieved. And that was it. I gathered up my things into my bag and said goodbye to Elizabeth. We have stayed in touch, however, and I know that while she still faces challenges, as we all do, she has made huge progress, especially in her business. I hope that in some small way, uncovering some of what lay at the root of her clutter helped her to stay clear.

Initially, the accumulation of coins appeared almost incidental to the work with Elizabeth. These small items were physically quite insignificant in the context of all the stacks of large boxes, bags and piles of clothes. And yet to me, they seemed symbolically representative of those small choices we make and whose impact builds up over time in our homes, our lives and our psyches. I suspected each time Elizabeth dropped a few coins into a box or drawer, she thought nothing of it. Likewise, each of her other unmade choices – is this pen worth keeping? Do I bin this completed notebook? – accumulated over time, steadily building up the disorder. By the end of a significant block of intensive work, we had been able to make all those postponed decisions and create the space and order she needed. But, as I told her, it was the incremental positive habits she needed to build that would enable her to win the ongoing battle with entropy in both her space and her head.

\*

There is something of a myth held by – and about – creative people such as Elizabeth: a romantic notion that chaos and disorder are part and parcel of being creative. I have a different view, one I share with the composer Igor Stravinsky, who said: 'My freedom will be greater and more meaningful the more narrowly I limit my field of action. The more constraints one imposes, the more one frees oneself of the chains that shackle the spirit.' There is a similar dynamic at play in our relationship with our spaces.

The less you have, the less you have to manage. So, when you create a sufficient degree of order and containment in your home – and this will vary from person to person – you liberate rather than restrict yourself. Instead of having to use your energy to battle with the consequences of entropy and disorder, you can focus on what is most important to you. With the clutter held at bay, your family, creative work, business, studies, personal development and new opportunities can take their proper place in your priorities.

You may need your home to multitask, but that doesn't mean *you* always have to. Creating containment and dedicating specific rooms, areas or pieces of furniture to particular jobs or types of activity can help your home function better. Knowing that when you are sitting at your desk, you are focusing on work, while another table is dedicated to, say, a hobby can be liberating. Most people find that defining those specific spaces makes it easier to focus more mindfully on one thing at a time.

Clutter can sometimes be a result of never saying no to others – to offers, requests, limits and decisions – and, as a consequence, actually saying no to your own needs. Are you someone, like Elizabeth, who feels almost compelled to say yes to others? As a result, do you find you are overburdened with commitments and rarely have the time or space to pursue what matters most to you? Or perhaps your home is full of things that people have offered you, and you simply were not able to say, 'No, thank you.'

If you struggle in the moment to say no when someone offers you something or asks you for something, one thing that can help is to say: 'Thank you/I'd love to help if I can. But I need to check something first. Can I get back to you?' This will give you a chance to consider things a bit more carefully. If, having given it some thought, you decide to say no, it's a lot easier to do so over the phone than it is face to face.

# Keepage

At a book launch, I spoke to Caroline, an old friend and business contact. She was telling me about a friend of hers.

'Mike needs help. He's drowning in clutter,' she said. 'Things aren't looking good, and his situation seems to be getting worse every time I see him. Can you help?'

It's not unusual for people to ask me to help someone they know, and it's always a tricky situation. It's painful to see someone you care about suffering. Especially if, with the clarity of an objective view, you believe you can see what the problem is. However, as anyone who has tried to support someone who is stuck knows, it's only possible to help another person change when they're ready and willing.

'I think you might know what I'm going to say: it's only going to work if he wants help. Do you think Mike is ready to make the changes he needs?'

'I don't know,' she replied, 'but I feel we have to try. I don't think he has fully got over the death of his father, but I really think that doing something with that house will help him make a shift.'

I have successfully worked with people who had been referred to me by friends and relatives, if they genuinely wanted my help, so I suggested Caroline contact Mike and ask if he was willing to talk to me. She emailed me a couple of days later and said he was, so, preparing myself for some barriers and resistance, I called him.

'Hello Mike. It's Helen Sanderson here.'

'Ah yes, Caroline's friend,' he said with the tone of someone who perhaps didn't want to talk. I wondered if the only reason he wasn't hanging up the phone there and then was that he didn't want to offend our mutual friend, but I knew it was also possible his reluctance could be down to fear or embarrassment, so I remained open to hearing if there was a way I could be of help.

'To be honest, I don't think Caroline needs to worry about me. But I'm happy to have a brief chat.'

'Okay, thank you. I know it's a tricky subject. Caroline mentioned that you're having a bit of trouble keeping on top of things at home. Are you willing to tell me a little about how you see the situation?'

'Well, I've collected some stuff, it's true. But it's nothing I can't handle right now.'

He paused for a moment, and I allowed him some space by not asking any further questions.

'I do have a lot of my father's things in the attic room,' he continued. 'I inherited most of his possessions, along with the house. But I've plenty of room here, to be honest.'

'I see. When did you lose your father?'

'Well, it was a couple of years ago, I guess.'

I was struck that Mike was unclear about exactly when his father had died; perhaps he was blocking out some aspect of the loss. I often encounter this kind of vagueness in my clients when it comes to the dates and timelines of events in their past. Holding on to possessions often reflects a resistance to letting go of life events, dreams or relationships. Unfinished business can take up a lot of headspace – and a lot of house room, too. I wanted to get a sense of how much of an issue Mike thought there was, so searched for a way to get underneath his defences without confronting him. If people are in denial about something, anyone who pushes them too hard to face the reality of their situation isn't usually going to be popular, and will often get the opposite result. I also suspected that Mike was minimising, as he had when he had talked about his father's property. 'A few things' often turn out to be far more than a few.

Whenever I asked an open question, Mike responded with short answers. I suspected that either he was feeling shame, or an internal voice was telling him he should be able to deal with his issues alone. I was, of course, sensitive and compassionate about this, knowing that when denial sets in, it is often because it is too difficult or painful for people to see the reality of their situation. If Mike really didn't want my support, or see he might need it, I wasn't going to push too hard. But as we continued our conversation, I could sense that he was starting to open up a little.

'It sounds like you keep a lot of other people's things there,' I said.

'I wouldn't say a lot, but I guess some . . .'

'It must all take up a lot of space. Do you ever think about letting some of it go?'

Mike raised his voice, and spoke more quickly. 'There's no way I'm getting rid of any of Dad's artwork.' Then, perhaps fearing he had been too aggressive, he continued more slowly: 'I'm sorry, I just couldn't.'

I sensed that I was walking a bit of a tightrope. Without a certain degree of encouragement from me, Mike might decide to stick where he was. But if I pushed him too much, he was equally likely to shut down completely to the whole idea of working together.

'I hear that,' I said. 'I promise you I don't see it as my job to force anyone to throw anything out. It is always your decision, especially when it comes to things that have real value and meaning. For me, decluttering is about mindfully connecting to what you have and what those possessions mean to you, just as much as it is about letting things go.'

I allowed a little space for connection to see if Mike had heard me and taken in what I'd said.

'That's reassuring,' Mike replied, and I sensed a softening again. 'There are a lot of memories in this place, that's for sure. Too many, maybe. I could certainly do with a little more room. I just don't know how to get started.'

At this point, I started to feel there was an opening that would make it possible for me to work with Mike. The first step in the process of tackling an issue you're stuck in is often accepting you've got a problem and that you can't solve it alone. Despite his initial resistance, by the end of our chat, Mike had invited me over for a longer conversation.

Mike lived in a three-storey, red-brick Victorian terraced house. Partially hidden from the street by a somewhat overgrown hedge, it shared a tiled pathway and small front garden with the house next door. A rather dishevelled-looking motorbike was chained to the wall of the front porch, and I had to manoeuvre past it to reach the front door. I rang the bell and waited. After a minute or so, a tall, handsome but anxious-looking man appeared. He was wearing a collarless shirt, his receding hair tied back in a ponytail. He half-opened the door and peered round the edge to greet me. I had imagined Mike would be okay with meeting after our call, but he looked nervous.

'Hello,' I said taking half a step back and trying to be

as unthreatening as I could. 'I hope I haven't arrived at a bad time.'

'No, it's not that. I'm sorry to waste your time, but I'm wondering if this is such a good idea.'

'It's okay,' I said. 'I know this can be a little nerve-wracking. Remember, I'm just here to see how I can support you. There's no judgement, and you can ask me to leave at any time.'

Mike opened the door and stepped back. 'Okay. I guess you'd better come in.'

I readied myself, half-expecting his home to be in a state of total chaos. However, the entrance and hallway proved to be fairly tidy, if a little tricky to traverse. Just inside the front door, a bike hung on two large hooks on the wall, and below that was a long but tidy row of boots and a black motorcycle helmet with a pair of padded leather gloves perched on top.

'Sorry, a bit of a squeeze, I know,' he said. 'I don't have a lot of visitors.'

I followed Mike into the house. The hallway was lined with numerous black-and-white photographs, along with many larger frames leaning with their faces against the wall. The photos were beautifully framed, but quite dusty. I sensed they hadn't really been looked at for some time. One particularly struck me, and I paused to admire it. It was a powerful portrait of a chef I remembered watching on TV in the nineties. He looked purposefully into the camera, his weathered hands holding a handful of artichoke heads.

'These are wonderful,' I said. 'Are they your work?'

'Yes. They're from way back,' Mike replied as he continued walking, apparently unable to receive the compliment, and clearly not wanting to talk about the pictures.

As we entered the living room, Mike motioned for me to sit on a large leather sofa, one end of which was piled with roughly folded clothes.

'Have you had a chance to think about our conversation, and do you have any ideas about the house and how I might be able to support you?' I asked.

'I don't know … I guess if I can get rid of some junk and clear a bit of space, I might be able to get on with a few of the things I keep putting off. Create a bit of momentum.'

'That sounds like a great idea. I think getting some things moving will be really positive.' I was aware that the house had a certain heaviness about it, a feeling of being stuck, although I didn't want to say that. 'Do you have a sense of what might be causing this lack of momentum?' I asked.

He shrugged. 'I'm not sure. I feel like I've made quite a few positive changes over the last few months, though. I took on a new part-time contract, and I've been going to this self-help group. But whenever I come back home, I feel stuck and bogged down.'

'So, you feel you're in a bit of a rut and that something needs to change here to help you get out of it?'

'Exactly.' Mike looked at me a little more intently, I guess appreciating that I had understood him.

Mike told me a little more about his life, describing several career setbacks that had clearly taken their toll. Reading between the lines, I could tell there had also been heartbreaks, and he hinted at some alcohol use that may have been a way of self-medicating his pain and sense of isolation.

When I meet people, I often notice how their home environment reflects an aspect of their personality that has become distorted: some part of them that either hasn't found its full expression or has not been integrated. As a result, there is some psychological process being played out that has become manifested in the home. Mike's situation, I suspected, was a classic example of this. He was clearly a very talented, creative man, who nevertheless hadn't managed to make an abundant living from his art. I could feel the depth of his despair in our conversation, his feelings and perception of his failure as a man, a husband, an artist. I wondered if perhaps some trauma in his past had stolen his ability to move forward and left him stuck instead in a painful present. What was left was a sweet but suffering soul and a smouldering creativity that stubbornly refused to leave.

'I can help you to shift some of this, provided you are ready. The key question is, can you see yourself working with me?' I asked.

'Yes, I guess so,' he said. 'I know I need to get this place sorted out, and now's probably the time to do something about it.'

Something in Mike's tone of voice and body language gave me the impression that he was saying those words to himself as much as to me. I guessed that he had probably said similar things to himself many times in the past without following through.

I knew it would be tough for Mike to make the shift in behaviour on his own. And I also knew from experience that, if he'd agree to take some big initial strides with me, we could get things moving and create a bit of energy and momentum. With that impetus, I hoped, he might then be able to continue the work on his own.

As we talked, I felt a powerful desire rising in me to say to Mike that his avoidance and habit of telling himself the story 'I will do it tomorrow' was killing his spirit. To tell him that it was a trap and that he was in denial. I resisted this impulse, though, as he hadn't explicitly described any procrastination.

Mike stood up, rather abruptly. 'Do you want to see the rest of the house?'

I followed him out of the room, unsure if this offer reflected a genuine interest in my input, or simply him wanting to get my visit over with quickly.

I trailed behind him as he strode ahead up a steep flight of stairs to the first floor, catching up with him by a door on the landing. 'Err, this is my room. That's where the real problem is, I suppose. It's . . .' His voice trailed off, so I didn't quite catch the end of the sentence. I sensed him shrinking away into some deeper part of his self.

I peered into the dark room. A heavy pair of deep-blue curtains, open just a crack, were drawn across the window. It was hard to see much, but I could make out clothes, books and art materials scattered everywhere. I asked Mike to flick the light switch.

'Sorry, the bulb's blown,' he said.

Struggling to push the door back, he stepped over a bag that lay on the floor and drew back the curtains. The additional light revealed a partially made bed covered in clothes. Elsewhere around the room were dozens of bags and boxes, along with more stacks of frames. There were several piles of books on the bedside cabinet.

As soon as I saw that room it was clear to me that, despite his efforts to bring about change, part of Mike was shutting down. I knew at that moment just why his friend had reached out to me for help. It was very apparent Mike was drowning, and that some vital part of him was lost. I became very aware that the pressure was on. Mike had begun to let me in that morning, and had shown me a lot of trust. But for how long would he be open to help?

Although Mike said that the problem lay in his bedroom, I wasn't so sure. I often find that the source of my clients' pain and 'stuckness', and the key to unlocking these, is uncovered in unexpected places. This usually requires some careful and thoughtful digging. In this sense, my work is almost a kind of archaeology: there is a lot to sift through, but at any point you can uncover treasure – a key link to the past, to that person's history.

As we made our way around the rest of Mike's house, I noticed more and more paintings. Almost exclusively landscapes, some hung on the walls but many were leaning against pieces of furniture or lying stacked in piles. In one of the bedrooms, I stopped to admire a large painting of reed beds that beautifully captured a sense of the grasses blowing in the wind. We stood looking at the painting together.

'I inherited all Dad's artwork along with the house when he died.' Mike stared at the painting and seemed to be drifting off somewhere. 'I don't know what to do with it all. Dad could be a difficult man, but I loved him, and I know how much this work meant to him.'

'So, I imagine it is your way of respecting him and his work, keeping all the paintings and other possessions. Perhaps it would feel like a dishonouring of the love you feel if you let any of it go?'

Mike didn't answer, but I could sense his agreement

'It must have been really hard to lose him,' I said.

Mike looked down at the floor and closed his eyes for a moment.

'Do you think your dad would want you to hold on to all his work and old equipment if he felt it might be blocking you from living your life and pursuing your photography?'

'I don't think of his work as getting in the way,' said Mike. 'It's my issues that are stopping me, if anything.'

I could see Mike was barely coping, with both our conversation and with his life. I also worried that he was getting steadily closer to collapse. I find it helpful to think of clutter as decisions that haven't been made, and the physical accumulation often mirrors a build-up of unaddressed practical or emotional issues in someone's life. We know that, as piles grow, the likelihood of them falling over increases. Well, it's the same psychologically. The more we allow issues to build up, the greater the chance that the whole psychological stack will come tumbling down. So, I felt it would help Mike if he was able to understand more about why he might be in the position he was.

'I hear that your situation feels manageable, but you also said earlier that maybe now is the time to take action. This suggests to me that there may be a conflict between different parts of yourself.'

Mike thought for a moment. 'That may be true. It certainly sometimes feels as if there are conflicting needs within me.'

'That's very much part of most people's experience. Those aspects of yourself can also perceive the world in a way that reinforces their agenda, so to speak. In relation to your home then, I think it's important to consider that things might not be quite as manageable as you say. And to be aware that they might get on top of you in the future.'

Mike gave a deep sigh.

'I went to see someone a few years ago in a similar situation to the one you are in now,' I continued. 'She decided not to deal with her clutter, which was fine. But last year, she called me again. Her husband had left, and her career was really suffering. We were able to sort things out, but it took a lot more time and pain than it would have done if we'd tackled it the first time around.'

I was a little surprised to notice that Mike had a tear in his eye, and, although he didn't say anything in response, I knew he was touched.

'I can see that was a painful subject. Are you okay to carry on and look at the top floor?' I motioned to the set of stairs at the end of the first-floor landing.

'I'm not sure that's necessary, I think you've pretty much

got the picture,' Mike replied. He turned to head back down to the ground floor.

From his demeanour, I suspected there was something there that he was ashamed of or wanted to protect from my gaze. Wanting to help him confront his denial about the full gravity of his situation, I gently encouraged him to let me see a little more.

'It really helps if you can show me the whole picture,' I said. 'I can offer you better advice if I've seen the rest of the house.'

'Okay. I guess it won't hurt to take a quick look. I warn you, it's a bit untidy.'

Somewhat reluctantly, he led the way up the narrow stairway.

The attic studio was chaotic. Art supplies, paintings and photographic equipment lay around everywhere. It looked and felt as if no one had been up there for a while. Mike moved around the space carefully, pointing out a few things in a somewhat detached way. The longer I was in his presence and the more I saw of his house, the stronger my impression grew that he hadn't really created a home. He was, in fact, more like the curator of a museum, preserving his late father's paintings. Tragically, his own hopes and dreams also seemed to be on hold. I worried that Mike was living so much in the past that he couldn't possibly embrace the future.

I felt real empathy for Mike and connected to a deep sadness in myself as I saw how trapped he seemed. I really wanted to find a way to support him to change his living situation, but I could sense his resistance so strongly it was almost tangible. Nevertheless, I tested the water a little.

'Can I ask if you know why you are holding on to that old computer hard drive? Or this scanner?'

Mike walked over to the desk and contemplated the dust-covered scanner, pausing for a moment. 'I guess it's like the longer I've kept something, the harder it is to let it go.'

'As if it has earned its space in your home somehow? That it has taken up residence, a bit like a squatter?' I suggested.

'Exactly. It's kind of like my head is telling me, "If you've held on to it this long, it must be important." It's almost as if it's come to deserve its place through just sticking around.'

'Ahh yes, I see. You could say it has earned "keepage",' I said with a smile, and a little lightness entered into our interactions for a moment as we laughed together at the made-up word. I do this sometimes. I think it's a reflection of my way of looking at the world and people's psyches as if I'm an explorer. When I come across some unusual plant specimen or creature in the psychological jungle, I like to name it in a way that helps me make sense of it.

So, thanks to Mike I had a new word: keepage. Definition: Quality of possessions, usually redundant, in which we have invested money and much time and effort in housing, so that, despite the absence of any easily ascribable value, they are nevertheless hard to let go.

I get that people often have a powerful emotional desire to hold on to things they don't need, but it doesn't make sense practically. Generally, junk just accumulates this 'keepage', which can also be shorthand for: 'I am going to bloody well keep this! Because if I let it go, I can't justify having held on to it for so long.'

We headed back down the two flights of stairs to Mike's living room. I have developed a kind of sixth sense for when people are ready to take steps towards change. Sadly, despite the connection I felt we had made, I doubted that Mike was likely to make a commitment to dealing with his situation right then. Nevertheless, I explained my working process and set out my recommendations. I left him to consider if and when he wanted to get started.

We made our way to the front door and Mike showed me out, thanking me politely for my time. I prepared to say some parting words, but before I could speak, the door clunked shut. I didn't feel that Mike was being rude; I simply took it as a further sign of his need to keep himself barricaded away from the world. And perhaps, too, from the potential for unsettling change that I may have represented. As I walked back to my car, I reflected on how he had been both reticent and yet also given to these bursts of enthusiasm. This kind of stop-start behaviour can be typical of people who are caught between conflicting needs or other psychological forces.

I had an email from my friend Caroline a couple of weeks later.

> Hi Helen,
> I'm sorry, Mike has turned down the offer of help.
> He told me he is going to make a start on his own. Which I know probably means he's not going to tackle the problem.
> I'm not sure what else I can do right now. I feel really sad and anxious about him.
> Thank you for trying.

It was a real shame, but I wasn't surprised. Mike had begun to open up to me, but I'd had a strong sense that he wasn't in the right place to take the hand that was being offered. He was clearly still too caught up in denial and resistance.

I replied to Caroline, asking her to try not to worry and acknowledging the concern she felt for her friend. I reminded her, and myself, that we had to leave Mike to find his own path. At least he knew there was help available.

It's not unusual for people to say they are going to tackle

their clutter and reorganise their homes on their own. I'm sure some of them do, and I understand that the investment in outside support is something not everyone is willing or able to make. I also think that not allowing themselves support means they can leave things as they are and avoid facing the painful underlying issues.

I was disappointed that Mike wasn't able or willing to work with me, and I couldn't shake this vision of him in his troubled space. But, as with everyone I speak to in the course of my work, I was deeply touched by and grateful for having met him. I realised that letting me see inside his home was a massive deal for him, and a significant first step that I greatly respected. I also appreciated his reminding me that I can't help everyone. Some people have a complex and traumatised past that is often reflected in their relationship with their space, and which means it is deeply challenging for them to do the work, make the changes and face the skeletons in their closet. Mike was simply not ready.

*

If, like Mike, you suspect you might be in denial about your clutter, here are a few tell-tale signs:

- Avoiding talking about the issue or changing the subject.
- Ignoring the advice and concern of loved ones.
- Rationalising your situation or behaviours, perhaps by thinking or saying, 'I'm too busy and stressed right now to deal with this. I'll tackle it later/next week/when I've more time.'
- Pointing out how cluttered others' homes are as evidence that you don't have a problem.

- Having stints of being tidier and more organised for a week or two, then going back to old patterns.
- Making a commitment to decluttering and then, when the time approaches, suddenly finding reasons you can't do it or other more important tasks and not following through.

If you identify with more than one of these, it may be time for an honest chat with a trusted friend or a professional.

You might also find it useful to take my online assessment, which will help you better understand your relationship with your home and identify the best strategies to improve this. You can find it at helensanderson.com/clutter-score.

# Walls that talk

I received a fascinating email via my website one day:

Dear Ms Sanderson,
My name is Angela
I am just about to turn forty, and I keep thinking the greatest
gift I could give myself was:
NOT **A**:
A trip around the world to South America ... the Pacific coast
and the Galapagos, the giant tortoises.
NOT **B**:
A cruise to Norway ... Yes, I know it's cold, but the fjords, north-
ern lights and colours for my art.
NOT **C**:
A saxophone ... an instrument that I have always wanted to
learn how to play ...

But, wait for it.
**D**:
Somebody ... somebody who doesn't know me, who lives far
away from me, and wouldn't see me again ... (I wouldn't bump
into them in Sainsbury's)
Somebody who could come into my home and help me – I mean

really help me – to get it tidy again: in order. In order for me to
love my home again.

To create a space ready for the conception of a new life. I'm not
talking about a baby; I mean a new life for me.
Can you help?

This stopped me in my tracks: not only the poetic writing
style, but also the candid content. I immediately thought,
*Here is someone who is clearly passionate about life, full of
ideas and aspiration, yet in real need of support.* I replied to
the email and arranged to meet this intriguing woman. The
story that unfolded over the course of our work is difficult
to tell and may be upsetting to read, but my intention is to
share a message of hope.

Angela lived in south-east London. Her parents, I discovered, had come to England in the 1950s, part of the Windrush
generation. They had settled in the area, worked hard, saved
hard and bought their home in the early 1980s. Angela had
gone to school and grown up in this area, and when her parents moved back to the Caribbean, a decade before we met,
she had taken over the whole house. As our work progressed,
it became apparent that even though she inhabited every
room, in a way it remained the family home, as she had never
fully made it her own.

We'd arranged our first meeting on a weekend, and as my
car was in for a service, I took the tube across town. Angela
lived just off a busy main road, bustling with Saturday morning shoppers. It was a bright spring day and Turkish, Polish,
South Asian and Caribbean stores lined the street, their
makeshift stalls spilling a whole world of fruit, vegetables
and brightly coloured fabrics out on to the pavement. The
aroma of jerk chicken, olives and spices filled the air, along

with the sound of Urdu, Polish and other languages I couldn't quite place.

As I turned off and walked down the terraced street, the sounds, colours and smells gradually faded and were replaced by quiet, and the brilliant white blossom of the trees that were dotted either side of the road. Angela's house was much like the rest, except the outside brickwork had been painted a deep pink. Although I had warmed to her email, we had only spoken briefly on the phone, so as I made my way up her garden path, I wondered how this meeting would be. Would Angela and I get on, and how would she find the process of working with me?

The front door was behind a wrought-iron security gate, and there were also sturdy black metal bars over the ground-floor windows. I pressed the bell. A few moments later, a tall, big woman in a boldly patterned dress opened the door and greeted me with a warm smile. 'You must be Helen, lovely to meet you.' There was a vivacious and playful energy to Angela's tone of voice and facial expressions, and I warmed to her immediately, my concerns about whether we would build a rapport quickly melting away.

She took a deep breath and stood with her palms together in front of her chest as if in prayer. 'Okay, let's go in. *Please* don't judge me. I have tidied up a bit, of course, but it's still a mess.'

I followed her into the front room. It was certainly crammed with stuff. By the entrance stood two seriously overloaded bookshelves, flanked by a pair of tall CD racks that were spilling their contents on to the floor. At the far side of the room was a brightly patterned sofa, one end of which was piled high with books and magazines. Layers of clothes were draped over the back and arms. The sofa faced a very large TV in the corner, which stood on a low unit filled with DVDs and yet more books. Beside this was a large drum adorned with shells, and several very overgrown houseplants. Opposite the bay window, glass doors led to a second down-stairs room. Beyond that, I could just make out what looked like a large kitchen extension.

As I looked around, Angela just stood there in the door-way, as if afraid to move, a little red in the face and shifting her weight uncomfortably.

'It's bad, right? I just don't understand how it got into this state. I'm pretty professional and organised at work – I even manage a small team of people. But when it comes to home, I'm a disaster. I cringe if I imagine what my colleagues would think if they saw this place. It's just so embarrassing.'

While I understood why Angela might feel shame, I wanted to encourage her to take a more compassionate attitude towards herself. 'Try not to give yourself a hard time, Angela. Yes, you've accumulated a lot of clutter, but you've recognised that and reached out for help. That's a huge step. Perhaps you can try congratulating yourself instead? This is where the journey to a more spacious and nurturing home begins, and we start to get things clear and organised for you.'

Angela looked like she was about to cry. 'Thank you for saying that. I'm not a bad person; I know I'm not. But I do get so frustrated with myself when I see my place in such a state. Let's be honest, it is pretty awful, right? I just feel really stuck, and don't know how to get started. Is there any hope for me?'

It's not uncommon for people to use me as a clutter barom-eter, but I am rarely interested in that. It's not the amount of clutter someone has that matters to me, but the impact it is having on their life.

'Absolutely. Some people I've worked with had a bigger task on their hands.'

Angela laughed. 'I find that hard to believe.'

I wanted to encourage Angela, but at the same time, I knew that pretending things were not that bad wasn't going to help. It was obvious that she had a serious clutter problem, and it was clearly having a big impact on her wellbeing. In order to help her, empathy was important, as was getting real and making an honest assessment of how things were and what needed to be done.

'It's true, and everyone has their reasons for why things are the way they are. But that's not to deny you have a serious issue here. Let's take a proper look around, so we can formulate a plan of action.'

We began our tour of the house, and it quickly became apparent that the issue wasn't confined to the living room. Some people contain their clutter in one or two places, but each room we came to was equally disordered and overflowing with clothes, cardboard boxes and full plastic carrier bags. What I saw confirmed my initial gut feeling that this was going to be a long-term project. We made our way back to the living room where we sat down to talk more.

'I was very struck by a phrase you used in your email. I can't remember the exact wording, but it was along the lines that you want to transform your home to be ready to conceive a new life; a new life for you.'

'Yes. That's right. I have so many ideas: to travel, write more poetry, to paint, but they all seem to be buried under all this stuff. I just want to know why I can't seem to take control of it.'

'Tell me if I'm wrong, but it seems to me there is a part of you that wants to create that is in a bit of a power struggle with another part that doesn't and for whatever reason is drawn to accumulate instead.'

Angela was listening carefully and nodded vigorously. 'Yes! That's exactly how it feels. Why would that be?'

My intuition was that now wasn't quite the time to delve

too deeply into Angela's psychology. At the same time, I wanted to assure her that we wouldn't only deal with the surface, but would also address the underlying issues.

'Well, there could be all sorts of reasons, and we may uncover some clues to help you understand that as we go through my process. My role would be to encourage, support and nurture that creative, aspirational part, while giving some empathy and security to the other part that perhaps wants to keep you safe. How does that sound?'

'Good. I was feeling quite nervous about all this, but now I'm starting to feel more excited than afraid. I really do want to make a change.'

'I can sense that. I'll be honest with you, there is a lot to do here. You don't need me to tell you that. But if you are willing to make this project a priority, we will get your home sorted out.'

Angela sat more upright in her seat and looked intently at me. 'I'm in. When can we start?'

My intuition and experience told me that what Angela needed was for us to get straight into action, so when I returned a couple of days later, I immediately grabbed my decluttering bag and started to unpack what I'd need to get started. I cleared some space on the floor in front of the sofa and set out the decision cards.

'Right. You set yourself up there and I'll put things here for you. Try not to overthink it; your job is to focus on quick decisions, like it says on the cards: Bin it, Recycle it, Action it, Keep it, and so on.'

Angela sat on the edge of the sofa and read the back of the 'Keep it' card, where I have included some tips. I was glad she seemed enthused by my energy.

'Okay, I've got it,' she said. 'Just don't put too much in the "Keep it" pile, right?'

I laughed. 'That's right. I'll be watching you carefully!'

I was pleased that we seemed to be really hitting it off, and hoped little bits of playful banter such as this would help to keep her energy levels up.

We dived into the work, starting in the living room, and pretty soon had built up a good head of steam. The piles of possessions kept coming off the shelves, out of drawers and from surfaces all around the room.

'Hey, this is fun.' Angela smiled as I handed her yet another stack of DVDs from the TV unit. 'Who'd have known I was such a fan of naff nineties sitcoms!'

But between the jokes, the odd phrase made me suspect that underneath her vivacious persona lay a lot of pain and sadness. I began to wonder if her home was a reflection of some inner turmoil.

One drawer of the TV unit was filled with greetings cards: a combination of blank cards and envelopes wrapped in cellophane, along with piles of old birthday and Christmas cards she'd been sent. I carefully lifted out a large stack and carried them over to Angela. She was still part way through sorting through the DVDs.

She collapsed back on the sofa with a groan. 'Oh my gosh. Not more, please. I don't think I can cope with all those cards right now.'

I have a delicate line to tread in my work between injecting purpose, focus and energy and overloading people. I need to be sensitive to their emotional state and not push too hard, while remembering they have employed me to help encourage them to do things they cannot tackle alone.

'It's okay, I understand it's hard work. Let's take five. Shall we have a cuppa?'

Angela headed off to the kitchen and I started to separate out the packets of greetings cards, grouping together the loose blank ones to make her part of the task a little easier. When she returned, carrying a cup of tea for me along with a can of diet Pepsi, we sat down on the sofa together.

'Is it getting a bit too much for you? I know I can be a hard taskmaster. But I push you out of a belief that you can do more than you might be telling yourself.'

'That's okay. I need motivating. It's just all those cards from family over the years – they bring up a lot for me.' Angela reached out and picked up a sweet from a bowl on the coffee table in front of us. 'Don't get me wrong, I have a lot of love for them, but I often feel this massive pressure to, you know, play happy families. Do you know what I mean?'

I nodded.

'It's like, just carry on and act as if everything is hunky-dory,' she continued. 'But there are certain people I just don't want to send cards to, if I'm honest. They always send one to me, of course, and then I end up having to reply late or feeling guilty and ashamed or something. Sorry, I know I'm wittering on a bit, aren't I? And they are only cards ...'

'It's okay, I understand,' I said. 'It's not the cards themselves; it's what they represent for you, the feelings they bring up. It's not easy to play along with these superficial niceties when there are things beneath the surface.'

'Exactly. Things never get talked about, then they send a stupid card, and suddenly everything is meant to be okay.'

She picked up her drink and, with a couple of gulps, finished off the can. Then she crushed it flat against the table and threw it into a wastepaper bin just across from her. It landed in the basket with a loud rattle.

'You know what, apart from the ones from my mum, I'm chucking all those cards away.'

'Okay. If you want to talk more about things, we can take another pause. For now, though, are you ready to get back to work?'

I looked at Angela and noticed she was stifling a yawn.

'How are your energy levels?' I asked. 'I know it's been an intense first morning.'

She turned her eyes down and away from me and reached for another sweet. 'I have to confess, I got up at 4 a.m. to tidy up. I felt I had to do what I could to make things a bit more presentable, or I wouldn't have been able to let you in.'

'You didn't have to do that. I can understand that you might feel embarrassed, that's perfectly natural. But remember there's no judgement here.'

The shame Angela felt was clearly immense, but I realised that the courage she had shown by letting me in the door was even greater. I reflected on this as I carried out a couple of bulging rubbish bags and set them down beside the already full bin on her driveway.

Despite her tiredness, Angela worked really hard to let things go, but I'd be lying if I said it all went smoothly. We cleared a lot that first day, yet there were also several very large 'Keep it' piles. As I was preparing to leave, I noticed that Angela was looking at them ruefully. Now was the time to encourage and acknowledge the positive steps she had taken rather than dwelling on where she'd struggled.

'You've done an amazing job today. Don't worry, we can revisit some of these decisions next time.'

One of the biggest hurdles for Angela was her bedroom, which we began to tackle the next time we met. Just as she had inherited the house from her parents, so she had taken over their bedroom. It still had their old 1960s lampshade, which I encouraged her to change. Angela told me she had moved the bed to a different position to make the room feel like her own, but there certainly seemed to be something going on in this space, as it was the part of the house that Angela most struggled to keep under control.

We started work on the bedroom cupboards, letting go of towels from two generations, bed linen Angela no longer needed, shoes that she didn't wear and clothes that didn't fit. It took a while before we could see the floor, but slowly, with persistent work, we were able to reclaim that room and start to create containers, allocating drawers for tops, jumpers, trousers and underwear.

Tucked away at the back of a drawer, I came across what appeared to be a package of some kind, wrapped in a piece of old bedspread. When she saw me pulling it out, Angela hurried over to me. 'Ah, I'll take that.'

'Ahem, and what exactly is that, young lady?' I joked in a teacherly tone. 'Remember: no stone unturned.'

She chuckled. 'You really are ruthless. It's just a few things I am keeping safe for some relatives. But I guess it wouldn't hurt to open it up and take a look.'

She put the package on the bed and unwrapped it carefully. Inside was a large brown box file, tied up with several wrappings of old-fashioned parcel string. Inside was a collection of old post office and building society pass books, along with some bank statements and cheque stubs.

'I know it seems odd, but this is the best place to hide them,' she said. 'They are safe in here.'

I was struck by a thought that flashed through my head: *What else are you keeping hidden? And are you safe in here?* I didn't say anything, though, as so far all I had were my intuitions.

I encouraged Angela to get the secret documents out of her bedroom. We found a more appropriate and secure home for them downstairs in a lockable filing cabinet I'd suggested she buy to store paperwork.

As we worked, Angela kept saying to me, 'This is huge Helen, this is really huge!' And I could feel the significance for her of the work we were doing, without knowing all the details of what it was. But it was hard going, for sure. Angela still made the occasional playful remark, but overall, her mood and energy had grown more sombre. I'd set her up on a chair by the side of the bed, but she seemed restless and agitated, shifting around in her seat and even getting up and walking out on a couple of occasions. Something in that room felt very heavy, and bringing it back to order wasn't proving easy, so I made a suggestion.

'The energy feels quite stuck in here. Are you open to doing something different and seeing how it works if we reposition a few pieces of furniture?'

Changing the physical arrangement of a room can facilitate a new way of being in a space, so I often envision and share a new way of configuring a room as a way to help create a shift.

'I think it would help practically, but also allow you to see the room differently,' I explained.

'I'm not sure,' said Angela. 'I've had it this way for years.'

'Exactly, that's my point. I think if you do this, you will more fully claim your space and make it your own. Perhaps your bedroom can become your sanctuary, somewhere you can truly rest and be yourself?'

Angela glanced around the room a little nervously. 'I can see where you're coming from, and I suppose it makes sense. But isn't it going to be a lot of work?'

I was again aware of a dilemma. From the perspective of a coach, who had been brought in to help declutter and reorganise her home, I wanted to encourage her to push through her doubt. But I was also becoming increasingly aware of a sense that something in her past may have been manifesting in the room, so the therapist in me wanted to

ensure that Angela was in control and the one making decisions – especially ones that could have deep significance for
her psychologically.

'I can tell that you're a little nervous about my suggestion,
and that's perfectly okay. My feeling is that it might really
contribute to the shift you want to make. Are you willing to
give it a try? If you don't like it, we can easily move things
back to where they were. You'll be surprised how quickly we
can switch things around.'

Angela thought for another moment. As is often the case,
she was probably experiencing a dilemma that, in a sense,
mirrored mine: an inner conflict between a part of her that
wanted to make a change, to move towards those dreams that
she'd shared with me from the very start, and another part
that was focused on keeping her in safely familiar territory.

Then I saw a twinkle in her eye, which I took to be the
adventurous, aspirational part of her, the poet and artist
perhaps. 'Okay. Go for it, girl! Let's do this.'

So, with an energising sense of momentum, we started
to rearrange the room. We began by moving a tall dressing
table that had stood in front of the window and finding a new
home for the portable TV that had sat on top of it. This let
some more light into the room, and also created extra space
for a beautifully upholstered chair that had emerged from
beneath layers of discarded clothes. In the process, we liberated an exercise bike that had been wedged behind the door.
To add a greater sense of peace to the room, we assembled a
lovely altar on the dressing table with all Angela's collected
crystals. When the rearrangement was complete, there was
certainly a different feel, as I'd hoped, although there was
a lot more to do, with two bedside units and the underbed
storage still to go through.

We agreed to do some more work on the room during

our next session, but when we came back to it the following week, it seemed to be in almost as much chaos as it had been before we'd started. I thought to myself: *When I said last week, we could put things back to how they were, I meant the arrangement of furniture, not everything back on the floor.* Perhaps my disappointment registered on my face, because Angela looked a little embarrassed. I immediately felt the sting of self-criticism. My intention is always to be compassionate and non-judgemental, but sometimes I fail. This was one of those occasions. I suspected that part of my frustration came from my growing awareness of how significant the bedroom appeared to be and my sense of having failed Angela.

'I'm sorry, I just seem to have trouble keeping things in order.' Angela looked questioningly at me. 'Why aren't you judging me?'

'It's okay. I understand that deeply engrained habits aren't going to change overnight. And I know you've got a lot to deal with, and this bedroom is clearly particularly tricky for whatever reason. Let's keep clearing space and working through things, shall we?'

It was absolutely right to keep working on the practical side, but I was also clear that for Angela to achieve a long-lasting change, we needed to try and discover what was really going on in that room. My concern was that if this wasn't brought into her awareness and tackled to some extent, the decluttering and reorganisation of the bedroom would become a recurring task. Not only that, but Angela's habits and ability to self-care would not be resolved, either.

'What's the story with the bedroom?' I asked in a gentle tone, picking up a book that I knew for a fact we had put in a bag of charity donations during my last visit. 'Things seem to keep going back to how they were.'

Angela looked a bit sheepish and turned away. 'It is all just too embarrassing. I wish I could keep it tidy.'

'I'm wondering what this room is trying to tell us?'

'What do you mean?'

'Perhaps there's a part of you that has a story to tell, and maybe that part is using the mess as a way of trying to get your attention.'

Angela screwed up her face quizzically, looking confused. 'I'm sorry, I don't really know what you mean. Can you explain a little more?'

'Of course; let me put it slightly differently. If your room was tidy and your life was fully functioning, would you think there was anything wrong? Would you stop, ask questions, reach out for help and listen?'

Angela sat down on the edge of the bed, her arms wrapped around a red velvet cushion she had just picked up from the floor. 'That's a good point. I suppose not.'

'So, maybe what's happening in this room reflects some part of you that is showing up here and communicating to you how she feels. Perhaps she is keeping the room messy to get your attention, so that you'll listen to her?' I gave her a moment to let the thought settle, then continued. 'This may sound a bit out there, but maybe we can improvise a sort of role play where you speak as if *you* were your room?'

'I don't think so,' Angela said, shaking her head and squeezing the cushion more tightly.

'Okay. I'm guessing that maybe that would be too much for you right now?'

'No, it's not that. I understand that it might be helpful to look at any underlying issues that might be there. It's just . . . I really don't know what they might be, or how to start.'

I admired Angela's courage, remembering how difficult it had initially been for me to address some of my most personal challenges. We had established an understanding that I'd help her with more than just the practical issues, and I wanted to gently encourage her.

'I know this sounds a little bonkers, but bear with me. If you're not sure how this might work, how about if I play the part of your room? Would you be willing to explore what I think it might be saying? It's just a game of make-believe we'll play to try and get a little deeper into what's underneath.'

Angela nodded to indicate she understood and was willing.

I crouched down on the floor. 'I am the mess in this room,' I said. 'Look at me! You can't ignore me now. I will trip you up and embarrass you and make you feel horrid.'

Angela laughed. 'That sounds about right.'

I continued: 'I don't care if you don't like me, but I am not going away. I live here too, you know.'

At this point, Angela sat more upright and put down the cushion she'd been holding. Then she took over the role play. 'Yes. Someday you will notice me, and listen to me and take care of me – someday!' Angela's mood shifted here. 'It's true,' she said to me, stepping out of the role play. 'I know I have rejected her too. I've pushed her away, and now I can't live with her.' There were tears in her eyes as she spoke. 'I think I know what this is about. This has been helpful, but I'd like to stop for now.'

'Of course. I can see it's upsetting to look into that place.'

As I'd imagined, it seemed there was certainly something deeper troubling Angela. Clutter can be a burial ground for trauma or loss, and I suspected this might be the case here. We'd had a brief glimpse into what might be going on, and I knew she would probably need some help to unravel it, so I encouraged her to get support to explore things further.

'I can see that whatever this issue is, it's very painful. Let's think about what it is you need to help with this, and what support you could get. I'd strongly encourage you to speak to a psychotherapist or counsellor if you think that will be helpful.'

'I have thought about that before, but I've been scared to open up the past. Maybe now is the right time, though. I'll give it some thought.'

'You do that. There are some things you can do for yourself as well. I'm also wondering about how you could start to listen to this child who communicates by making a mess, to take care of this little self. What sort of things do you think she might find nice to do?'

Angela picked up the cushion again and thought for a while. 'I could go swimming and sit in a hot tub. I love how warm and cosy they are.'

'That sounds great. What else could you do?'

'Maybe I can just cuddle up in bed with this part of myself and listen to some relaxing music.'

'That sounds nice as well. Maybe give it some thought and see what else suggests itself to you.'

'I will do. Thank you – that was really helpful. I guess it's time to move on, though?'

It was near the end of the day, and we had just enough time to clear the decks after the session. I was pleased that Angela was thinking more about ways in which she could nurture herself. With each session, as we cleared more and more clutter from her home, she was showing an increasing interest in this type of self-care.

Later that week, I was sitting at home with my laptop and cat on my lap when I received another email from Angela. It wasn't uncommon for her to send me thoughts and reports between sessions, and she sent this musing in her usual poetic style.

Hi Helen,

I really wanted to write to you after our session last Monday.
So many things have been going through my head
since we rearranged the bedroom and had our talk.
This work is mighty, mighty powerful!
I'm holding this mental image of blossom on a tree.
Fresh green buds, bright blue sky.
I have a sense of ease, of peace and connection.
It's hard to describe, but there's this feeling
of a gentle, compassionate and peaceful order.
I've rarely had a feeling of flow like this in my life before.
No longer the same sense of separation,
of a split between my home, my body, my soul, and nature.
This may not last, I know.
I may awake tomorrow to the return of deep-blue darkness
and grief.
But this morning, I see clarity, space, possibilities.
The inner critic quiet, I can relax in this place, in this body.
I feel profound gratitude and the beginning of self-love
speaking in the absence of that old self-hate.
This is deep, Helen. That's all I keep saying ... feeling.
This is deep stuff!
Thank you for your compassion, which is holding me.

I was really moved to hear of the powerful internal shifts
that were clearly taking place for her. I was also touched by
her obvious appreciation of the work we were doing. In this
very intimate journey we were undertaking together, where
I was privileged to have been given the trust to guide her
towards a happier home, she was showing me how important
and how deep this work can be, how transformational and,
potentially, how life-changing.

After another couple of sessions, it felt like we were making more sustainable progress in the house. As more stuff was unpacked and either reorganised or taken out of the house in the form of recycling, rubbish or charity donations, Angela seemed to be becoming more relaxed, positive and energised. She told me she had found a therapist, who she'd been seeing once a week, and that it was really helping.

I often leave 'homework' for clients, so they can maintain some of the momentum we establish on the day. So, I suggested that Angela sorted and categorised her photos between sessions. I knew this wasn't going to be an easy task. During our first session, I had discovered a large archive box full of photos in the back of a storage unit in the living room. Over the weeks, we had added a lot of other photos gathered from various places around the house. There were photos of her and the rest of her family, pictures from her childhood as well as from college and work: different parts of her life, all mixed up. This felt fragmented and scattered. Often when people have things jumbled up like this, it is because they want to keep themselves from seeing something clearly, and this reinforced my sense that there was something in her past that Angela was trying to bury. Was this an attempt to lose painful parts of her life in the chaos, to consign certain memories to the depths of her unconscious? Somehow, collecting them all into one place felt to me symbolic of her beginning to integrate her scattered sense of self. I hoped that in her own time, and with the right support, Angela could begin to put herself and her memories back in order.

This gathering of things from all over a house is like finding bits of jigsaw that have got lost, or putting parts of a child's toy back into the box. I find myself doing this a lot, and it often reminds me of games I loved as a child: bringing all the pieces of the puzzle together and feeling satisfied as they click into place.

In between sessions, I got another email from Angela:

Helen, I felt like a giddy teenager when I came downstairs
this morning.
I pinched myself. Was it a dream?
I just cannot get over the transformation of the house.
The energy, the vibe . . .
How I feel when I enter it: proud, calm, at peace.

If these walls could talk.
What they have witnessed, what they have held,
Now starting to be released into a new space.
No wonder I can't sleep . . .
Thank you.

But those photos, man, it's too much, too intense.
So up close and personal.
A whole lifetime of memories condensed in a box.
Maybe we should let them be?
But I know they have to be sorted . . . help!

Angela was letting me know that the task I had set her
was too much for her to do alone and that she needed
more support. And so, I suggested that we used some of
our next session to sort them out together. She responded
simply: 'Maybe.'

As I sat in heavy traffic on the way to Angela's the following week, I recalled our email exchange and wondered if she
might choose to avoid dealing with what was clearly difficult
for her. However, when I arrived, the large box of photos was
sitting on the table.

'Okay, I'm ready,' she said, with a forced smile. 'You really
mean it when you say no stone left unturned.'

It's always a difficult thing to sort through photos. Each set, its own little folder of memories. With old photos, I find the strips of film negatives can be even more evocative, containing as they do the actual physical imprint of light from that past moment. As you open and pull out each batch of pictures, it's like another chapter of the past is exposed. You are never quite sure what you are going to find, what is going to come up. I suggest that people don't spend too long looking at the pictures, as it is easy to get lost in memories and drawn into the past. Not that there's anything wrong with nostalgia; it's just not the best way to sort through them, as it can end up taking weeks that way. So, we started to work our way through the box quite quickly, taking out the photos and spreading them out on the table, sorting them into sets.

I could tell it wasn't an easy process for Angela, but we were making steady progress. She seemed fine with the more recent photos. Opening one batch and looking through them, she began to giggle to herself. 'Helen, you have to see these from the work Christmas party five years ago.' She handed me a couple of the pictures. 'What was I wearing?!'

It must have been a fancy-dress party, as Angela was dressed in a hilarious Bo-Peep costume, surrounded by a group of very drunk-looking colleagues dressed as various farmyard animals.

'Oh yes, very stylish. Are you sure you don't want to frame this one?' I teased.

Whenever we came across any older photos, a blue mood seemed to descend, however. Still, we persisted, sorting the images into categories that made sense for her. An hour or so into the process, I noticed that Angela had gone quiet. She was just sitting there, staring blankly at a photo she had picked up. After a few more moments, she turned it around and held it up to show me. It was of a beautiful young woman of around thirty, who was fit and healthy-looking.

'This was me.' She took a deep breath and paused. Then: 'This was me before he did that thing.'

She lowered the photo and made nervous but very deliberate eye contact with me. I think she wanted both to check that I understood the significance of what had happened, and to reassure herself that it was safe to continue. I returned her gaze and looked steadily at her to show her I would be able to contain whatever she wanted to tell me about. After a short while, I added a little nod of empathy to let her know I was with her.

'Do you want to tell me about it?' I said.

'Yes, I think I do. It's time for someone to know how much this hurt me.' She put the photo face-down on the table between us and paused for a moment before continuing. 'It was on my birthday, as I remember it. All the memories came flooding back, reminding me of all the times before, when I was growing up. In the days and weeks that followed, a doorway to my past seemed to have been flung open. I couldn't stop crying, and I started to remember things I didn't want to remember. Things that I guess I'd decided were best left buried, out of sight and out of mind.'

I felt a pain in my heart as the implications of her words sunk in. It was a deeply personal and difficult revelation to make, and naturally I was saddened, but not exactly shocked. I'd had a sense all along that there was something significant beneath the surface. Along with my great empathy for Angela, I was also very moved that she had shown such trust in me. In inviting me into her home and allowing me access to her most private and intimate spaces, she had also allowed me close to a place of trauma in her psyche. And as our connection and trust had grown, she had gradually become willing to open up and let me see into this deeply personal place.

'I'm so sorry, Angela. I can't imagine how that must have been for you.'

We sat together in silence while Angela cried.

After a few minutes, she took another deep breath, turned the photo over and looked at it again.

'I feel so ashamed of this, but I needed to tell someone. I realise that I can't keep hiding. In fact, I don't want to keep this secret anymore. The past needs to come out in the open, and then perhaps I can begin to move on and feel a bit better.'

'There's absolutely no reason for you to feel shame. You did nothing wrong, nothing at all. The shame belongs to the one who caused this hurt, not to you. You've carried this for a long time. And you're right, maybe it is time to deal with it now. To move towards forgiving yourself and letting go of any guilt or responsibility you feel.'

Looking down again at the photo that still lay on the table between us, I was struck by the young woman in the picture, who looked fit and confident.

'Tell me about *this* Angela,' I said.

She dried her eyes with a tissue. 'I was really happy then. I was fit, eating healthy food, doing a lot of meditation. Life was going well, and I was feeling good about myself.'

I could tell Angela was still fighting back the tears, and her voice wavered as she continued. 'I had moved away from home and made a break. I was starting a new life. For those few years, I felt I had really found myself. My studies, my writing and all the self-development work I'd taken on, really helped me to begin defining who I was. And then ...' She paused and reached out to take a sweet from the three-tiered cake stand that stood in the centre of the table. 'After that day, something in me snapped and my whole life seemed to come crashing down around me. I really started to hate myself. I couldn't stop thinking about what I must have done to make it happen again. It was just too much to deal with, and I think part of me decided to push it all inside. To bury it all for all these years. Look at me now; I'm a size eighteen.' She picked up the photo again. 'Where on earth did the person in this picture go?'

'She is still there, I'm sure. I see and hear her, especially in your writing.'

Angela began to cry again, and while I wanted to be there for her, I also sensed she might appreciate some time and space.

'I can see this is really hard for you. Thank you for trusting me with this. Why don't you take a little moment with yourself? I'll go and make us another cup of tea.'

I wondered whether to take the conversation any further, but I felt that the relationship I had with Angela was very strong. We had built up a lot of trust, and I could tell she was comfortable with me, so it felt safe to continue and put off the practical process of decluttering the photos.

Angela put her head in her hands. 'I still feel so ashamed.'

I quickly reassured her again. 'No, no, no. It's not your shame. You didn't do anything wrong. Absolutely nothing at all. You were a child.'

Angela cried and cried, and I just sat with her. Along with the sadness and grief, I felt that Angela was relieved to no longer have to carry so much of this secret. I hoped that this might be the beginning of a journey to set herself free. I knew that she had a good therapist who could help her untangle exactly what had happened and how it had impacted her life.

After some time had passed and the tears had subsided, I checked in with Angela.

'How are you doing? Shall we stop now and leave the rest of the photos for next time?'

'No. He isn't going to stop me,' said Angela. 'We keep going.'

I was really pleased she had made that choice, because I didn't want to remove myself from her right then. I wanted her to know we still had a connection, and that I remained there for her.

Angela really was one of the bravest clients I had worked with. Despite the trauma that had now become so apparent, she had such resilience and determination.

So, we finished our tea and continued to go through the photos. One of the first pictures we came across after the break was one of Angela as a young girl, cute in a white dress, on her way to church, perhaps.

'He took that one. It can definitely go,' said Angela, putting it far away from the others on the table.

As I looked at the image, there seemed such vulnerability, innocence and loneliness in the girl's eyes. And as we continued, further photos of this lost little girl appeared and were added to the pile. No wonder Angela could not face this task alone.

'What do you want to do with those pictures?' I asked.

'I want to burn them.'

'That sounds like a good idea,' I said, 'but can I suggest you do one thing first?'

'What's that?'

'Show them to your therapist when you talk to her about all this. And then, when you feel that this part of you has been fully heard, maybe that would be the time to burn the photos.'

'Okay. If that's what you suggest, I'll think about it. It feels hard, but I trust you.'

After the powerful emotions that had accompanied Angela's revelations, there was something comforting in returning to the practicalities of sorting the photos. Thankfully, most of those we looked through were of happier times. We were both emotionally drained, and the simple task of categorising the various images into piles felt quite soothing.

As we tidied up at the end of the afternoon, I contemplated what Angela had told me and recalled the role play we had done in her bedroom. Of course, beds and bedrooms were going to be difficult for her. The feeling of heaviness that often arose now made more sense and confirmed my guess that she had been using the clutter to bury something significant.

A few weeks later, I was at home hanging up some freshly laundered sheets when I got a phone call from Angela.

'Helen, he just died!' she blurted out.

'Who died? What?'

'He did, him, that man. I just got a call, he died last night! I can't quite believe it. I feel like I'm free. I probably should be feeling sad or guilty, but I just feel free! I don't have to tell any more lies. I don't have to make excuses not to take his calls. I don't have to defend my right not to let him come and stay. I don't have to pretend anymore.'

'Wow. It's quite amazing that this has happened right at this time. I'm hearing that it feels quite liberating.'

'Yeah, it's so weird. I've spoken to a few people and everyone is grieving. He was so charismatic, so loved. But I knew the darker side, and *I* am celebrating. This is so big, such an amazing gift. Who'd have thought that clearing my clutter and moving some furniture around would be the start of so much change? I said this was deep shit, but it is scary shit too!'

Naturally, this news had made a big impact on Angela. We talked for a while and, as she told me more, she certainly sounded lighter. But I also sensed a lot of anger and sadness rising to the surface, so I encouraged her to arrange an extra session with her therapist later that week.

The following Monday was the final session we had booked together. Angela was still energised by the events that had unfolded, but her mood was more subdued than it had been on the phone. Towards the end of the day, we talked a little about what had happened and its impact on her. Along with the feelings and thoughts to process, Angela had to carefully consider what she would do about attending the funeral.

'I feel like I've got a huge choice to make: do I go to the funeral or not?'

'That is a big decision, how are you feeling about it?'

'Well, I discussed it with Mandy during our last therapy session. She said that maybe it might help me mark an ending and close that chapter of my life.'

'Okay, and what do you think?'

'I think she's probably right. I think I'm going to do it.'

We completed the work in the living room, which was the last space still to clear, organising the mountains of CDs ready to be digitised, and even trimming back a few of the overgrown pot plants. As I was packing away my bag, I paused to survey the now almost-unrecognisable room.

I pulled out my phone. 'I'll send you some before-and-after pictures so you can see how far you've come.'

It was great to see that the once overloaded bookshelves now had space for some treasured ornaments. Pride of place went to a couple of smiling photos of Angela as a young girl with her mother. She had bought some beautiful silver frames for these, and my heart lifted as I saw them. There seemed something deeply powerful represented by this apparently simple act. I felt it symbolised that Angela was now able to give her vulnerable inner child the safe haven she craved – and also that she no longer felt she had to keep that part of herself hidden away.

I gave Angela a long hug as I was leaving. 'You've done an amazing job here. You are very welcome to stay in touch. I love hearing how people are doing.'

I am deeply indebted to Angela. My time with her reinforced my belief that clearing space and shifting things around can sometimes bring about a profound shift in someone's life.

A month or so later, I had an email from Angela.

> So much has changed, Helen.
> I went to the funeral in the end, like we discussed.
> I wanted to see him in the ground. Buried for good.
> And for myself to be out there, for the healing to continue.
> To show and know that I survived.
>
> Afterwards, back to his old house for the wake.
> Hot sun. Cold drinks and sandwiches in the back garden.
> What a head-fuck. Everyone laughing, talking about how great he was.
> Well, not everyone. Not me.
> I went inside, into his tumbledown house, to leave a message.
> I wrote on a tiny piece of paper, rolled it up and pushed it into a crack in the wall:
> 'You did wrong.'

As I read this, I thought to myself: *Wow, what an amazing woman. What a way to reclaim your power and place the responsibility where it belongs.*

\*

If you have been deeply impacted by some traumatic event in your past, I'd strongly recommend you seek help from a counsellor or psychotherapist. This can be hugely helpful. There are contact details for some reputable organisations in the Resources section (page 285).

Are you aware of a sense that something seems to be blocking you from moving forward in life? It may be that difficult or painful experiences from your past are behind this. They could be expressing themselves indirectly or in a way of which you aren't entirely conscious. You might find it helpful to think about how the content and configuration of your home could be mirroring these aspects of your inner life. Your home may be trying to tell you something, so use your intuition to listen for the symbolic meaning and then take action. For example, much as some people discover that perhaps they have put on weight as a way to make themselves less desirable and avoid intimacy, others will accumulate clutter to shield themselves from the world. Ask yourself, what might be making you reluctant to let anyone in? How might you be using clutter to barricade yourself away and create a place of safety?

A key part of overcoming an impasse in your home life is realising you are stuck, and being able to reach out for help as Angela did. This reaching out will be different for each person. For you, it might mean opening up to a trusted friend, joining a self-help group, or contacting a professional therapist or coach. Whichever you choose, it's important to know that you don't have to deal with everything alone. Help is out there, and if you decide you need it, I hope you find the care that works for you.

# Grounded by Mum
## at fifty-three

Jan's life had come to a standstill. I received a call from her in mid-November, as the last leaves were falling and we were moving into winter. My work tends to quieten down at that time of year, picking up again in the New Year when people have got through the joys and stresses of Christmas and are making resolutions for change. But Jan seemed very eager to get going. I looked at my phone after getting in from a session with another client and noticed several missed calls from a number I didn't recognise. Just as I was closing the front door behind me, the phone rang again.

'Oh great, you're there,' came a somewhat flustered voice. 'I called a couple of times already. I'm sorry to bother you, but I'm getting a bit desperate. I really hope you can help me sort out my flat. I have to find a way to clear some space, but I just seem incapable of making time to actually tackle it.'

I wanted to help ease this caller's anxiety, so spoke slowly and with empathy. 'What is your name?'

'It's Jan.' I could sense her relaxing and slowing down a little.

'Okay, Jan. I can hear you are struggling. That's okay. It's perfectly normal, and that's what I'm here for. I'm happy to talk about how I might be able to help. Perhaps you could start by painting me a picture of your situation? What's going on in your home?'

'I just feel overwhelmed. I live with my elderly mother, and it's as if I don't have room for anything anymore. Everything seems to be piling up, and it's getting me down. In fact, everything is getting me down, but if I could just deal with this bit of my life, I think I might be able to cope better ...'

'It sounds as if you are under quite a bit of pressure, Jan. I'm guessing there are a lot of demands on you.'

'I suppose there are. But, like I said, if I could just deal with all this clutter, it will give me space to think and get clear in my head.'

Her words – and her tone – were carrying a lot that probably would need to be unpacked. Usually, on my initial call with clients, I try to dig a little deeper and get a clearer picture of what the underlying issues might be. But with Jan, my sense was that this wasn't going to happen over the phone. She sounded too flustered, and had, so far, only asked me for practical support, so I decided to focus on that. I checked my diary. As I'd had a cancellation at the start of the week, I was relatively free.

'As it happens, I've a day available tomorrow,' I said. 'How do you feel about meeting then?'

'Oh yes, that would be wonderful. Mum will be out, so tomorrow would be perfect, actually. Thank you so much.'

The sense of relief at the other end of the line was tangible. After discussing my fees and a few practical details, we agreed I'd visit her the following morning – and I added a mental note about Jan's comment regarding her mother to the other things I needed to be mindful of.

Jan lived in Putney, south-west London. Her flat was on the ground floor of a nice-looking red-brick terraced house. The two-storey terrace extended either side of Jan's, and the style was repeated in the houses opposite. This, along with the wide pavements, meant the street had an open, light feel. The house itself was quite close to the pavement. Freshly painted black railings enclosed a small paved front garden filled with a collection of neatly trimmed evergreen shrubs in large pots. A small pile of swept leaves lay beside the low brick wall that separated the garden from the street. Along one side of the short, mosaic-tiled walkway that led to the front door stood an evenly spaced row of four standard bay trees in ornate planters.

Jan, a short lady in her early fifties, greeted me with a smile. We made our way along the short entrance hall and into the flat. I wondered if there would be a contrast between the neat, shared entrance and the state of the flat behind Jan's front door, but once inside, it was immediately apparent that this space was also pretty tidy. The rooms were well-proportioned and nicely laid out, if quite full. The flat was fairly narrow at the front, but extended back a long way. At the rear, it opened out into a bright garden room that spanned the full width of the flat. A pair of French windows opened on to a delightful walled garden with a small patio area and beds containing some beautiful winter-flowering shrubs. A mature apple tree stood in the centre of a well-manicured lawn, with a few bright yellow leaves that had clung on through autumn, along with a couple of apples that I guessed had been missed in that year's harvest.

I turned my attention back to the interior. At first glance, I couldn't see much clutter. Yes, there were a few piles on the sideboard and things spilling out of some cupboards, but I wondered why Jan had sounded so desperate when she'd called me. I trusted that this would emerge naturally during what I call the discovery session: the in-depth conversation I have with all my new clients to start to find out what the underlying issues are beneath the piles, the chaos or the 'stuckness' they feel in their life.

We sat down with a cup of tea in a pair of wicker chairs by the window overlooking the garden.

'It's a lovely flat. How long have you lived here?'

'About ten years. I moved in after my divorce. Before that, we had a lovely old house a few streets along.'

As soon as we began to talk, details of Jan's past life and current troubles came pouring out. I had the impression she had been holding in a lot that she wanted to share with me. We talked about the years of marriage, the ending of the business she had run with her husband, his series of affairs, the divorce, the children leaving the nest, the old house – their beautiful family home. As each subject was opened and we began to examine it, more and more emerged.

From a married life that seemed characterised by expansiveness, via strife when much of what she held dear had fallen away, Jan now found herself in a two-bedroom flat with a permanent fellow resident, her elderly mother.

'Mum has quite bad arthritis and had a hip replacement a few years back that didn't really go that well. There are good days, when she is able to get up and about. But she often spends days at a time in bed watching daytime TV while I bring her cups of tea.' As Jan told me this, she began to cry softly.

I handed her a tissue. 'That must be hard for both of you.'

There is often a simple and profound benefit that people gain from finally being heard. This can be as important as any of the practical work that I do with them.

'It's awful to say, but I feel like a prisoner in my own home. Mum just needs so much of my attention.' Jan dried her tears and started to collect herself again.

'Where is your mum today?'

'She's playing cards at the local bridge club. She goes there every Wednesday, thank goodness. It is the only time I seem to get any space to myself.'

'I'm guessing it must feel a bit like being a grounded teenager again,' I offered, and again, with this subject opened, there was more that Jan needed to tell me, this time about her childhood and her current relationship with her brother.

'I was the oldest of two children, and was always the one who took on the responsible role. My brother isn't around, and has kind of washed his hands of Mum. He doesn't say anything, but it's like he thinks because I'm living alone, I can take care of her.'

'Caring can very much be seen as the traditional province of women.'

'Exactly – and my brother has some very traditional views, I assure you,' said Jan, with a knowing look.

I really felt the weight this woman was carrying, the suffocation and the grief. It was clear to me that we needed to honour the losses Jan had experienced in her life – there were many – as well as addressing the unwanted additions.

'I know sometimes life just doesn't seem fair,' I said. 'It takes away things that we value and want and leaves us with things we don't. But this is where you can start to take control, on the smallest, most basic level, beginning with the clutter in your home. And as you think about what you want to keep and what you are ready to let go of, and start to re-organise it all, I think you'll find it will help you process some of what you have shared with me. But let's start to deal with the accumulation of possessions and just see what happens.'

We booked some sessions into my diary, fitting in around 'mum-sitters', and then started to work on the flat. We began in the garden room. Along one wall was a tall set of built-in cupboards, and I began by opening the doors and pulling out some drawers to get a better sense of the scale of the work. Jan's home fell into the category of what I call 'tidy clutter', meaning that there was a hell of a lot of stuff neatly packed away in storage boxes and in every available space. To a visitor, everything looked pretty tidy on the surface, but open a cupboard and inside were stacks of containers, each one packed full. Occasionally, the contents were carefully categorised, but the majority seemed to be collections of random bits and pieces.

I pulled out three shoe boxes and a large plastic container from the lower shelf. Opening the first shoe box, I found it was home to a seemingly haphazard selection of objects: pens and pencils, bottles of vitamins, a brass cigarette lighter, a tape measure, nail files and clippers, paint charts and carpet samples. The next two boxes contained old letters and photographs, piles and piles of them. And I could see that the clear plastic container was filled with multi-coloured glass beads and jewellery-making equipment, unmade creative expressions. I carried the boxes over to the table where I had set Jan up with some of my decision cards: Keep, Recycle, Memory Box, Bin, Action, Don't Know.

'Okay, what I want you to do is to simply take out each item in turn and allocate it to one of the piles. Follow your gut instinct. If you are spending too much time on anything and really aren't sure, just place it on the "Don't know" pile for now. The most important thing is to maintain momentum.'

Jan nodded and began to diligently sort the items as I'd suggested.

Storing things away can be a great way to create space in your home, yet somehow the presence of an over-full cupboard is very different to that of one that has some spare capacity. Even when stored out of sight, the items seem to have a presence and psychological weight that pervades our perception and experience of the room. And it's not just the quantity; the way they are organised can also have an impact. Part of our psyche seems to have to work to hold an inventory of what is there. This is undoubtably a relic of our biological past.

Out in the garden, I noticed a squirrel running busily about, burying acorns in the flowerbeds. If you watch them carefully, you see how much attention they pay to where they've buried their stashes of supplies. Their very survival, of course, can depend on how well they recall where they have secreted away the food, so there's an evolutionary value to that capacity to retain an inner inventory. But, as with everything, it comes at a cost. The squirrel has to rush around, busily maintaining its store, checking and remembering where each acorn is buried. Our minds pay a similar price. This is where the value of a good organisational system comes in. When you know that all your light bulbs, spare plugs and fuses are in the lower right-hand drawer next to the fridge, you don't have to allocate headspace to remembering that a specific one is in the toolbox and another somewhere under the sink. I call this the planting plan or a mind map: a way of helping my clients to know how to find their way around their home and where to locate things. Many of my clients long for this kind of order, and often refer to the saying 'a place for everything, and everything in its place'. They know that they lose time and mental wellbeing looking for items such as lost keys, and can often end up buying several versions of the same thing because they simply cannot remember where they put them.

Throughout the day, as I opened further cupboards, pulled out more boxes and began to unpack them, the scale of the task became clearer. Jan was pretty decisive when it came to making choices about her things, though, so we made good progress. In the afternoon session, I pulled out yet another plastic storage box, put it on the floor and began again to decant the contents on to the table.

'Oh, God!' said Jan. 'Not more photos. I think we can just put that one back as it is.'

When people say, 'We don't need to go through that one,' it is a red flag. I generally ask them to go through everything. While it may be that someone has carefully packed a box and knows exactly what it contains, not going through it can also be a strategy to avoid looking at things that they are resistant to dealing with.

'You've done brilliantly, Jan. Why don't we keep going and finish this last one? "No stone left unturned," as I like to say. Once boxes go unopened, and are put back where they were, it may be years until they are looked at again. So, it's important to grasp the opportunity to reassess them while things are in flux.'

'I guess you're right.'

I was pleased. In those 'out of bounds' areas or containers, important things often lie, waiting to be processed.

Jan began to leaf through the photos. 'These are from the years just after my divorce. Oh wow! This is me in New Zealand with my childhood friend Sue.'

She handed me the picture. A younger Jan was standing in walking gear on a stunning mountainside, with a broad smile on her face.

'It looks like you had a great time.'

I looked up at Jan and saw she was gazing quite wistfully out into the garden. After a few moments, she turned her attention back to me and the room. 'Yes, life seemed so full of possibilities back then.' She picked up another pile of photos. Underneath it was a walking map and a copy of *The Rough*

*Guide to New Zealand*. 'I was actually thinking of moving out there. The trip was meant to be me testing the waters, so to speak.'

'It sounds like it was a time when you were striking out for independence,' I said. 'What made you decide not to move?'

'My dad passed away, so I had to put all my plans on hold for a while.'

'Oh, I'm sorry. So, these pictures must bring up painful memories as well.'

Jan shrugged in a gesture of resignation. 'It's just another of those things that life hits you with. I had to cut my trip short and head back home to be with Mum. It wasn't long after that she moved in here.'

'I hope you don't mind that I encouraged you to open up that box.'

'No, that's fine. It's good to see that picture with Sue. And there are things in there that I don't really need any more. That map and guidebook can go in the bin, for sure. No chance I'm ever going to use them.'

'Maybe not, but it sounds like that was a significant time for you. Perhaps these are good candidates for your memory box?'

I had set aside one of the plastic containers to serve as a temporary memory box, where Jan could collect meaningful or sentimental items that she wanted to hold on to. She decided to put the map in there, along with the photo on the mountain. The piles of other photos were slimmed down and returned to the container, which now had room to take other photos and freed up space elsewhere.

We'd been decluttering for several hours by now, and the room was quite a mess at this point in the process, as it often is. There were empty boxes stacked up in one corner, piles of old newspaper that had been wrapped around ornaments, bags of recycling and items to be donated. And, of course, the more manageable piles of things that were being kept, ready to go into new homes around the flat. In order to get to a new order, I usually find I need to take the client through a stage of chaos. I have to hold a vision of how everything will be organised and know that it will all fall into place at the end of the day.

As I completed reorganising the greatly thinned-down contents of the large wall unit and prepared to leave that day, there was a tangible sense of a different energy in the room. On the surface, the cupboards looked just the same as they had when they were filled with clutter. But there is some way that the physical and mental space created in the process changes the mood of a room. Knowing that there is space brings with it a sense of ease and possibility. I like to think of it as the silence between the notes in a piece of music. The spaces in between are so important. Without them, you just get noise; but with them, you get music.

Jan stood up and surveyed the work we had done. 'Wow, things feel so different.'

I put away the last few things, and together we carried half a dozen bags of charity donations along the corridor to put them in the boot of Jan's car. I find it's a good strategy to get things out of the house quickly once decisions have been made, in order to avoid any temptation to revisit them.

As we opened the boot and began to carefully load the bags into the car, a black cab pulled over to the kerb outside the flat.

'That's Mum!' Jan said anxiously, dropping the bags she was carrying and hurrying over to help her mother out of the back. The strikingly dressed elderly lady who emerged from the taxi didn't quite match the image of a frail, dependent person I'd constructed from Jan's description. Jan's mother

wore a boldly patterned blouse beneath a rather stylish wool-
len coat, along with a bright-cerise silk scarf that billowed in
the wind. Jan helped her mother step down from the vehicle,
but once she had both feet on the ground, she moved determinedly on alone towards the front of the flat. She walked
slowly and a little unsteadily with the help of a stick, slightly
favouring one leg.

'My goodness, we had a devil of a time getting across the
bridge this afternoon,' she said to Jan, who reached into the
back of the cab to retrieve a couple of large shopping bags.

Her mother called after her. 'Don't forget that blue one
on the seat.'

Jan had already grabbed the bags and was paying the
cabbie in cash from a purse she had pulled from her mother's handbag.

'Ah, you must be Helen. Nice to meet you. I'm Margaret,'
Jan's mother said.

She put out her hand. 'I trust you're helping my daughter
to put her house in order. I jolly well hope she hasn't thrown
away any of my birds.'

'Of course not; we've kept any of your things to one side
for you to take a look at. Can I help you, Margaret?'

She waved me away. 'No, don't make a fuss, dear. I'll
manage.' She turned to Jan, who had joined her by the front
door. 'You've got all those bags, haven't you?' she said.

I rearranged some of the bags of charity donations in the
boot of Jan's car to make room for the ones she'd dropped,
then closed it and headed back into the flat to see if Jan and
her mother needed any assistance.

The pair of them were still little more than halfway along
the corridor.

'Here, give me those bags, Jan,' I said.

Together we carefully steered Margaret into the garden

room and towards the dining chair at the head of the table, where she gratefully sat herself down with a groan.

'Phew, made it. Time for a nice cuppa, I think.'

Jan hurried off to the kitchen. 'Yes, I'll put the kettle on, Mum.'

'Getting around is not getting any easier, I can tell you,' Margaret said to me.

She pulled a copy of the *Telegraph* from one of her bags and set it down on the table, open at the partially completed crossword page. 'My hip's been giving me hell this afternoon. It's no fun getting old, I can tell you, my dear.'

'I know, time catches up with all of us, doesn't it? My mum's a similar age to you.' I put the last of the cards back into my decluttering bag, along with some pens and sticky notes we'd been using.

'You're not leaving already are you, dear? Why don't you join us for a cup of tea? I picked up a cake from the bakery on the corner, they're usually rather good.'

I was eager to get on the road and beat the worst of the traffic, but by the sound of it, it had already started to build up on Putney Bridge. I looked to Jan, who had come back from the kitchen carrying a tempting-looking cake. I didn't want to intrude.

'You're very welcome to stay,' she said. 'I'm sure Mum would love to talk to you. I'll make a pot for three.'

The prospect of a slice of that cake did appeal, and I was also interested to get to know Jan's mother. Jan hadn't said much about her as we'd worked, but she was clearly a powerful presence.

'Excellent! You must tell me what you've been up to.' Margaret smiled, picking up the paper. 'Now, what's a name for a horse-drawn carriage? Six letters: H, something, something, S, something, something. So, what's my daughter been telling you about me?' she continued, and then, in a quieter tone as Jan returned to the kitchen. 'I do worry that I'm a burden on her. It's true I can't do a lot of things for myself, but she does worry so. I have my bad days, but I'm not helpless, you know.'

'I can see that, Margaret,' I replied, wondering what a bad day was like for her. 'Is it "hansom"?'

'Is who handsome?'

'No, the crossword: hansom cab.'

'Yes, of course. Pass me that pen, will you?'

I handed Margaret a silver ballpoint from a pot that stood on a place mat in the centre of the table. 'How long have you lived here?' I asked.

'Oh, since not long after my Fred died. It's five years this month.' She filled in the missing letters with a slow and shaky hand. 'I loved having my own place, but it felt so empty without him, and everyone kept telling me I couldn't really manage on my own. Right, that means twelve across starts with an M.' She scanned down the list of clues with her finger. 'You'll know this one, Jan: Belgian surrealist painter, eight letters.'

Jan had returned carrying a tray, on which stood a trio of mugs and a large teapot emblazoned with blue tits, a robin and various other garden birds.

'Ah, wonderful! You used my favourite pot. We don't have a lot of visitors, so we rarely get to use that one, Helen. Cake?'

It had been nice to meet Jan and her mother. As I drove slowly home, the traffic not having cleared as I'd hoped, I had plenty of time to process the events of the day. I was struck by the contrast between Jan's description of her mother as needy, and the strong-minded woman I had just met. What exactly was going on in the relationship between them, and their relationship with the space they shared? I guessed that

Jan had bought the flat as a place for a single woman. It was certainly a bit tight for two people, and in order to accommodate the needs of her mother, Jan had probably decided to cram quite a lot of her possessions away. Did this mirror the ways in which she was also setting aside her own needs? The situation was clearly complex, but I trusted that the process we had started would shed more light on things, and perhaps help bring some resolution.

We had our second session the following week. Margaret was at her bridge club again, and Jan and I cracked on with the work that needed to be done. This time, we focused on the far end of the room, where Jan had squeezed in the desk from which she ran her business. We greatly slimmed down the contents of her filing cabinet and were able to relocate a lot of her client files from the desk surface into the space we'd liberated in the wall units the previous week. The day was fairly uneventful, but Jan was quite engaged with the process and embraced the opportunity to make some extra room to work.

The week of our next session, however, I got a call from Jan. She sounded alarmed and distressed. 'I'm sorry, Helen, I have to cancel tomorrow. Mum has had a fall.'

'Oh, no! Is she okay? What happened?'

'She decided to go out into the garden on her own this morning when I was making breakfast. It was still a little frosty and she slipped, fell down the steps and hit her head. The ambulance seemed to take forever to arrive, and then they decided to take her into hospital for a scan.'

'I'm so sorry to hear that, that is worrying. How is she doing?'

'They said she would be okay, thank goodness. Nothing broken, but she has some nasty bruises and mild shock, which is why they thought it best to keep her in overnight.'

'That must be a relief. I expect it was quite a shock for you, too. Are you taking care of yourself?'

'Oh, I'm fine. I'm back at home, you know how strict they are with visiting hours. I just feel so guilty.'

'Why? It sounds like a complete accident.'

'I don't know, I just think I should have been more careful and watched her.'

'You can't be there twenty-four-seven, Jan.'

'I know that, but she seems so vulnerable and needs a lot of care. More than I can give, maybe. I've spoken to her health and social care teams so many times, but every request for help has fallen on deaf ears. They say she isn't in enough need, and we can't afford a private care home, so that isn't an option. In any case, every time I've raised the idea with Mum, she has met it with a clear "No". Anyway, let's not go into that now.'

I felt great empathy for Jan and her mother, who seemed trapped in what appeared to be a lose-lose scenario. Margaret was lonely and unstimulated, and increasingly needing full-time care, more than Jan could provide. Jan, meanwhile, felt trapped: she needed to rebuild her life and grow her business, but was left without the time and resources to do so, and also seemed to struggle to prioritise her own needs.

'It sounds like a really difficult position to be in. If you want to talk it through, we can chat next time we meet.'

'Thank you. And I'm sorry again about having to cancel.'

'Don't be silly. Just let me know when you're ready to start again. I hope Margaret makes a swift recovery – and remember to take care of yourself, too.'

I really felt for Margaret and Jan, but hadn't been entirely surprised when I heard the news. Her mother had looked quite unsteady when I met her, and I know things like this sometimes happen when you start stirring up the energy of your home and your life and begin to instigate change. I've repeatedly witnessed how things start to change in people's lives when they begin to deal with the clutter and start clearing space: making room for their future, as I like to call it.

A week or so later, Jan called me again to say that she'd like to recommence our work on her flat.

'How is your mum?' I asked.

'She's okay, thank you. It was only an overnight stay in the hospital, thank goodness. She has decided to go away for a couple of weeks and stay with my uncle. He's driving up from the south coast to pick her up this weekend.'

There was a sense of relief in her voice that I imagined came from a combination of her mother being okay and the prospect of a break from her caring duties.

When I arrived for our next session, Jan's demeanour was definitely more relaxed. As I followed her into the garden room, she asked, 'Can I take you up on your offer to talk about Mum before we start, Helen?'

She made us each a cup of tea and we sat down at the dining table.

'I really notice how much less stress I feel with Mum not here, and knowing that her brother and his wife are taking care of her,' Jan began. She settled back into her chair.

'I can see that, Jan. It's quite noticeable. Don't underestimate how much emotional pressure comes from feeling so responsible for her all the time.'

Jan leaned forward and took a biscuit from the Willow pattern plate she'd set down on the table between us. 'I think I'm beginning to acknowledge that it is probably too much for one person on their own, especially when I'm trying to get my business off the ground at the same time,' she said. 'Maybe now is not the time to be doing that. What do you think?'

'I understand, of course, that you want to make sure your

mum is properly cared for. But do you think that putting your business on hold is going to solve the issue? You said the other day that she needed more professional care. Are you going to be able to give her that, even if you aren't working on your business?'

'She does, Helen. It just feels really hard to contemplate handing over her care to anyone else. I really want to keep her safe.'

This was obviously a big dilemma for Jan. While I knew it wasn't my place to advise her on her mother's care, I was happy to be a sounding board and sympathetic ear. I also couldn't help feeling this situation and the clutter issues in her home were interrelated. These things very often are. I suspected that more would be revealed as we continued to work and move things around in the flat.

'It's a tough position to be in, Jan, I know. My intuition is that the best thing to do right now is to persevere with this project of getting the practicalities of your home sorted. That feeling of being stuck was the main issue we identified, and it was obviously something you felt was important to address in order to give you a greater sense of agency. I'm sure you'll know the right thing to do with your mum as the picture becomes clearer.'

This short conversation seemed to be enough for Jan, so we finished our tea and got to work. We decided to start tackling the tall glass-fronted display cabinet that stood in the corner of the living room. The upper shelves were packed with china figurines and glass ornaments. Many of them were birds: chaffinches, robins, tiny hummingbirds, multi-coloured enamelled peacocks, and a veritable colony of glass penguins.

'You must really love birds,' I said.

She laughed. 'I do, and so does Mum. Some of these are hers, actually. And you know how it is: mention to one person that you like birds, and people start to give you them for Christmas and birthdays. Before you know it, you have a virtual aviary in your living room. A lot of them aren't really my taste, but I'm not sure if I can let them go.'

'That's okay, it's your choice. But I'd like to suggest we still go through them anyway, even if we just get them out and dust and tidy the shelf. I think you'll find it really helps to know what you have, to handle and review everything. Once you touch things, you tend to know if you want to hold on to them.'

'Agreed. Actually, I'm not too fussed about those plates behind the birds – in fact, I never really liked them.'

So, we began carefully taking out and organising some of the delicate ornaments that had literally been gathering dust. The upper shelf was quite high up, so I got a little footstool from the kitchen. As I positioned it in front of the cabinet and made to step up on to it, Jan began to look anxious and stopped me.

'No, let me do that,' she said somewhat suddenly, getting up from the sofa where she had been sorting through the ornaments and moving hurriedly over to the cabinet. Checking herself, she continued, 'It's just that they are really delicate.'

'I hear they're really precious to you, Jan. It's okay, I'll take good care of them.'

'Please do, they're my mum.'

I noted the Freudian slip, one of those little errors in speech when we reveal some aspect of our unconscious.

'Let me take care of this; your mum's things will be fine, I promise.'

Jan looked reassured, if still a little nervous, and she returned to the sofa while I continued up the steps and took a closer look at the top shelf. In the corner was a china figurine of a sailor standing at a ship's wheel. He was surrounded by another collection of birds of all sorts. In front of them was another set of figures: a frog, a badger and a rat in human clothing. *Ah*, I realised, *it's not a frog, it's a toad!* They were the characters from *The Wind in the Willows*.

'Do you have a duster? They've accumulated quite a bit of dust here.'

Jan hurried out to the kitchen to get one for me. I guessed she was happy to have something to do to distract her from her anxiety.

I very carefully transferred the figurines into a small box so I could carry them down from the shelf and over to where Jan was sitting. I wiped each one carefully with the bright yellow cloth she had given me before handing them to her. After my second trip back to the sofa, I noticed Jan was in tears. I squatted down quietly beside her to reassure her that she wasn't alone with her feelings. After a few moments, I said gently, 'These must bring up a lot of memories.'

'It's not that. It's just these ornaments. They're like Mum, aren't they? So fragile and vulnerable.' She pulled a tissue from her pocket. 'Especially now she is getting so weak. I feel that I have to be responsible for keeping her out of harm's way. But maybe I'm being overprotective, or putting too much onus on myself. What do you think?'

'I understand the dilemma. I can get really anxious about my mum's welfare too, especially when she wants to carry on doing the things she did in her fifties. She's in her eighties and still likes to zip around the farm on her quad bike. We all recognise the impact a helicopter parent can have on a child. I wonder if there is also a sense in which, when the roles flip and the child becomes the carer, we too can be overprotective. In our natural desire to keep them safe, maybe we can end up holding them captive.'

Jan nodded. 'It has an impact on me too, Helen. I'm

thinking back to what you said about me being like a grounded teenager. I can see that, in a way, I'm being restricted by my attitudes. I choose to care for Mum, yet at the same time I'm feeling resentful towards her, which is the last thing I want.'

As we worked, Jan and I continued to talk about her mum. Later, during a tea break, we discussed some of their options. Jan told me that following her mother's stay in hospital, the powers that be were finally starting to pay more attention. They were beginning to acknowledge there was a problem and to accept the need to address it, as was her mother. I am a great believer in finding win-win scenarios. Now it appeared that such an option was opening up. It seemed Jan was becoming more open to the idea that it could better serve both of them if her mother was living somewhere she could more easily get the professional care she would increasingly need. As our conversation earlier had revealed, Jan was also more able to acknowledge that her mother, although someone she loved dearly, had become someone who was clipping her wings and holding her to the nest. I understood that this was probably a challenging and painful realisation, and wanted to acknowledge the dilemma that Jan felt.

'As I told you, my mum is a similar age to yours, so I know how hard it is to balance the care needs of a loved one with their desire for independence. But it's also important to consider your own needs. Just as we've been doing physically in the flat, you can start to create space for yourself by letting go of how you relate to your mother.'

Jan looked a little disturbed, so I explained myself further.

'To be clear, that absolutely does not mean discarding the person themself. The form this takes is different for everyone, for each unique relationship. But the common thread is often about more fully understanding the way that we relate to the person, the established role that we may have unconsciously taken on long in the past, or have evolved into over the years. And it's also about being open to redefining that relationship in a new way that works better for both people.'

'That makes sense. I can see the way I've become trapped here; I just don't know how to change.'

'It's not easy, that's for sure, but a good place to start is to examine and let go of the accumulated ideas, stories and resentments that we connect internally with that person and that we can see no longer serve us. Particularly with key relationships, when we are able to be a different "us" with that person, we can often move into a new phase of our lives. At that point, we may choose to redefine that relationship.'

Jan nodded. 'I can see how I've become quite stuck in this role I've taken on.'

'It often happens that the other person will initiate the change themselves,' I told her. 'If our new way of being with them is no longer meeting the need that we previously served for them, they may look to someone else to fulfil that role. Or perhaps they find other ways to get those needs met, or even discover they don't really need them met at all.'

In subsequent decluttering sessions over the next couple of weeks, Jan told me about further conversations that had taken place between her and her mum, and also with the medical team. It sounded as if the shift I had noticed had continued apace. I know how tricky it can be trying to reconcile an elderly relative's need for independence with what you feel is in their best interests. There was clearly an important change happening, and changes of this type are seldom easy. In fact, they usually entail a struggle: a battle, even. And often, alongside this, we face a battle between conflicting parts of ourselves.

In what was scheduled to be our final session, Jan's mobile rang and she went out into the hallway to speak. I heard raised voices, and when she returned to the room where we were working, she was clearly disturbed and quite angry.

'I don't believe it,' she said. 'That was the man I've been renting a garage from. He's just told me I need to clear out the things I've got stored in there; he wants it back. And he's pressuring me to do it before the end of the month. I guess this isn't going to be our last session after all.'

There had been no previous mention of a garage, but this didn't surprise me. It is not unusual for people to have secret places that they don't tell me about. It can be like the alcoholic who keeps a bottle hidden somewhere to protect their addiction.

What did feel positive to me was to hear Jan's anger. This seemed to point to her being more assertive and recognising what she wanted. Maybe she was starting to put her needs first instead of those of others all the time.

The garage was only a couple of minutes' walk from Jan's place, so we paid a visit to assess the work. It was one of a row of four set back from the road, with brightly coloured up-and-over doors. Jan unlocked the padlock, and together we heaved the door open. Thankfully, the garage wasn't packed as full as some I've seen, although there was certainly no room for a car in there. In one corner were a row of large, heavy-duty cardboard boxes, each with 'John' written on them in a large black marker. They were dry, as was the garage itself, but marked with water damage, so I guessed they had been stored somewhere else and subsequently relocated. I went to move one and it was very heavy, too heavy to lift, so I dragged it out a little towards the centre of the garage to take a closer look. It had been carefully sealed with packing tape, but due to the passage of time and the old water damage, this peeled off easily. Inside, the box was tightly packed with vinyl LPs.

'Are these your husband's records?' I pulled out an album by an obscure blues guitarist I'd never heard of.

'Oh, no. Martin didn't leave a single thing behind when he left,' Jan replied, somewhat bitterly. 'No, these are my brother's. He was quite an avid collector in his twenties.'

'I can see that,' I said as I opened another of the boxes. I could count at least five more elsewhere in the garage.

'I really don't have room for them in the flat, which is why they're out here. But every time I mention it to John, he kind of changes the subject.'

'Doesn't he have room to store them himself?'

'The thing is, he lives overseas, so I'd have to pay to get them shipped out to him.'

'They're his things, Jan. Surely he should arrange and pay for the shipping?'

'I know, but he's my little brother. I always took care of him growing up.'

Another piece of the picture was emerging. Her brother was out of the country, and all the responsibility for their mother's care, along with the care of his youth – as represented by the record collection – had fallen on Jan.

'If he doesn't take responsibility for his collection, where are you going to store it all, Jan? As you've already said, there's no room in the flat.'

'Well, we've cleared out those shelves in the garden room unit now, maybe they can go in there?'

I could see that one of Jan's old patterns was beginning to reassert itself, and I wanted to help her see this so she could make a more conscious choice.

'Can you see what's happening here? You've just done all that work to create some space for yourself and now you're proposing immediately giving it away to your brother.'

'Oh my God, you're right. It seems that I'm holding a lot for other people.'

'Exactly. Maybe it's time you start to put greater focus

on taking care of yourself and thinking more about your needs?'

'That makes sense, I just don't know how to tackle it with John. Like I said, he just avoids the subject if I ever bring it up. Do you have any suggestions?'

I thought for a moment. 'Perhaps, instead of having a conversation, you could write an email. It can help keep some of the emotion out of the interaction.'

'Right. I just don't know what to say. Even though he's in his forties now, he's still my little brother.'

'Maybe you can say something along the lines of, "I'm sure you are very busy, but I'm under pressure from the garage owner, who really needs me to clear everything. With Mum in the flat, there's just no space at home. So, I need you to arrange to have your record collection picked up. I know you've a lot on your plate as well, so if I don't hear from you by X date, I will get a collector to take them away and I will send you the money."'

I noticed I was being a bit directive, but in some cases, that is part of the support I give: helping people to overcome the obstacles they encounter while striving to move forward. Jan was pretty organised and capable, but one area in which it appeared she wasn't confident was setting boundaries. Throughout our work, I was encouraging her to think about this, and to understand that it's better for everyone if you are clear about your needs.

In the New Year I was back with Jan and we began clearing the garage together. Faced with the prospect of losing his record collection, her brother had kicked into gear and arranged for a friend of his to pick up the boxes, meaning there was less to tackle than I'd initially imagined. And the majority of the remaining boxes were things that, if Jan hadn't had the garage, would probably have gone direct to a charity shop or the local tip. She had probably simply used the garage as a staging post to get things out of her home, while not having to actually make a commitment to letting them go.

I reminded her: 'Clutter is decisions that haven't been made. So, instead of making the decision to take things to the tip, and to confront your brother, you've left this stuff here. And you've been literally paying for it, in the form of garage rent, ever since.'

It was a crisp January day, so I was grateful there was not a lot of sorting to do. For the majority of boxes, it soon became apparent that it was simply a case of opening them up so Jan could reassure herself that there was nothing she wanted to keep. She picked out the occasional item and we took a couple of boxes back to the house for her to sort through. Other than that, we made rapid progress, and shifting the boxes around kept us warm.

To speed things along, I had arranged for a man and van to collect all the unwanted items. So we stacked the boxes outside the front of the garage, along with larger items, such as two rusted old lawnmowers and a tired-looking exercise bike. Jan had initially floated the idea of a yard sale, but when I pointed out that would mean she'd have to stand around in the cold all day, she quickly forgot this.

Jan had cursed the garage owner for forcing her to deal with its contents, but I was sending out gratitude. I understood that, at its core, a key part of this whole project for Jan had been to establish clearer boundaries between her personal needs and those of her loved ones. The work in the garage had been another opportunity to do this and further let go of a past that was clogging up her present. The things around her represented commitments that both defined and restricted who she was and how she could live her life. Some needed to be acknowledged, honoured and let go, so that she could more fully embrace and appreciate what she had chosen to keep.

A few months later, on a bright spring morning, I was taking it slowly and doing my monthly admin. I took the chance to write a follow-up email to Jan to see how she was doing, and within a few minutes of pressing 'send' my mobile rang.

'Hi Helen, it's Jan. I just got your email and thought it would be easier to ring. Things are going pretty well, thank you. My business has really felt like it's taking off over the last month and I'm feeling much more focused.'

I was immediately struck by how very different this person sounded to the one I had first spoken to. Her tone was more relaxed, but energised and positive. I'd caught glimpses of this Jan during our work together, but this felt new.

'That's great to hear. How is your mum?'

'She's okay, thank you. She was given an assisted-living residential place a couple of months ago. It's close enough for me to visit regularly and she seems really happy there. I miss her, naturally, but in all honesty, we are both much happier. She says in an odd way, it feels like she has some of her independence back.'

'I can understand that,' I said. 'I'm sure there is something hard in changing from the mother who cares for your child to the one being cared for by them.'

It was only a short call, but it was lovely to hear from Jan, and after I put down the phone, I found myself reflecting on her situation. With so much packed carefully away in every available space, it was almost as if she'd believed she had to keep everything in her home exactly as it was in order to hold her life together. I'd had a sense of a powerful internal voice saying: *Do not disturb the status quo. You must stay as you are, in your responsible, selfless role in order to not lose your mother.* I could see how the idea of letting go of that position, of everything she had constructed to buttress herself, was scary. The prospect of no longer having the security created by that role could quite possibly have felt like it would mean losing her whole identity. Yet when she was able to trust herself and let go of some of what felt so essential, her core spirit was freed and became better able to flourish.

*

Clutter builds up in our homes, our lives and our psyches for many reasons. For you, it may be fear or unwillingness to let go, some inner refusal to acknowledge that for some things their time has passed, or perhaps simply the comfort of the familiar. I think often we know, deep inside, that if we begin to shift things around, it will bring change: perhaps in a form or direction that we are afraid won't be what we want. So, in an attempt to maintain the safety of what we know, we choose instead to keep all our possessions exactly as they are. And there they remain, collecting dust and resentments. This may appear to work for a while, but the only guarantee in life is change. What this rigidity invariably ends up creating is stagnation.

  If you are able to understand there is something at your core that is separate from any of the roles or identities you have taken on, then you can be more open to trusting how life will unfold, and, as a result, you can be more willing to let go of what no longer serves you. Are there objects in your life that feel so critical that the idea of not having them fills you with dread? One thing that might help is what I call the 'I am not my . . .' meditation. It's quite simple. Find a quiet space and time, sit comfortably, close your eyes and take a few deep breaths. Then, when you are ready to start, say quietly to yourself: 'I am not my book collection. I am not my curtains. I am not my shoes. I am not my mobile. I am not my designer sofa.' Continue taking this inventory of all the possessions that surround you in your home. Simply by reminding yourself that you are none of these things, you create a little space between them and the essential you.

You can download some free audio meditations at helensanderson.com/secret.

# In his father's house

I received a call one summer day as I was on my deck, trying to stay cool. The garden was in glorious full bloom, and I had decided to sit outside to make the most of the gentle breeze while I caught up with some admin.

'Hi there,' said the man on the phone. 'I wonder if you can help. I really need some support to sort out my dad's house; it's full of so many years of clutter. Can you tell me a bit more about how you work?' He sounded quite upbeat. His voice was gentle, but confident and clear. I wanted to understand how I might support him, but I also felt cautious, as I've learned to be when people call me regarding another person.

'Certainly, I'm very happy to do that. Firstly, though, can I ask if your dad knows that you're calling?'

The line went quiet for a moment.

'My dad died last year.'

A little rush of guilt and embarrassment hit me. 'Oh dear, I'm so sorry. I didn't realise.'

'No, no, that's okay. Please don't apologise. I didn't explain myself properly. I've taken over the house, or at least I'm trying to. It's hard because his presence seems so strong in the place.'

'I can imagine. It's all quite recent, then? You must still be processing it all.'

'I suppose so, yes. He had been ill for some time, so it wasn't entirely unexpected. It was still a difficult time, though, of course. Then I inherited his estate, which pretty much was this house. I moved in towards the end of last year, but I'm still not really sure what I'm going to do with the place.'

'I'm guessing there are lots of emotions tied up in it all. Is that the main thing that's proving difficult?'

'There are lots of memories, of course. But it's not that so much. Like I said, there's so much stuff in there, but also the whole house itself is just a bit of a puzzle.'

He had me at that word: puzzle. I love working out ways to solve the spatial and organisational problems created by our homes, so my curiosity was now fully engaged.

'I'm intrigued. Can you say more?'

'Where do I start? It will make more sense when you see it, but I'll give you some background. Dad bought the place not long after he arrived in the country, back in the late fifties. It began as this spacious, four-storey terraced house and gradually, over the years, he turned it into a warren of small studio flats, which he rented out. It started as a way to earn extra money to supplement his income, and gradually, as family moved out and more and more rooms were added, it developed into a full-on business. He did all the work himself. Everything from building walls to divide up the rooms, to making custom-built beds and tables to fit into the odd-sized spaces that he'd created. When I say he did the work himself, I mean he literally crafted everything with his own hands.'

'Wow, it sounds like you've taken on quite a place. How exactly can I help?'

'I'm still thinking about what my options are, and I'd

love to get your thoughts on that. For starters, though, the priority is to get the place clear and organised. There's so much stuff everywhere, and it just feels stifling. I want to get it done efficiently, but also to approach it all in a mindful way. I read some of your blogs and I liked how you talked about Zen. I know this is going to be about more than just practicalities, and it's clear that you get that. It's the holistic approach you describe that attracted me; I need someone who can help with the pragmatic aspects: the interior design *and* the psychological side.'

'Great, that's certainly how I work best. As you say, I strongly believe that all those aspects of a home are interconnected.'

'Exactly. As I've tried to get the place sorted, I've become increasingly aware of that. In my professional life, I'm pretty together. But it's weird; whenever I attempt to move this forward, I very quickly start to feel stuck and overwhelmed.'

'That's very common, and I can definitely help you overcome that. Do you have an idea of timescale for this project?'

'That's the other thing. I work in the music business, which means I'm travelling a lot. My calendar for the rest of the year is super full already. So, as well as expertise in getting the place sorted, I need someone to help me stay focused on the project. Otherwise, I know I'll just get overtaken by work commitments and it will drift.'

Although Chris was clearly a busy man, I had no feeling of being rushed by him. I sensed we were very much on the same wavelength and that he understood what I could bring to his situation. So, mindful of his time, I skipped some of the usual preliminaries I go through on a call and suggested we met up in person so I could take a look at the house. Despite our busy schedules, it turned out we both had a few hours free later that week.

Chris lived quite close to me, so a couple of days later I made the short walk to his place. It was mid-August and the heat of the day had already started to build as I turned into his street. The house was in quite a dense urban setting, close to a busy road. The terrace was separated from the street by a short bridge that led from the pavement to a steep set of stone stairs rising up to the front door. I walked across it, passing a little iron gate to the side that opened on to another set of stairs down to the basement. Reaching the top of the flight of steps, I was confronted by a confusing array of doorbells and buzzers. Unsure of which one to ring, I pulled out my phone to give Chris a call, but as I did so, the door opened and I was greeted by a good-looking young man with tawny skin and a shock of wet, tousled hair. He was dressed in a black pair of jogging bottoms and a T-shirt, and a towel hung around his neck.

'You must be Helen.' He put out his hand with a broad smile. I was struck by his warmth and openness, and I sensed a generosity in his being that immediately drew me to him. He invited me in, and we made our way along the hallway, where a roll of new carpet lay alongside the stairs, carefully wrapped in plastic. I had a sense of work in progress.

'Excuse my appearance, I just got in from a run,' he said, pulling the towel from his shoulders and briskly drying his hair. 'It's good to get out before it gets too hot at this time of year.'

'No problem. Do you want to start by showing me around, then we can talk about your goals and priorities?'

He draped the damp towel over the banister. 'Sure, why don't we start at the top and work our way down?'

We headed up to the top, third floor. As we ascended, Chris told me a little of his history in the house. 'As you'll see, it's a huge place. This was a very rundown part of town in the fifties, so I guess Dad must have been able to pick it up very cheaply. He couldn't have had a lot of money when he arrived in the country. When I was a kid, our family occupied the whole house, along with assorted aunts and cousins at different times. Then, as my relatives began to move out, Dad saw the potential in the place and started to turn over more and more of the house into little flats and bedsits.'

We continued to climb up through the house, passing rolls of wallpaper and paint pots that were piled around the landings. On each floor were myriad rooms. As Chris had described, the house was definitely something of a warren.

'After I moved out, Dad only lived on the ground floor and in a couple of the smaller bedrooms upstairs. He increasingly gave the house over to the business rather than himself.'

We reached the very top floor. A pair of large rooms with pitched ceilings were set into the roof.

'Dad had plans to put in some dormer windows up here to create a little more headroom, but when he looked into it, he realised it was a bit beyond his skillset.'

We paused, slightly breathless after the long climb of three flights of stairs.

I looked around the first room. A very robust but somewhat Heath-Robinson bedframe, fashioned out of unpainted planed timber, stood against one wall. There was a similar one on the other side of the room. Other than the bedframes, a painted bentwood chair and a faded poster of Madonna taped to the wall, the room was unfurnished. A strip of timber was nailed to the floor, running down the centre of the room. There was another strip directly above it on the ceiling.

'This is what's left of the dividing wall Dad put in,' Chris told me, tapping it with his foot. 'I'm part way through taking it out.'

At the far end of the room lay a pile of timber and broken plasterboard, partially covered with torn floral wallpaper.

'There's no real decluttering to do in here; I just wanted to show you the space.'

Taking care not to trip on the timber, I crossed the landing to take a look at the room at the rear of the house, which was similar.

'These could be really nice rooms, couldn't they?' I said. 'Especially if you added some headroom. That was a good idea your dad had.'

Chris picked up a couple of empty beer cans from the window ledge. 'Yeah, I think so. I'm getting quotes from some guys I know to put in those dormer windows he always talked about.'

We headed down to the floor below and into the largest room at the front of the house.

'This my music studio,' said Chris. He moved over to a big mixing desk, which was covered with dials and lights. He flicked a couple of switches. The low hum that had filled the room subsided. The room was packed with professional recording equipment: several pairs of loudspeakers, an Apple laptop, a couple of keyboards, turntables, a large reel-to-reel tape deck, and numerous other pieces of gear that I didn't recognise. Two large wooden shelving units were piled high with tapes and CDs and a huge collection of vinyl records. Chris took a record from one of the turntables, placed it carefully in its sleeve and filed it away in the shelving units.

'I thought about maybe making the smaller bedroom at the back of the house into an archive room and relocating a lot of the old tapes and vinyl there, so I have more room to work in here,' he said.

We went to take a look at the small bedroom, which was certainly in need of clearing. There was a lot of spare furniture piled up in there, along with a large stack of cardboard boxes and several old suitcases.

'I'm not really sure what I want to do with the small room next door to this one, either. These two rooms will probably be a good place to start decluttering, though. There's a load of stuff from my old flat that I moved in when I took over this place last year. I never got round to unpacking most of it.' Chris tore off a strip of tape to open one of the boxes and looked inside. 'A lot of this is probably junk and can go, but there's also a load more vinyl I'll want to keep.'

As we explored the remainder of the house, most of the rooms were in a similar condition to the ones I'd seen so far. Each of them contained different layers of objects that had accumulated over the years of multiple occupation. Firstly, there was the legacy of what Chris's father had built in the house, along with those remaining possessions of his that had not been given to other family members. Then there was a random selection of items that I assumed had been left behind over the years by previous tenants. Finally, there was the furniture and boxes of belongings, some sealed, some partially unpacked, that Chris had transferred from his old flat. It was a complex scenario. A good metaphor is that of the palimpsest: a document on which a text has been written, over which one or more subsequent writers has superimposed further writings. The house struck me as very much like this. His father, the various tenants who had occupied the rooms over the years, and now Chris himself had each inscribed elements of their own stories into the spaces.

Practically, there was certainly a lot of work to do. What many of my clients want initially is support and encouragement to get unstuck. But having spoken to Chris and taken a look around, my impression was that what he most needed from me was help to find clarity: to decide how exactly to move forward and make changes in a way that would best support his goals and aspirations.

'I think I have a good sense of the lay of the land,' I told him. 'Is there a place we can sit and talk? Ideally somewhere with a little space that feels away from the clutter in the house.'

'We can try the back garden; there's some room out there.'

We moved through to the rear of the house. I had hoped it might provide a little green oasis where we could work on a clear vision of what Chris wanted to achieve. But even outside, there was no escape from the clutter. More of a backyard than a garden, the area was quite large, but certainly did not feel spacious. It was filled with rusted old fridges, freezers and microwaves. The whole scene put me in mind of an elephants' graveyard.

Despite the number of old appliances out there, it wasn't exactly chaotic. Rather than being dumped, it felt as if everything had been carefully, almost ceremoniously, placed. I think this highlights something important to understand about clutter. When things accumulate, there is often quite an intentional process at play. Frequently this is not entirely conscious, but may instead be driven by hidden psychological forces and patterns. A vital part of the work I do, alongside clearing the physical objects, is to bring those aspects into the light of awareness, where they can be examined and processed. This psychological uncovering is vital. If the forces in question remain in the shadows, they will inevitably find expression in the repetition of those patterns of behaviour that caused the clutter to accumulate in the first place. In Chris's case, of course, some of the patterns and much of the clutter were his father's. I suspected, however, that he might have inherited some of his dad's behaviours and attitudes along with the property.

'Dad couldn't throw anything away,' Chris told me. 'He always believed he would find a use for things – and, often, he would.' Given the ingenuity and resourcefulness I'd seen demonstrated in the house, I didn't doubt this. However, it was clearly never going to be the case with an old fridge that had presumably been moved outside because it had stopped working.

Despite the slightly disconcerting presence of all the old white goods around the garden, there was at least blue sky above and a cool breeze. In a clear area of unkempt lawn, I saw that Chris had set up a few garden chairs and a little low table. Given the heat of the day, this was certainly preferable to the stuffy atmosphere inside the house. We sat down and continued our conversation.

'How do you feel when you see all this stuff here?' I asked.

'Nothing much.' Chris shrugged. 'I guess I've got used to it, to an extent. That's just how things always were at home. One thing I have noticed since I've moved back in here, though, is that I sometimes feel quite small and disconnected from my body.'

'That's interesting. Can you say a little more about that feeling?' I asked, curious to learn more about what might be going on.

'It's hard to describe exactly. I guess it's a kind of . . . mental escape,' Chris replied, obviously looking quite deep within himself for an answer to my question. 'It's as if I'm shrinking away, maybe, withdrawing into somewhere dark and warm. That's why the yoga and running that I'm doing are so important. I find they really help me reconnect to my body.'

Chris closed his eyes and straightened his back, sitting more upright. He took a couple of deep, controlled breaths and then exhaled steadily. Opening his eyes again, he slowly rotated his head and took in the slightly bizarre scene that surrounded us. It was as if he was trying to see it all afresh. There was a marked contrast between his calm, centred state and the environment he was living in. I imagined it was quite an effort of will to maintain this stillness, and I wondered if he was always this collected.

'I really don't feel anything, to be honest,' he continued. 'Around all this, the house, the whole situation. There's no shame, certainly.'

'Nor should there be,' I interjected. 'Your father was obviously extremely resourceful. That quality is one of the things that helped him develop the property and build the business. His personality clearly had a huge impact on shaping how this house is. Just walking round earlier, I had a powerful sense of him. But from what you described just now, I wonder if his presence makes it harder, in some way, for you to be fully yourself: the way you might be at work or when you had your own flat?'

Chris looked up at the back of the building. 'Maybe. There is so much of my father in this house. And it's not so much the possessions he left behind, it's also the work he put into this place, into building it up as a business.'

'I can sense that. For you, I'm guessing it's almost as if his spirit, his essence, is built into the very fabric of the house.'

'Perhaps, I've not quite thought of it in that way.'

'If that was the case, it would be natural that the idea of changing that, breaking down and taking out much of what he built, would feel quite a challenge.'

Chris let out a deep breath. 'You're probably right. When I think about selling the place or turning it back into a family home, it does somehow feel disrespectful. Almost like a betrayal.'

This dilemma was clearly a key issue for Chris.

'I understand that you really value the way he created all this to provide for himself, for you and the rest of the family. How he made the most of the skills and resources he had.

Do you really think it's a betrayal of him, though, to want to build on that?'

'I guess not. It's just he seemed so wedded to this place. So proud of what he'd done here.'

'And rightly so. He established an amazing foundation for you – but do you want to be held back by that? I never knew your father, but I can't believe that's what he'd have wanted.'

'No, of course not. It is complicated, though.'

'I understand completely. Can I ask, how was your relationship with your dad growing up?'

'Quite good. But as boys and dads often do, we clashed a bit, especially when I got older and wanted to pursue my work in music. As you can imagine, he was all, "Why don't you get a proper job, instead of wasting your time with this nonsense?"' He related his dad's phrase in a West Indian accent. 'I didn't always fully appreciate Dad,' Chris continued, 'but towards the end of his life, we became closer. When he saw me getting success and good money from my work, he respected that and often told me he was proud of me.' He paused for a moment. Then: 'I don't remember ever telling him I was proud of him, though, certainly not as much as I wish I had. Perhaps at the time I didn't really understand or appreciate what he had done.'

'That must be hard. I can see how that might be a further reason you feel reticent or conflicted about taking action that could seem like you are tearing down his legacy.'

Though he was a big guy, there was something boyish about Chris. He projected a positive, youthful energy, but there was not that deeper-rooted confidence that you sense in a man who has truly travelled on his own journey. With his successful career, Chris had certainly set off on his, but I sensed there were still internal forces binding him to his childhood relationship with his father. I often find that when they are too enmeshed with their parent's values, people can remain stuck and struggle to find their own way in the world. Both honouring and cutting some of the unhelpful ties, to his father in particular, might be critical to the work we would do together: something that could enable Chris to make a fuller break and move on in his life with more independence.

'We can certainly look at some of these psychological aspects if it's helpful,' I said.

Chris nodded.

'But setting them aside for now, on a practical level, what are your priorities?'

'I'd really appreciate your input into the layout of the place, but to begin with, let's focus on creating more space. There's just so much stuff that it's hard to see the wood for the trees. I think that's the first thing I need, to help me get some clarity on what comes next.'

When I arrived for the first session, Chris invited me through to the backyard. Around the low table where we had talked, half a dozen guys of about his age sat engaged in lively conversation. Music was playing from inside the house, and the table was covered with bottles of beer, cans of soft drinks and a full ashtray. 'We're having a yard-clearing party,' Chris said. 'I figured it was a good way to get it sorted.'

This was a really positive start to the process. There was clearly nothing in the yard that Chris was going to keep, so there was no role for me in this area for now. Chris had cleared a route from the garden to the front door, so it was a simple matter of getting rid of everything. A group of strong, healthy guys was exactly what was needed.

'Come on boys, it's time to earn your beer!' Chris called from the kitchen door.

With a little reluctance and some grumbling, the group

stood up and set to work. 'I'll leave you guys to it,' he said. 'Try not to break anything in the house.'

Chris and I headed upstairs and started work decluttering the first-floor bedroom, as we'd agreed at our previous meeting. The sound of raucous but good-natured banter, along with the occasional expletive, echoed up the stairwell as his mates manhandled all the fridges and freezers through the house and on to an opensided truck parked outside. It was quite a noisy process, but in less than an hour, they had completely emptied the yard.

'We're off to the tip, Chris!' came a cry from downstairs.

'Cheers, guys!' Chris called after them, and the clamour gradually subsided as the group spilled out of the house and on to the street.

As we unpacked and steadily worked our way through the stack of cardboard boxes from Chris's old flat, we talked about his plans for the house. Although he was full of ideas, it was clear that he was still trying to figure out what he really wanted.

'Part of me wants to make this my permanent home, but I'm not even sure if I want to stay in the UK. A lot of my work is overseas now,' Chris told me as we carried a small wooden desk through to the room next door.

'Do you have a sense of what might be causing this uncertainty? In other ways, you seem very clear and focused.'

'Don't get me wrong; I'm really grateful that I've inherited this amazing legacy. But in a way, it also feels like a great burden, you know.'

'In what way, exactly?'

'I suppose I have this sense of my dad's presence, this expectation that I'll carry on his work and keep things how they are. Since I moved back in here, I notice that sometimes I feel as if I'm still a little boy in my father's house again.

It's like I have to follow his rules and live by his values. You know, Dad never wanted to spend money on anything; he'd always try to do it himself. And if he did buy something or pay anyone else to do some work, he was always looking for the cheapest option. I'm not really like that. I like to buy myself nice clothes and eat out at decent restaurants. And for work, I always buy the best equipment and bring in the top people to work on my music projects. But here, as soon as I walk in, it's like I completely lose that expansive side, that generosity toward myself.'

'Is that true? I mean, you've brought me in, for example. I hear what you're saying, though. It sounds a bit like, around your dad, and in his house especially, you never fully grew into adulthood. I find the same thing sometimes when I'm around my mum; a lot of people do. And, of course, our parents can quite naturally tend to treat us a bit like children when we go back home. It's really easy to slip into the role of being the child and not the adult.'

Chris nodded. 'Yes. Even since Dad passed, I've continued to feel a bit like that here. At the funeral, I had a sense of stepping up when I made a speech, thanked everyone for coming and so on. I remember one of my uncles saying, "You're the man of the house now." But when I came back here that evening, I felt like a lost boy in this huge place again.'

'Naturally, there's a lot contained in this house for you psychologically and emotionally, as well as all the physical clutter. This is where you grew up, so it's bound to be filled with all sorts of memories. And with your dad passing quite recently, you have a lot to process. When you think about your position, that now you are the one who gets to make the choices, how does that feel?' I slid a box of LPs over to him to sort through.

'Well, it feels good, in a way. It's great that I've got this place, there's a lot I can do with it; but I also feel pressured.' He pulled out a handful of LPs and began to leaf through them. 'I don't want to sound like a spoilt brat. Of course, I appreciate what I've been given. It just feels like a big responsibility.'

'I get that. It's right to have gratitude for what your parents have left you. And it's also important to acknowledge the downside: the curse of that gift, in a way. From what you've told me, in a way it is also holding you back from creating your own life as an independent person.'

'You could be right; it's certainly complicated, and I do have mixed feelings for sure. Maybe that's something we can talk about more some time. It would be good to get a clearer idea of what's going on; something is definitely making it hard for me to make decisions about the place.'

During that first session, we achieved a lot. The majority of the boxes in the two rooms contained more of his vinyl collection. As a musician and sometime DJ, he kept most of them, although we did fill a couple of boxes with records he had borrowed from a friend years earlier, ready to be returned. Decluttering is not necessarily about getting rid of things. I prefer to think of it as getting clear about what you have, reconnecting to what has meaning and value to you, and making choices about what will help you live your best life going forward.

As we emptied each box, he flattened it out and added it to a pile on the landing. It was very satisfying to watch this steadily grow throughout the day, and there was a great sense of achievement as we stood on the landing at the end of the session and surveyed the two small front rooms on the first floor. Aside from the desk and a couple of chairs, both were now pretty much empty and ready for whatever came next.

When I left at the end of the day, I passed several boxes of charity-shop donations in the downstairs hallway, and an impressive stack of cardboard for recycling and numerous bags of rubbish stood by the bins at the front of the house. It had certainly been a productive day, and we continued to make good progress in the two sessions that followed.

The next time we met, we began by turning our attention to a large understairs cupboard on the ground floor.

'I haven't really looked in here,' Chris said, 'but I'm pretty sure it is absolutely chocka with Dad's old tools and decorating gear.'

He opened the panelled, stripped wood door, and as he did so, a large orange bucket filled with rags and a couple of paint rollers tumbled out on to the floor. We moved them to one side and looked in the cupboard. As Chris had suspected, it was piled high with DIY equipment including a pair of paint-covered stepladders, a large workbench and numerous pots of ancient-looking paint.

'Okay, let's just get everything out and see exactly what we've got,' I said. 'I suggest we put all the paint straight by the front door to go out. I doubt if any of it is much good now.'

'Right,' Chris replied. 'I'd like to check it all though; maybe there's some we can use.'

He took out the stepladders and stood them against the wall in the hallway.

The cupboard was a bit of an Aladdin's cave. The further we went into it, the more 'treasure' appeared. The treasure in question being Chris's father's vast collection of tools, paints, tubes of sealant, paintbrushes and rolls of wallpaper.

'Ah, this might be useful,' Chris kept saying as we pulled out more and more from under the stairs.

'It's your decision, of course, but I'd ask you to really think about whether you are likely to use any of this paint or wall-paper. It seems that you and your dad have quite different tastes.' I handed him a couple of rolls.

He partially unrolled the paper. 'Oh wow! This is what I had in my bedroom as a kid.' He laughed and showed it to me. It was covered in colourful images of comic-book super-heroes: Superman, Batman and a slight goofy-looking Robin. 'You're right; there probably isn't any point in keeping most of this stuff,' he said. 'But I might actually hold on to these rolls; it's pretty cool seventies retro. I remember when Dad decorated my room with this. I think he even took me along to the wallpaper store and I chose the pattern.'

I looked into Chris's eyes. The laughter from a few moments earlier had been replaced with a hint of sadness.

'He was a good dad. Although he could be an awkward so-and-so, I do miss the old bugger.'

It took most of the morning to work our way to the back of the cupboard. Reluctantly, Chris had to admit that the vast majority of the DIY gear and most of the tools weren't going to serve any useful purpose.

As we took a lunch break, I began to talk more to Chris about what he wanted to do with the house.

'Now that we're making progress with the decluttering, are you beginning to get a clearer picture of what comes next?'

'To be honest, I still don't really know,' Chris said. He took a drink from his glass of water. 'What with being so focused on getting things cleared, I've lost sight of what my long-term plans might be. There are plenty of ideas floating around, but I'm really not sure what direction to go in.'

'There's this exercise that I find really helpful sometimes when clients get to this stage. If you like, we could do a little visioning process at the end of the afternoon. It might allow you to get some clarity around how you see your life unfolding and the ways in which this place could best serve you to help make that happen.'

'That sounds really interesting, thank you. Yes, let's do that.'

So, once we had finished carefully replacing and arranging the greatly slimmed-down contents of the understairs cupboard, we moved down into the basement. This was one of the clearest spaces in the house, and had a large empty wall that I thought would be ideal for what I had in mind. I always carry a selection of coloured sticky notes and marker pens in my declutter bag. I took these out and explained the plan to Chris.

'These are for you to write ideas on and stick them on the wall, to explore some of your different options. To begin with, in terms of the bigger picture, what matters most to you? What are the things you value most highly?'

'When I was a kid, I was inspired by people like John Lennon and Bob Marley,' he said.

'Okay, and what was it about them that you connected to?'

'I guess it was that their music always felt like it had a wider purpose: an agenda beyond just the songs they wrote. So I suppose that I would like to develop my work in music so it has wider impact and meaning.'

'That sounds great. What ideas do you have about what form this might take?'

Chris paused for thought. 'I like the idea of taking music into a healing space,' he said after a moment. 'I think the emotional resonance of music really has a kind of healing role in the world. I've also always liked the idea of creating some sort of communal creative space.'

He wrote 'CREATIVE HUB' in capitals on a large pink sticky note and stuck it in the centre of the wall.

'I imagine a place where the musicians and artists I work with can come together and collaborate,' he said. 'You know, how Andy Warhol had what he called his art factory?'

'That sounds exciting. What might it consist of?'

Chris added some more sticky notes to the wall around the note: 'music studio', 'music library', 'social space', 'communal yoga/meditation room'.

'Okay, so you have some ideas around the career and creative side, but what about your personal life? Where do you imagine that going?'

'I love travelling with work and quite enjoy living the bachelor life with my mates, but recently it's been wearing a bit thin. I've been thinking that maybe I'm ready to settle down and start a family.'

'Okay, so write that down and add it to the wall.'

Chris picked up a green marker and wrote 'marriage?' on one of the sticky notes.

We continued to draw out ideas in this way for some time. Chris embraced the exploration with a lot of energy and enthusiasm, and I noticed him becoming increasingly confident and animated as we continued. About half an hour into the process, he stood back and looked at the wall. It was painted a grubby magnolia colour on top of lining paper that was peeling away in several places. 'You know what, this whole side of the room needs to be stripped and repainted anyway,' he said. 'I quite like the idea of drawing directly on to the surface. I'll be back.'

He rushed enthusiastically out of the room and returned a minute or so later carrying a small box filled with coloured oil pastels. He began to draw directly on the wall. He took down the sticky notes and re-wrote the phrases, and then drew lines to connect related ideas together in groups. I prompted him with a few suggestions here and there, but I mainly took a step back and simply watched, enjoying the space he was taking up to consider his options. The broad physical gestures he was making as he drew sweeping marks across the wall felt

very expansive. When he had finished, we both stood back
and took in the scene.

'It reminds me of the plans they drew up in wartime control rooms,' I said. 'You know, where the different elements
of a battle or campaign are set out and configured?'

Chris smiled. 'Yes, I know what you mean. I was thinking
of it as a bit like a musical score.' He pulled out his phone
and took a series of photos.

Like many creative people, Chris had a tendency to be
quite divergent and scattered, which was reflected in the way
he was using the different rooms and spaces in the property.
In many ways, what we had just done on the wall mirrored
the process we were undertaking in the house, where we were
organising and bringing together the disparate elements into
a more meaningful and coherent whole. I didn't push him to
make any decisions; we were simply mapping out his options.

'The exercise has certainly sown the seeds of a lot of possibilities,' I said. 'Let's leave them to germinate here on the
wall in the basement, and in your mind, while we complete
clearing and reconfiguring the house. I find that by simply
doing, our thinking becomes clearer.'

A degree of contemplation and discussion are central to my
work, but it is also characterised by a lot of action. I find it
important to build up a good head of steam. There is something about the momentum established in this manner that
helps break through the years of accumulated 'stuckness'.
There are things to be said for a slow and gentle pace, and I
know this works for some people. But in my experience, it's
not the most effective approach for those who have become
profoundly enmeshed with their clutter. When moving at a
slow pace, it is much easier to come to a standstill, to get
caught up in distractions and find yourself standing there,
contemplating the view. So, I aim to work, if not quite at

an unsustainable sprint, at least at the brisk, steady pace of a middle-distance runner. My clients and I run together as a team, with me as the pacemaker, keeping things moving towards the finish line. As a result, there is a contrast and deeper stillness when we do come to a natural break and pause for a while. And in these moments, when we stand calm in the eye of the storm and contemplate the flux around us, my clients sometimes have significant insights: inner break-throughs, born in the stillness of the battle we have been waging with their stuff.

In our next session, we focused our efforts on the room that Chris had decided would be his bedroom. I could see why he had chosen this particular room. The largest on the second floor, it featured two generous sash windows that overlooked the newly cleared yard. The rear gardens of the terrace backed on to those of the next street along, so there was a great sense of space. We opened both windows to let in some fresh air and stood looking out over the upper branches of the mature trees. In the distance, beyond the tops of the houses opposite, clouds scudded across the London skyline.

There was something expansive in his choice of room. Chris had given himself permission to take one of the best spaces as his bedroom, something I suspected his father would never have done. This was another room that had pre-viously been split into two. Chris had taken out the dividing wall, but it was still partially filled with storage containers and ramshackle pieces of furniture.

Many of the houses I visit have been split up into flats, or the rooms divided into smaller spaces. I see it as a reflec-tion of how our lives have been compartmentalised and our families divided up. Sadly, with the increasing demands for accommodation, utility wins over beauty more and more, but it was never what these townhouses were intended for. They were once spaces with high ceilings and large rooms, where people had room to breathe. Places where families could share time together. Now they are so often chopped into saleable little parcels, the buildings as fragmented as our domestic lives. So there was something inspiring and expansive about the way Chris was reverting this house back to its original configuration.

'I think I'm going to make a bed to go in here,' Chris said, his voice energised from the work we had been doing. Here was the resourcefulness that he had learned from his father. And yet, admirable and valuable as that characteristic is, I was struck that what he was suggesting was another one of those make-do, makeshift solutions. Unlike the choice of room, this did not feel very expansive or visionary. I wondered if he was still partly seeing the house through the frame of his father's perspective.

'Well, that's okay. You could do that,' I said. I wanted to challenge Chris to think differently, without squashing his enthusiasm. 'It would work on a practical level. But on your vision board, you talked about getting married. Would that be the sort of bed that you want your future wife to climb into?'

'I hadn't thought of it like that,' Chris said. Stopping what he was doing, he turned back to the window and clouds in the distance. He just stood there motionless for a while. I could see that what I'd said had affected him.

'You're right,' he said finally, turning back into the room. 'I think that's my dad talking, not me. The kind of woman I want to be with deserves more than that.'

'And so do you,' I added with a smile.

Chris nodded. 'I'll have a think about it. I'm sure I can afford a decent bed.'

I returned to emptying out one of the large storage containers, which it turned out was filled with a random selection of faded and dog-eared magazines. I wondered if what Chris had said was a real 'I'll think about it', or more of the 'I'd rather not' kind.

So, I was pleased when, at the start of our next session, Chris pulled out his iPad. 'Here, let me show you the bed I've ordered.' He handed the tablet to me and I swiped through the images of the bed on the screen. It was beautifully crafted from solid oak with elegant, curved lines.

'That's the kind of bed I want to share with my future wife,' he said.

The short conversation about the bed didn't seem that significant at the time, but as we continued to talk and work together, it became clear that it had brought about big shift in Chris's thinking. He referred back to it a couple of sessions later.

'Do you remember when I suggested making a bedframe, and you asked me "Is that the bed that you want your future wife to climb into?" I think that was a really pivotal moment for me, when I realised some of the ways I was unconsciously doing the same things as my dad. But I can see that, actually, my situation and my life are very different to his, and I don't have to be living a make-do life.'

And he absolutely didn't have to. Here was a thirty-year-old man with a flourishing and lucrative career, who had also inherited this valuable property. Practically and financially, there really wasn't any reason why he had to continue in that family vein, except for the fact that it was all he knew. He'd been operating in part on the basis of an internal script. In psychoanalysis, a script is a set of beliefs or expectations, often acquired unconsciously in childhood, which may drive our choices and decisions as adults. I suspected that one of

Chris's scripts was: 'There will never be enough, so you have to make do.'

This shift in Chris was positive, then, but there was still more work to do. Alongside the decluttering and redesign of the house, there was a parallel process of supporting Chris in continuing to move on and connect to a stronger sense of his adult self: to let go while honouring his relationship with his dad and the legacy he had left him.

Many of us have some version of this conflict. Do we take what has been given or left to us, both physically and psychologically? Is it a gift or a burden? Children who inherit a family business in particular often experience a clash between loyalty to the family and the livelihood that their parents have built up, and the desire to find their own path, their unique individual expression in life.

During a break in our next session, Chris initiated a conversation about whether or not to 'declutter' the house itself out of his life.

'I was thinking about that planning session we had in the basement last month. The plans for a creative hub and all that are inspiring, and I could certainly do that here. But I'm wondering if perhaps I should just sell up, move on and let that go?'

'What has led to that thought? When we spoke before, you seemed pretty excited about the idea.'

'I've been thinking about it a lot over the last few weeks. I wonder if I am trying to make a business out of this place, just as my dad did? Even if it is a very different one. Perhaps there is simply too much of my father's life's work built into this place for me to ever be fully my own man. I loved my dad, but if I'm honest, part of me wishes he'd never left me this place.'

There was a sudden tension and tightening in my gut when

I heard this. I took a moment to acknowledge to myself that I was feeling irritated before I replied. 'I guess a key question to ask yourself is whether your decisions are coming from a sense of obligation and duty, or if they are based on what you really want for yourself. This is an incredible gift your father has left you. I think it can be very anchoring for someone with your type of personality. Like a lot of creative people, you can be quite scattered and struggle to focus because you see so many possibilities everywhere. But I understand that the downside of this anchoring is that it can also feel quite restrictive.'

Chris thought for a moment and took a sip from his cup of coffee. 'I see what you mean,' he said. 'Since I've moved in, I've noticed how this place grounds and supports me. And you're right, it does also come with a burden of expectation. In a way, it reflects my whole relationship with my dad. Despite a few run-ins, he was very involved with my life and quite supportive. Once he realised how serious I was about music, and that I was making a real career out of it, he really encouraged me, and even gave me money for equipment. But I probably sometimes made choices because I thought they would please him, rather than just doing what felt right for me. I don't know, maybe I'm still doing that now. What do you think?'

The emotional reaction I'd had initially continued to build as I answered his question.

'I think only you can answer that, Chris. The great thing is that by having an awareness of your tendency to do that, it can become more of a choice than something you just do unconsciously. Another thing I'd say is that when you consider your options, remember that if you choose to, you can create that grounding sense of home and place in a new location. Selling up could be a way to let go and leave behind what no longer serves you, physically and psychologically. Maybe you'd prefer somewhere more compact and in a different location, and a place without all the childhood associations. But it could also be empowering to stay put and transform this house into the place *you* want it to be, just as we are doing now.'

'Yeah, there's certainly a lot to consider. I need to do some more thinking before I make a decision, but you're right: it is good to know I have choices. Thank you.'

As I walked home that afternoon, I reflected on the disturbance I'd felt during this conversation. It didn't take long for me to realise that at the root of my reaction was envy. The highly desirable neighbourhoods in which some of my clients live can certainly generate a sense of longing, but that wasn't exactly it here. There was certainly a degree to which I was galled that Chris's father had left him the rental property, whereas my father's business had passed to my eldest sibling. But more than that, it was the paternal support that Chris described that had impacted emotionally. In contrast, my own father had often felt unavailable, even a little detached. Like all psychotherapists, I work with a supervisor. Their role is to support me and ensure I aspire to the best level of professionalism, by acting as an impartial third party in my therapeutic work. This helps reduce the risk of serious oversight and gives me a space to reflect on my feelings, thoughts, behaviour and general approach. Although it is not therapy per se, my work with decluttering clients often moves into deeper psychological territory. And when work such as this impacts on me personally, I find it invaluable to discuss things with my supervisor. It can be difficult to mask my personal reactions at times, and in fact I am not of the school that thinks the therapist should be a neutral, impassive observer. Rather, I believe there is value in being seen as human and flawed, and showing yourself in the therapeutic process, as this helps establish trust and authenticity in the relationship. There is, of course, always a tricky balance to be struck: I need to show myself openly, but not allow my personal reactions to get in the way of our work. This is where the support of a supervisor is especially relevant. It helps me to more fully understand the impact the work is having on me, and also to get clear about what might be helpful to share with my clients and what is better dealt with in my own process.

Our next session was one of the last I did with Chris. We had completed the basement and all the upstairs rooms and were now working on clearing and reorganising the large ground-floor room at the front of the house. It was a beautiful space, with high ceilings, ornate Victorian plaster coving and a huge bay window that flooded the space with light.

'What about this chair? Do you want to keep it?' I asked.

Chris looked at the tired-looking armchair I was referring to. 'Yes. I know it's a bit tatty, but I like it.'

'Okay,' I said. Taking a closer look, I saw that, aside from the threadbare arms, it was quite a nice chair. I was very aware of Chris's tendency to mirror his dad and repair and make do. But there was certainly potential in this piece of furniture. 'I know that sometimes I've encouraged you to do the opposite, but maybe in this case, you could get it reupholstered and re-varnish the wood, give it a new lease of life?'

'Yeah, that's a great idea,' Chris said. 'Dad always used to sit and watch the football from here on a Sunday afternoon. That was one of the few times he'd allow himself to take a break. Other than that, he'd always be beavering away at something ...'

As Chris's words tailed off, I could see that he was wrestling with some deep emotions. As I mentioned earlier, running alongside the whole project of working on the house was a reassessment of his relationship with his father and a processing of grief. Much of the time, this project had been a practical and intellectual exercise, but as we neared the end, it was clear from his reaction that there was still more emotional work to be done. So, we made ourselves some hot drinks and I just sat with Chris while he talked more about his dad and the loss he felt.

After we'd finished our drinks and our chat, I took a look around the room. The sets of built-in shelves either side of the fireplace had been full of old paperbacks, stacks of papers and VHS tapes. Now, they were pretty much cleared, and were home to Chris's books. There wasn't much more to be done in the room, and I started to vacuum the carpet. Chris moved the chair so I could clean underneath. As he did so, I saw what looked like a scrap of paper on the floor. Chris had obviously noticed it as well, and bent down to pick it up. As he turned it over, we both saw it was an old photograph.

'Oh my God, that's my dad!' Chris exclaimed. He examined the picture for a while and then handed it to me. Looking confidently out from the faded photo was a smartly dressed man, probably around the same age as Chris was now. He was shorter than I'd imagined, but I could see a pride and resolution in his eyes that chimed perfectly with the image of the man I'd built up in my mind. This was one of those very moving, profound and sublime moments that happen sometimes in my work. Neither of us said anything, but there was something communicated in the look we exchanged. It told me we both shared the feeling that this picture somehow showed that his father's loving presence had been there with us the whole time.

It's not unusual for me to experience this type of almost otherworldly moment with clients. We are immersed in everyday reality, pushing through the obstacles of life and the clutter that's been left to them or that they've accumulated. And then something from the parallel psychological realm seems to bleed through and become manifest in the physical world. Some may say these are merely coincidences, but I prefer to think in terms of what Carl Jung called synchronicity: 'the simultaneous occurrence of two meaningfully but not causally connected events'. Among his patients, Jung observed that synchronicity often happened at times of emotional intensity and upheaval, often peaking right before a psychological breakthrough.

'You know what, Helen? I think I'm going to shelve the idea of selling and stick around in the house for a while. Sure, there are a lot of memories, but I feel I've really taken ownership of this place now. What's left over from my dad is what I've chosen to hold on to.'

A year or so later, I spoke to Chris again. I was delighted to hear that he was going to become a father. He had decided now was the right time to put the house on the market and relocate to west London. He planned to set up a new home there with his partner and their child. 'I know Dad would understand me selling up. It just makes sense to move, as it's closer to her family and better for my work,' he told me. 'I'm sad he won't be around to see his grandchild, but his legacy will give us a great start in life.'

*

Moving into a different home can allow us the opportunity to redefine who we are. I think of it as like when a snake sheds its skin as part of its growth cycle. Yet often, as Chris had done initially, people simply box up their old lives and unpack them pretty much as they were in a new location. Others end up keeping boxes of their possessions packed away indefinitely in a loft or spare room. There's nothing wrong with that, of course, if it's done as a conscious choice. But if your life is not exactly how you would like it to be, why not take the opportunity to reassess? Whether you are moving house or just reorganising your current place, everyone will benefit from taking a fresh look at their home.

We tend to think of ourselves as fixed, but in many ways, who we are at forty or fifty bears little relation to us as twenty-somethings, starting off in life. Our beliefs, behaviour and even our values can change radically over time. It can be reassuring in all this flux to have a fixed point, a North Star by which to navigate our lives, and our homes and the possessions within them can play that role. But do you want to continue to be defined by the objects and environment that you built around yourself many years ago? This is especially important to consider if the choices you made at that time weren't made particularly mindfully. Perhaps you simply opted for the latest fad, or what was easiest in the moment? Maybe you've just stuck with places and things you were given or inherited? And it's not only homes and possessions we inherit. Do you find yourself behaving around the home in ways you recognise from your parents that you swore you'd never repeat? Or perhaps, if you think about it, do you suspect you might have gone the other way, and do the polar opposite of what you saw growing up? If these patterns are a little unconscious, chances are they don't really serve you as fully as a more mindful way of being.

Becoming more conscious of your behaviours and choices around how you create and inhabit the spaces in your life can be very helpful, and you may gain some useful insights by reflecting on where or from whom these patterns derive. From this clearer perspective of where you are now, and perhaps with a little more insight about how you got there, why not take a step back and set aside time to create a fresh vision of how *you* want your home life to be?

If you would like to try a version of the visioning process I did with Chris, you can download a free template and worksheet from helensanderson.com/secret.

# Nothing on the floor that doesn't have feet

Our homes and the spaces within them should be there to serve us, but my clients can often feel as if they are slaves to their homes. When the places we live are poorly designed and disorganised, they hinder our ability to nurture ourselves. A bad layout can reflect and contribute to a difficult relationship to the home. The space will drain our energy instead of supporting us, and this can have a significant impact on our relationships with those we share our homes with, especially our kids. Children are particularly sensitive to their environment and will feel this strongly, although, like us, they may not be aware of exactly why they are affected. I often work with parents who have young children. Understanding and trying to help meet the needs of a child is a passion of mine, and an area where I did a fair bit of work in a previous career. I learned that for children, having special time with their parents' undivided attention is a precious thing, and the value of this should never be underestimated.

Maria, one of my early clients, taught me a lot about the positive impact that optimising our space can have on family relationships. She was a busy mum who had the tricky task of being not only supportive and caring, but also having to set boundaries and contain her daughter's emotions. This is a tricky balance for any parent, but with a child that arrives with a painful early life and resultant challenging behaviour, it can become a dance that is exceptionally difficult to do. Maria's daughter Sadie was a particularly special child: she had been adopted, and brought with her a lot of issues they were still working through. The love that Maria had for her was obvious, and although their journey together was tough, the commitment she offered Sadie was unwavering. Sadly, it seemed that there was often little energy left for Maria to cope with the demands of her home, and almost none to devote to herself and her own needs.

When Maria first called me, it quickly became apparent that she was struggling to cope. 'I really need help, Helen. I'm afraid my house has gone to pot. It's pure chaos, there's clutter everywhere, and I just don't know where to start. It all feels so overwhelming.'

From her agitated tone, it was clear she was at her wits' end, so I offered her some reassurance. 'I understand exactly what you are experiencing, Maria. And it's okay, believe me. I can help; that's what people like me are here for.'

I heard Maria take a deep breath and her speech slowed down a little. 'Just to reassure you, it's not like I'm a hopeless case. There aren't huge heaps of stuff, it's just very disorganised. But the more I think about it, the more paralysed I feel. And the more likely I am to end up in bed with packet of biscuits.'

Whenever someone tells me something of this ilk, I always wonder if there might be some depression in the mix.

'Are you serious about going to bed with biscuits?'

'Oh yeah, absolutely. I'll definitely grab a packet and head off upstairs at times. I do love my duvet.'

'Okay. Do you do that a lot?'

'More than I'd like. Once my husband, Paul, has left for work and the kids are out of the door and off to school, I look around the house, and sometimes it all feels too much. I don't know what's wrong with me. I really want to be a good mother, to give them a nice, nurturing place to come home to. But when I see the state of this place, I feel that I'm just not doing a good enough job. I keep going over it in my head, trying to work out what I've done wrong to create so much clutter, and how I can sort it out. But no matter how much I think about it, I get nowhere. I just end up coming to the conclusion that I'm useless, or simply a bad person.' She began to cry.

Having heard a similar, self-critical voice in my own life, I knew how crippling it can be and felt a deep empathy for Maria. It is unlikely that anyone can think themselves out of a vicious circle like the one she described. Firstly, because it takes practical action alongside thinking, and secondly because it is usually the thinking, or some internal psychological process, that is contributing to the build-up of clutter in the first place. Importantly, though, Maria had taken the courageous step of asking for help. And by doing so, she was admitting that she was stuck, and that significant action was needed to get things back on track.

I sought to reassure her. 'This is very common; please don't beat yourself up. You're not a bad person, you've just got caught up in a bit of a negative pattern. I see this a lot. You will be okay, but some proactive action is needed. What's great is that you've reached out for help; don't underestimate that. In fact, you could give yourself a pat on the back.'

My words seemed to be helping, and Maria was able to collect herself a little.

'Yeah, I definitely need help,' she said. 'I don't want to keep finding myself back in bed comfort-eating.'

'Of course not. I'm sure you know that while the duvet and biscuits quieten down the bad feelings for a bit, they can also feed this cycle of defeat. And that may undermine your confidence that you can take care of yourself in a healthier way.'

'Absolutely, that's what seems to happen. And it's not just me I need to look after. I just feel so bad when I'm getting the kids ready for school in the morning, and we have to run around playing "find the homework". When I think about them coming home to this mess every day, it's really upsetting. My eldest, John, is fine. He's a teenager and doing well at school. Outside that, he spends a lot of time at football practice or playing his online games. He seems fairly settled, although I don't see a lot of him. But little Sadie finds life pretty challenging, so I especially want her to have a nice place to come back to, I really do. I know how much she needs it, but I'm really struggling to do it all alone.'

'It's okay, Maria, I understand. Try not to give yourself too hard a time about this. Why don't we set a date for me to come and visit, and we can talk about how I can help you get things sorted out for you both?'

The following week, I headed down to south-east London, where Maria and her family lived. It was a large 1960s semi-detached house, part of a cluster set around a central communal grass area. Designed with a nod to the Modernist style, the façade featured several large steel-framed windows and wooden panelling painted in bright colours.

I followed a short path across an area of lawn that hadn't been mowed for a while, and rang the bell. The front door was glazed with obscured glass, and through it I saw a blurry form approach along the hallway. Maria opened the door to greet me. She was a short woman, dressed in stonewashed jeans and a sweatshirt, her long chestnut hair tied back in a ponytail.

She invited me inside. 'I'd say sorry for the mess, but that's a bit of an understatement, as you'll see.'

The small entrance hall was dominated by a precarious-looking coat rack. It was overloaded with coats, jackets, scarves and bags, and looked like it would topple over if asked to bear any more weight. Beyond the hallway, the front of the house was a large open-plan living area. Towards the rear was a generous dining room that led through to a decent-sized kitchen. For some of my clients, having limited space can contribute to them becoming cluttered, but having lots of room can also be a problem. Despite – or perhaps because of – the space, Maria had certainly managed to strew her stuff around. Like a well-buttered piece of toast, things were spread into every corner, and on top of almost every available surface.

We made our way upstairs, past a pair of duvets that hung over the first-floor banister. Maria showed me around two upstairs bedrooms, both of which were equally cluttered and filled with piles of boxes. Most of the surfaces were covered, and layers of clothes hung on many of the chairs, doors and radiators.

'I realise I've said this already, but I'm so sorry for all the mess. You can see why I called you.'

'That's okay; you don't need to apologise.'

'Sadie's room is at the end there.' Maria pointed towards the door. 'To be honest, I was already starting to lose control of the house, but it got worse after we adopted Sadie. When she moved in, she brought a load of emotional baggage, which takes a lot of time and energy to deal with. I'll tell you more another time.'

'It must be nice to have her around, though.'

'Of course. I wanted to adopt for years, so it was brilliant to bring her here and offer her a stable home. But it is a challenging relationship. When she's not at school or out with her friends, she spends most of her time in her bedroom.'

We stood at the doorway and looked into Sadie's room. Maria had clearly made an effort, and it was less cluttered than the rest of the house, but in its own way, it was still pretty chaotic. Sadie's books and art materials were piled haphazardly on the dressing table, and clothes were spilling out of the wardrobe.

John's bedroom was on the other side of the landing. I stuck my head in and was immediately struck by the contrast with what I'd seen so far. It was noticeably tidier than the rest of the house. His computer games and books were lined up in order on a high shelf above his desk, and a small stack of neatly folded football kits sat on the end of a perfectly made bed. It's fascinating how some children take on their parents' habits and patterns around the home, while others go in the opposite direction.

'I can see why he doesn't like to spend time with me,' Maria said, somewhat shamefaced again as we turned away from her son's room and back into the chaos of the rest of the house. 'Who would want to live in all this mess?'

Returning downstairs, what struck me the most was the dining area. Despite the open-plan layout of the house, this room was surprisingly dark and dingy. As I entered, I felt a bit like I had just walked into a war zone. It wasn't just the general chaos and disorder; there was a palpable feeling of collapse and depression. Although it was a decent size, there was very little free space due to the combination of excessive clutter and its jumbled layout. An extendable dining table was stacked high with piles of clothes, magazines and used crockery. There was a sofa, a large, black leather recliner and various other chairs, also covered in clutter. Looking up, I noticed that several of the bulbs in the recessed ceiling lights had blown, partially explaining the gloom. If ever a room could be described as depressed, this was one. I suspected it was little more than a dumping ground on the way to the kitchen, so I was surprised to hear Maria say that she did use it.

'At the end of the day, after I've fed Sadie and helped with her homework, sometimes all I can manage is to collapse in front of the TV and try to blank out the mess.'

I wasn't surprised she was feeling down. The mood of the room had affected me immediately, and I could only imagine how it was for her to live with this, day in and day out. Although my clients often say they don't notice the cluttered state of their homes anymore, I am never convinced. I knew that, however accustomed to its disorder Maria had become, the condition of the room would still have a significant impact on her state of mind. It was likely to be a constant reminder of how she was struggling to stay on top of things. Perfect fuel for the rampant inner critic I'd heard her voice a number of times.

'Where do you usually eat?' I asked.

Motioning towards the front of the house, she said, 'In the lounge, on the sofa in there.'

I was struck that the pair of French doors between the lounge and the dining area didn't open fully. The reclining chair Maria sat in to watch TV was in the way. It was almost as if she had started to barricade herself in. I felt I hadn't arrived a minute too soon. The restricted flow through to the kitchen was made worse by the piles of obstacles you had to clamber over. The kitchen and dining area are places we feed and nurture our bodies, our family and friends.

For Maria, it seemed unlikely many of these things were happening here.

'It really gets me down to see everything like this,' Maria confided as we stood and contemplated what had once been the dining area. 'It's just got embarrassing, and I don't want to let anyone in anymore. I can't bear the idea that people will judge me and think I'm not a good mother, so I feel that I have to hide how bad it's got.'

She slumped down on one of the dining chairs and looked round the room again.

'I remember how it was when Paul and I first moved in. We were full of hope and energy, and we put so much effort into creating a homely space. Now I feel as if I'm sinking into this deep, dark hole. My GP says I'm depressed and gave me some tablets, but I don't like to take them.'

It didn't surprise me to hear that Maria no longer invited friends over. Isolating yourself from others can be a classic sign of depression, and of course is very common when people feel shame about their home. The fact that she had named her depression felt positive to me, though, as it meant I could acknowledge and address the issue more directly.

'I know what those dark feelings are like. They can be so isolating, and I can understand why you couldn't face dealing with the clutter alone. There is a way out, though, and taking back control of your home can be the start of that. We can get this place back to how you remember it – better, in fact.'

Maria sat a little more upright in the chair. 'I'd love to believe that. I just worry that the horrible way I can seem to attack myself will kick in again. It's so hard to stay positive when that takes over.'

'It's okay,' I reassured her. 'You have me as a defender and advocate on your side now. Tell your inner critic we'll see her in court! We won't let your depression defeat us.'

I don't often use a fighting metaphor when it comes to illness. I would hate to imply that people who don't get over a disease are somehow losers who haven't fought hard enough. But in this instance, I thought it might help Maria to see her depression as an adversary she could take on, rather than as something she was a victim of and could never change.

'How does Paul feel about the state of the house? Does he know you've called me?'

'Yes – actually, it was him who suggested that maybe we needed to get some help. He's quite an easy-going, tolerant guy, and like me I think he's just got used to it. He works very long hours and when he's home, he tends to just watch a bit of TV and then go to bed early. He's usually up and out of the house before any of us are awake.'

As we continued to contemplate the dining room, I kept looking at the large black recliner. To me, it personified despair and melancholy. People talk about living with depression as 'wrestling with the black dog'. Perhaps, in this case, it was a big, chair-shaped one? And I wondered if, rather than wrestling with it, we could just get it out of the room – in fact, out of the house altogether. Getting rid of the recliner wasn't going to magically heal Maria's depression, of course. But I hoped that, symbolically and practically, removing it might help kickstart the process of change we were about to embark on.

'Apart from the late-night TV, do you use this chair much? It seems to dominate the room somewhat.' I guess I was being diplomatic, because it was clear the room was mainly being used as a dumping area.

'Not really. It was a good one, though, when we bought it.'

'You could donate it to charity, or Freecycle it. Are you open to letting it go?' I asked, feeling that if there was an elephant in the room, this was it (sorry for mixing my metaphors here!). 'Freecycle is a fabulous online community where someone will come and collect your stuff and give it a good home – much less hassle than selling stuff online.'

'You know what? Yes. Let's get rid of it. I don't really like the person I become when I end up slouched in it.'

I had expected resistance, but Maria seemed ready to embrace the change. When things are stuck, I might facilitate a short, imaginary dialogue between a client and their possession. I find this often helps them understand a bit more about their attachment to it. But in this case, it clearly wasn't necessary. To me, this was a positive indication that, despite her low mood, Maria was ready to tackle what needed to be done, for her and for Sadie. Some clients are very tangled up in resistance and have an ambivalence about getting rid of their clutter. Others, like Maria, are more ready to change, but just don't know how to make it happen. Perhaps they simply need an expert helping hand, someone to guide them through the practical and psychological challenges they'll encounter.

We spent the rest of that first meeting clarifying Maria's goals.

'As you've already told me, you want to get on top of your home and clear all this clutter,' I said. 'But once that's gone, thinking about the new future we are making room for, how would you like your home to be?'

Maria took a deep breath and exhaled slowly. 'I'd really love to know I have a place for everything to live. To feel things are held and contained, instead of just spilling out everywhere.'

'That sounds great. And what else?'

She paused for a moment, then said: 'What would be really special would be to create a lovely space so we can sit together as a family, to eat and just spend some time together. I'd love that.'

The suggestion really touched me, and I smiled at Maria. 'That is such a great vision. I can just imagine you sitting here together.'

Having established a clear picture of what we were aiming for, we agreed a plan of action, and scheduled in an extended series of day-long sessions. It was going to take some time to turn things around, but with the additional motivation of helping mother and daughter connect more, we were both inspired to make it happen.

When I arrived for our first proper session, the black recliner had gone, and it seemed to me that Maria looked a bit lighter already. Perhaps not only from letting go of the chair, but also because she had reached out for some help. It is not always true that change comes from the inside first. When you change your outer, physical environment, your inner reality can change, too. Time and again, I witness people dramatically alter the conditions of their inner lives by changing the organisation and energy in their physical environment. I hoped and suspected this would be the case for Maria, too.

By taking action and donating the recliner, Maria had begun the process of change. Having made this initial shift, the task ahead of us seemed just a little easier. A cluttered room can be a bit like one of those Mystic Square puzzles, where you have to slide the tiles into the empty space in order to rearrange them and reveal the image. In this case, the key thing had been to create that bit of empty space so the rest of the things could be shifted around to help us realise the vision we had defined. I know some people extoll the virtues of tackling things small pieces at a time, but that doesn't work for everyone. When people are really stuck, I find it often helps to tackle the biggest challenges first. I think about the scenes in movies when new arrivals in a tough prison go up and start a fight with the biggest guy in there. I guess, in the same way, my strategy is about showing the house or the clutter who's the boss.

I began, as always, by setting up my decluttering prompt cards and containers around the room, and placed one of the dining chairs in the centre for Maria to sit on.

'Okay, if you're ready, I'd like you to sit here.' I rested my hand on the back of the chair.

Maria moved over somewhat hesitantly and sat herself down on the edge of the seat.

To put her more at ease, I continued light-heartedly: 'Right. You are the head honcho, the CEO, chief decision-maker. You only have one job, but it is the most important one: to decide which pile to put each item into. Keep, donate, sell, recycle, bin, action, and so on.'

Maria smiled. After a nervous pause, she said, 'Okay … I'll give it a go. What if I'm not sure? I'm a bit rubbish when it comes to making decisions.'

'That's okay. Being more decisive is a muscle that you can build through practice. Trust me, you'll soon get the hang of it. If you really aren't sure, use the "don't know" pile and we'll come back to it later. But use it sparingly, please.'

With the process established, we threw ourselves into the mammoth task at hand. Maria did struggle at first. But as the morning progressed, old toys, clothes, papers and food supplies were steadily designated to different piles. By mid-afternoon, things started to go much more quickly. We grouped possessions that Maria chose to keep in logical piles, ready to be relocated to more appropriate places around the house. And we carted unwanted stuff out of that room by the bagful. Out to the bin, recycling containers or to the car, so they were already on their way to the charity shop. Gradually, from beneath the clutter, the table surface began to emerge, and soon after that, so did a dining space.

'When we're finished with this project, I suggest you think about creating a House Charter, some basic ground rules that everyone agrees to abide by to help maintain the order we are creating.' I picked up yet another bag from the floor. 'One good rule might be "Nothing on the floor that doesn't have feet".'

Maria laughed. 'I like that.'

Towards the end of that first session, the front door slammed. It was Maria's daughter Sadie, arriving home from school. A nervous-looking, slightly built girl, with her hair in a long plait poked her head around the door.

Maria had dropped what she was doing and stood up as soon as she heard the door. 'Hello, love. How was school?' she asked.

'Okay,' Sadie replied brusquely. She dumped her oversized duffle coat and bag on to one of the living room chairs.

'I just need to make Sadie a snack. I'll be back with you soon, Helen.'

As they made their way past me into the kitchen, the little girl threw me a sly sideways glance.

A few minutes later, they emerged together from the kitchen. Sadie set down the carton of juice and sandwich she was carrying, and picked up one of my illustrated decluttering cards, examining it carefully. I created these to engage and inspire the inner child, so I find children are often drawn to them.

'There's more in the box if you want to take a look,' I suggested. 'Are you interested in art?'

Sadie shrugged. 'Yeah it's alright,' she said, dropping the card. She hurried off upstairs with her food.

'She had a pretty tough first few years with her mum, and

finds it hard to trust people, especially strangers,' Maria confided in a hushed tone. 'Sadie's been living with me for over three years, and the authorities still haven't been able to locate the parting papers from her family of origin. I'm trying to piece together all the details, but there certainly wasn't a lot of nurturing for the poor love. I had some sense of what I was taking on, of course. But nothing can fully prepare you for the reality of how that early trauma impacts a kid. She can be pretty wild at times.'

I don't want to give the impression that the condition of Maria's home meant that she wasn't properly looking after her daughter. She was clearly devoted to Sadie's care. But I began to wonder if the disorder in the home might be linked in some way to their difficult relationship. From what I'd seen of the house and heard from Maria, it was apparent that things in her household were breaking down. It certainly wasn't working optimally for either of them. Things needed to change here – and quickly, as mother and child were certainly facing some significant challenges. I really wanted to realise the vision we had established, and I thought that if I could help Maria uncover a little of what was going on beneath the clutter, it would help.

As we'd identified when we spoke on the phone, Maria struggled to nurture herself, but as I got a fuller picture of the condition of her home, I also began to consider whether the solution for her was also about establishing boundaries and containment. She had mentioned this herself, in more practical terms, when we set our goals in the first session. But my growing sense was that both her and Sadie would benefit from creating a home and spaces that could serve as containers for some of her daughter's inner turmoil.

As we'd worked through the room, clearing, ordering and sorting, I did what I always do and waited for my intuition to show me the best configuration for this space, this family. A layout that would better work for them. I struggled with this one, though. As I mentioned, the room had, for a long time, been little more than a rather wide and messy corridor to the kitchen. Corridor-style rooms are the most awkward areas to design, and I didn't want to get into the trap of putting everything around the edges. This is not only boring, but also never a great use of space. The week preceding our next scheduled session, a flash of inspiration came to me, and I excitedly emailed Maria.

*I have a cunning plan for your dining room. Can you get a few things before next Thursday? A TV aerial extension, some picture hooks, wire clips, some plants and a couple of lamps.*

I also suggested she take down the dark red curtains that were half hanging off the pole and made the room feel heavy, along with the net curtains, which had come with the house and she'd never made a conscious choice about. *Maybe you can get some wooden Venetian blinds to replace them?* I suggested and included a link to some affordable ones I had found, along with a few suggestions for some lamps.

When I arrived for the next session, I was delighted to see that the curtains and nets had gone. Not only that, the Venetian blinds had also been installed, and Maria had chosen some lovely lamps, which had arrived that morning. These were great signs that Maria was starting to become more proactive and engaged with her home.

'I never liked those curtains, anyway,' Maria said. 'Paul put up the blinds at the weekend. I'd forgotten that he was a bit of a DIY buff.'

What was especially lovely was that the blinds were raised so you could see a few daffodils potted up in a box on the windowsill, meaning there was not only light coming in, but also some beautiful flowers. There was something deeply symbolic in the opening up of the blinds, letting in the light. Oh, and she had replaced the blown light bulbs, too. There was a great sense of building momentum.

'Maria, what a star. You're on fire! The room is starting to look so much better.'

'Thank you. I have to confess, when you first said you were going to set me some homework, I wasn't happy. But actually, I really love the little projects you set me between sessions. I got really excited about choosing lamps and planting those daffs. It was also nice for me and Paul to have a little project to work on together over the weekend.'

Maria's zest for life seemed to be returning. I noticed that she moved with greater purpose and energy and was laughing more and more. In fact, we laughed a lot as we worked.

'Why on earth did I keep that? What was I thinking!' Maria chuckled, as she discarded the packaging from an ancient mobile phone that must itself have been long gone.

Now that we had cleared the floor and surfaces, there was space to move the furniture around. We both agreed that a large cabinet needed to be moved out of the front room. I showed her how we could move this heavy piece of furniture together, gently walking the corners on to a rug so we could slide it along the wooden floor.

Sometimes, I take a fun little device to my sessions with clients. It's a red button, like a quiz-show buzzer, and when you press it, it says, in a mechanical voice: 'That was easy!' It's a fun way to mark and celebrate small victories, especially those which are not, in fact, easy. The irony suits my sense of humour. Often when we actually deal with things we expect to be difficult, though, we discover they were much harder in our heads than they were in reality. After moving the cabinet, Maria and I both rushed to hit the button, laughing. The pair of us were so energised and enthusiastic. Seeing so many things change and so many improvements was truly motivating.

It was half-term break that week, meaning Sadie was in the house as we decluttered. She seemed more engaged and interested in what we were doing than previously. This time, she did want to look at my cards, and I noticed she was examining them carefully. Maria asked me if I could do a mini session with Sadie in her room and spend a bit of time showing her my process. Of course, Sadie wasn't able to make lots of big decisions about what to let go, but we did spend a bit of time reorganising her wardrobe and creating a photo wall of picture frames she had created. It was a special session, and such a privilege to be given not only the trust of Maria, but that of Sadie, for whom trusting did not come easily.

The following session, Sadie was back at school and we completed our work on the dining-room area. I moved the TV so it not longer stood in front of the stylish wooden fireplace that had emerged from behind the clutter. At my suggestion, Maria had bought a new bureau that fitted perfectly into the recess to the right of the chimney breast, replacing the ugly old computer console that had been there. We lifted the TV onto the new piece of furniture, along with a telephone, answering machine, DVD player, satellite box and Wi-Fi router.

Sometimes in my work, it's a case of two steps forward, one step back. In contrast to the previous session, Maria seemed quite flat and unresponsive. In recognition of her mood, I gave her a low-energy job: sorting through a pile of books she had decided to keep. This had been whittled down from the huge collection we had started with to a manageable number. I didn't know if Maria was a prolific reader, but she was definitely a prolific shopper. As she sat in an armchair sorting and categorising the books, I began to tackle the complicated jumble of power cables, extension leads and wires that fed all the electronics we had relocated. Tangled cables such as these are not uncommon in my line of work, but this was a particularly impressive example, and I'd had my eye on sorting it ever since I first spotted it.

'I'm glad someone is doing that,' Maria said. 'It drives me nuts, but I can never be bothered to deal with it.'

'Yes – I'm sorting out your communication channels!' I joked. I started to separate and untangle the writhing knot. 'How is Sadie finding all these changes at home?' I asked, as I unplugged the telephone cable.

'To be honest Helen, she's not doing so well. She was placed in a special school at the start of the year, and it's not been an easy adjustment for her.'

'I'm sure it hasn't been straightforward. And it's a lot for *you* to deal with as well, Maria.'

'It is – and I feel pretty unsupported by the local authorities. They say they're really busy, but it's as if they've washed their hands of us.' She dropped the book she'd been holding on to the pile by her chair and let out a deep sigh. 'It's all a bit of a mess, but that's what life is like, really – isn't it?'

'The new school must be better for her, though, if she's getting more specialist support.'

'I suppose so. I have noticed a few positive changes recently. She has a new teacher she likes, and she seems to sense the value in what we are doing here, and is responding to it. When she got in from school yesterday, she actually hung up her jacket behind the door instead of dumping it on the chair.'

We carried on talking about Sadie and her struggles at school as I continued to sort out the wires, rolling up any excess length and tying them together. I carry a little roll of Velcro just for this job. I repositioned the reorganised wires neatly out of sight behind the bureau, and tacked the extension wire around the skirting.

'That's better. It feels as if the room can breathe again,' I said, stepping back. That side of room looked pretty good, and, if not exactly enthusiastic, Maria seemed pleased.

As we stood there admiring our handiwork, the phone rang. I encourage my clients to switch their mobiles to 'do not disturb', as I find it helps to avoid this sort of distraction when decluttering, but this was the landline ringing.

'Sorry, this could be important,' Maria said, picking up the cordless phone and walking into the next room.

When she returned a few minutes later, she said, 'You won't believe this. That was the council, our social worker. They've found Sadie's papers! Details about her family of origin, the whole back story. They just turned up. We'll be getting copies soon.' She looked at the wires I'd untangled earlier and laughed. 'It's exactly as you said, the communications channels *have* been sorted.'

We looked at each other and smiled. Both of us could see how this apparently unrelated event seemed to reflect the increasing clarity and order in her life.

I'd never claim that making changes in your home has supernatural effects. But time and again during my work with clients, I witness what some may describe as coincidences but I prefer to think of as synchronicity. I don't know how it works, but when we unstick and re-establish flow in our homes, it seems to help other aspects of our lives flow more smoothly.

'I don't know quite how you did it, Helen,' Maria said, 'but it seems like you wove some kind of magic!'

It was good to see Maria's mood lifting, and with a little more positive momentum, we continued the work on the room. Our next task was to relocate the dining-room table, which, as I mentioned, had been out of commission. Once it was in position, Maria laid a boldly patterned tablecloth on top. It really was starting to feel like a home. At the far end of the room, at Maria's suggestion, we created a little art area for Sadie, using a small desk that we'd liberated from one of the bedrooms. I gathered up all her pens, paints and sketchbooks from around the living room and dining area, and organised them into some colourful containers. Then I carefully arranged a new lamp and the plants in the adjacent corner. If rooms had vocal cords, I would say it had started to sing.

When I'd first arrived in the house, my overwhelming impression was that absolutely everything was undefined and mixed up. There was no real sense that any room or area had a particular purpose or meaning any different from anywhere else. Food was as likely to be eaten in the living room or bedroom as in the kitchen. Clothes were equally liable to have found a home over the back of a dining chair as in a bedroom wardrobe. Creating the defined dining area was part of my intention to establish boundaries between different activities, and so add more structure to the lives of Maria and her family. Similarly, I hoped that collecting Sadie's art materials into one place would bring her a greater feeling of containment and safety, a sense that she had her own special place in the room.

There was just one more thing needed to complete the room. Maria had some really lovely artworks in the house. A vibrant red, orange and gold painting hung on the wall behind the door, meaning you didn't really see it when you entered. She also had a love of the Celtic tradition and had a wonderful picture of a family gathered around a fire. I took the pictures down and, with the new picture hooks, repositioned the bright orange one on the wall opposite the door, so it was the first thing you saw when you entered. It felt much better there, welcoming you warmly as you came into the room. The Celtic print went just above the table.

'That's perfect: it's like a calling together of the ancestors to bless the food,' Maria said. She stood back, looked at the print and straightened it slightly. 'I'm really committed to the idea of us eating together here at regular mealtimes. No more taking food up to the bedrooms or the front room.'

Before I left, we sat down at the table with a cup of tea, reflecting on the work we had done. We heard a clatter of keys and the front door opening as Sadie arrived home. As I've already mentioned, this was a child who was dealing with many challenges and carrying a lot of trauma from her very early life. I can only imagine how it must be for a young person who already has that degree of internal chaos to have a lot of disorder in their home as well. So, Sadie's reaction when she came home from school that day is something that will always stay with me. When she saw the room, there was a huge smile and a look of contentment on her face.

'Oh-em-gee! This room is dope,' she said, running excitedly around and looking at things. As Maria and I watched, we smiled at each other. It was like our inner children were also responding, saying, 'Yippee! Look at this room! This is really amazing, so wonderful.' It felt as if we had conjured this amazing space out of nothing.

Remembering I had relocated and organised Sadie's art supplies, I went over and sat with her. I showed her what I had done and where she could find everything. It felt important she was included in the process and orientated in the new space. She grabbed some coloured pencils and paper. 'It's totally lit. What should I draw?'

There was still a lot to do around the rest of the house and I carried on working with Maria on a fortnightly basis for a couple more months. Her energy and moods continued to go up and down, but she had revisited her GP, who'd prescribed some new medication. This seemed to be helping to level out her moods. Maria and Sadie continued to deal with the ongoing legacy of Sadie's traumatic early years, on top of the usual challenges that all parents face. Yet whenever I returned to their home out in the suburbs, things usually seemed a bit more harmonious. There were little signs, such as the way Sadie sat down and talked to Maria for a while when she came in from school, rather than disappearing upstairs immediately. And once, when I left, I looked back towards the house and through the front window saw Maria, John and Sadie sitting at the dining table together.

I don't want to paint an unrealistic picture of this as a simple happy ending. Clearing the years of accumulated clutter, along with the spatial and organisational changes, did have a significant impact. But on their own, they weren't going to be sufficient to bring about a complete transformation in this family. However, the process of clearing the house did remove some significant obstacles, and set the stage for Maria and Sadie to create some new ways of relating. When Maria said goodbye to me at the end of our final session, I think she understood this.

'I feel like I have a fighting chance now to be more of the mum that Sadie needs. We've done so much over the last few months, but I realise that now it's over to me. There are no more excuses – and the hardest part, perhaps, is just beginning.'

*

Defining clear personal and spatial boundaries is a key strategy that can help you nurture yourself and your home. Personal boundaries are basic rules about how you would like others to behave around you and how you behave towards yourself. For example, what behaviour you consider to be okay and what you don't, and how you will respond if someone oversteps those limits. Setting boundaries can help ensure your relationships are mutually respectful, appropriate and caring. However, boundaries are not just about protecting yourself or keeping people out: they are also a key part of defining your values. I'm not suggesting rules that are so rigid they get in the way of spontaneity or become a stick with which to beat yourself up. But like Maria and her family, most of us can benefit from having a House Charter that we agree on with those with whom we share our homes. You can download a free copy of my House Charter template and tips on writing one that works for you at helensanderson.com/secret.

You might also find it helpful to consider the ways in which you define and respect areas of your home. Take a step back, look carefully at your environment and ask yourself: what might this reflect? For example, if things are spilling out of a cupboard, is there something in yourself that you cannot contain or are avoiding containing? If you have filled a room that could be your art studio, craft room or writing office with junk from other parts of the house, why might you be restricting space for those creative projects? I often find the answers to this type of question bring invaluable insights.

If the configuration of your home feels chaotic, I recommend you start to establish some spatial boundaries in the place in which you live. Make use of the containment that each room, area or piece of furniture can create. Carefully considering the layout of spaces can be a key way of achieving this. Positioning furniture to practically and visually define specific areas in a room creates what architects refer to as positive space. For example, a table positioned at right angles to a wall will define a space behind it. These defining elements don't have to be continuous physical barriers: positioning a large plant or floor lamp can subtly suggest a boundary and the eye will fill in the gap. Along with the use of furniture, the choice of which smaller objects you keep in particular areas will also help create containment. We did this with Sadie's art materials: storing all her paper, paints and pencils in one place helped define that area as her creative space. Try to extend this by practising the tenet 'a place for everything and everything in its place'. In simple terms, this could mean keeping food in the kitchen and out of the bedroom, keeping paperwork in the office, or just putting the stapler back in the stationery drawer when you're done with it. It also means sticking to your House Charter, for example 'nothing on the floor that doesn't have feet'.

Having some clear personal and spatial boundaries in place can just make life simpler and give you greater freedom to relax and enjoy life.

# Holding back the years

As you read through the different tales in this book, I hope you are seeing that under many a pile of clutter there is a story. Often, the narrative has either come to a halt or is stuck in a loop, and needs to be brought to some kind of resolution in order for the person to move forward. Each time I help a client with this process, I become more and more convinced of this. Some stories are harder to uncover, more painful to hear, and so tougher to tell. This is one of those.

Felicity was a retired musician and music teacher. Our work together began, as usual, with a preliminary chat on the phone, and while I got all the facts that I needed to begin working with her, I had a powerful sense that, despite the presentation of confidence in her voice, there was something vulnerable about her.

When I walked into Felicity's house, an elegant Georgian property in south London, I immediately had a strong feeling that time had stood still in her home – which is not to say that it was antiquated or old fashioned. In the living room, for example, along with the beautiful original covings, picture rails and fireplace, there were some really nice pieces of modern furniture. A lot of thought had clearly been given to the interior design at one time, but now the place just struck me as a little lifeless. There was something of the museum about it all. Along one wall, a beautifully fitted set of bookshelves was filled with hundreds of books and magazines, mainly about music. Virtually two full shelves were taken up by a complete set of *Classical Music* magazine dating back to 1983, neatly arranged chronologically in labelled open box files. I scanned along one section, and not an issue was missing – until they stopped abruptly at August 2008, where a couple of empty files stood as if waiting for the rest of the year. There were also dozens of biographies of famous musicians and composers, along with histories of leading orchestras and famous music venues. It was quite an impressive collection, yet I had the distinct impression that none of them had been taken off the shelf for many years. Overall, the room felt like it was in a state of suspended animation.

I looked around the lounge again. My eye was drawn to a large antique Chinese sideboard. Dark and solid, it was lacquered with red and gold inlays against a black background. It looked slightly incongruous considering the mid-century style of most of the other furniture, but it brought a certain character to the living room, which I guessed was why Felicity had kept it.

As we walked through the rest of the rooms, talking, the intuition I'd had when we'd spoken on the phone persisted; there was a growing sense of something hidden in the house. Not necessarily physically, but in Felicity's relationship to the place. I was curious to know what it was, because I wanted to support her in finding some harmony again, and help her to move on from whatever it was. I also knew that I needed to accept that perhaps it would remain hidden, and that, as sometimes happens with clients, our work together might remain on a more practical level.

Felicity was a tall woman in her late fifties with long,

slightly fading red hair. She wore it drawn back tightly from her face, tied in a bun. I couldn't put my finger on it, but there was something rigid and defended about her. She seemed quite guarded, and our interactions tended towards being overly business-like. I'm not unused to this when I first meet clients, of course. Some people open up quickly, while others need to keep themselves safe until we have built up enough trust between us. That's not to say Felicity wasn't able to talk about her feelings and what she wanted. For example, during our initial call, she had told me she was suffering from depression and felt really stuck. But it all felt somehow one step removed, as if there was an invisible shield or barrier that she needed to maintain in order to keep something in her protected.

'What are your long-term plans?' I asked.

She gave a deep sigh. 'I feel very attached to this house; I've been here for so many years. But I really need to downsize. The cost of maintaining the old place is getting a bit much, and, realistically, I only use half of the rooms. It just takes a lot of energy to move, and I feel so down most of the time. And while I like the idea of relocating, whenever I begin to think about it, I really don't know whereabouts I'd move to.'

There was a sense of resignation in her tone that I recognised at once as typical of depression. It is such a disabling illness. At times, it can be like there's a voice in your head telling you that every idea, plan or dream you have is a waste of time, that it will never amount to anything. And if you hear that, day in and day out, you can begin to think it's true. It can feel like mental torture, and unless you are blessed with having people in your life feeding you some alternative information, you can easily become stuck in that one-dimensional reality.

'I understand how hard and painful that feeling of

"stuckness" is,' I said. 'But that's why you've called me, isn't it? I sense there's part of you that wants to start getting things back in motion.'

'I guess so. I just couldn't face dealing with all this alone.'

Anyway, regardless of whether Felicity was going to stay there indefinitely or move on, it felt vitally important to address the clutter and organisation of the house. The over-whelming impression I had was that her life had virtually come to a standstill. The longer I looked around, the more I noticed things that looked like they hadn't been touched for years. From the dusty photo frames on the mantelpiece to the piles of unopened letters on the table by the front door, the sense of stagnation was palpable. I couldn't see any way Felicity could move forward without addressing what I can only describe as the build-up of the past. What do I mean by that? I'm talking about the way that, if we allow things to accumulate without processing them, aspects of the past remain present in our homes and our psyches instead of receding naturally. This physical and mental clutter takes up valuable room in our heads and our spaces, and affects our capacity to both live in the present and move on into the future.

We agreed that the books and magazines in the living room needed to be weeded down and reorganised, but other than that, there were two main jobs. First, tackling a huge backlog of many years' worth of correspondence and paperwork. This was stored in various places around the house in a large col-lection of bags. And not just any bags: those giant blue IKEA ones. Secondly, to clear the back bedroom that Felicity had set up years earlier as her music teaching room.

We walked up the stairs and made our way to the rear of the house to take a look. There was a solemnity to the house and Felicity's manner, and it felt like there was nothing new anywhere. As we passed old prints and photos on the wall, my sense of the house as museum was reinforced. In an alcove at the top of the stairs was a blue Scandinavian-style vase containing a display of dried flowers. Any hint of life and colour they'd once held had long since faded to a dusty brown.

'I have to rent this room out,' said Felicity in a resigned tone as we stood in the doorway contemplating the old music room. 'I've been largely living off my savings for a while now, and I could really do with some extra money coming in. I suppose I have to accept that it has been years since I had any students in here, and I can't see myself ever teaching again.'

It was clear that music had been a huge part of Felicity's life. The room was home to a collection of musical instruments that she must have used for teaching, along with music stands, metronomes, tuning forks and various other trappings of her profession. To one side of the chimney breast were four sturdy built-in shelves, heavily laden with piles and piles of folded paper.

'What are these?' I picked up and unfolded one of them, and quickly realised they were musical scores.

'I really want to keep all these, they are such a big part of my old life.'

'Of course,' I said, 'but as you want to rent out the room, they will need to be sorted through, organised and relocated elsewhere in the house.'

'There's no room; that's the trouble,' Felicity said.

'Don't worry, we'll find a home for them,' I reassured her. 'You'll be amazed at the space we liberate when we sort through things.'

A rather tatty-looking green velvet Chesterfield sofa-bed stood against the wall opposite the door. The contrast between the quality of its design and its somewhat threadbare appearance spoke of how Felicity's abundant past had been overtaken by years of stasis and austerity.

'Do you want to keep this?' I asked, examining the fabric a little more closely to see if repair or reupholstering was an option. 'It's a lovely piece, but maybe it's had its day.' I pushed on the seat and noticed that the springs felt shot.

'Agreed. My sister slept on it last year, and by all accounts she didn't have a great night.' Felicity sat on the sofa and gave it a little bounce, somehow giving me the impression that she hadn't sat on it herself for quite some time. 'I can't imagine anyone wanting to rent the room with this to sleep on, but I don't know how to get rid of it,' she said.

When you are depressed, doing even simple things can feel like climbing a mountain, and although this task wasn't exactly simple, it wasn't that difficult, either. We chatted over the options she had. Call the council, sell it on eBay, arrange a charity collection.

After this first meeting, Felicity made a few calls and arranged for someone to take the sofa-bed, and when I arrived for the next session, it was no longer there. It felt like there had already been a shift, and that we had established a sense of momentum in the direction of her goals. Getting that room sorted so there was some money coming in was going to create some ease and flow, which was a priority for Felicity. While she didn't say so explicitly, there were signs around the house that led me to suspect she was struggling financially.

Setting aside its current state of clutter, the old music room was beautifully proportioned and quite generously sized. An ornate gilded mirror stood above the marble fireplace, and a pair of elegant sash windows opened on to the garden. I felt sure someone would love to rent it once it was sorted out.

The practicalities of the decluttering process went quite smoothly, and we worked together in an efficient and pro-fessional way. We began by putting all the music scores into cardboard boxes that we piled up on the landing, temporary storage until we found them a permanent home. Felicity had lots of lovely objects in the room. They were difficult things to say goodbye to, but she made her choices and kept the items that had most value and meaning for her. We talked a little as we worked, establishing more of a connection, but Felicity remained fairly guarded. I love to sing and had been a member of a choir for many years, so I attempted to start a conversation about her singing career, but Felicity was quite reticent. Recognising this might be a painful subject, I let it drop.

With all the scores boxed up, we moved on to the lower shelves, which were filled with wooden box files. These contained a large collection of programmes from classical music concerts. Each one had been carefully wrapped in a plastic sleeve for protection. Without even looking at the programmes, Felicity said, 'They're from my performances as a soloist; I used to travel a lot to perform and record. Just throw them all away. I never look at them anymore.' Then, after a short pause, in a slightly more melancholy tone, she said, 'That part of my life feels dead, anyway.'

This struck me as slightly at odds with her desire to keep all the musical scores, which flagged something for me. Although I generally encourage people to let go of things they no longer need, I'm also aware that they can get carried away in the process. A vital part of my work is to help people keep their precious memories intact and connect to what has meaning for them. The last thing I want is for people to discard possessions they subsequently regret letting go of. Inevitably, this does sometimes happen, so I always warn people that they may occasionally end up throwing away a few things that they later want. But I'm also keen to empha-sise that this isn't a reason to hold on to everything. On this occasion, I was aware that there may have been something pushing Felicity to discard these programmes. Perhaps her decision was more driven by the fact that she didn't want to go through the process of looking at them and awaken memories or feelings that she preferred to remain buried.

'Are you sure?' I said. 'These seem quite significant to you. You have held on to them for all this time and stored them quite carefully.'

'I just can't look at them now,' she snapped. Probably realising she had been a little abrupt, she followed this immediately with, 'I'm sorry. There are just too many memories, so much loss.'

'I completely understand. I think this collection might be what I call a "gremlin", meaning they hold a powerful emotional charge. What I suggest is that we put them away safely in some storage boxes and set you a reminder to come back to them in a while, say twelve months. How does that sound?'

'I suppose that makes sense,' Felicity said, carefully picking up one of the programmes.

'Is that one important to you?' I asked, sensing that she was reconnecting to some meaningful memories.

'Not really.' She shrugged and put it carefully back on the shelf. 'Just wondering where to store them. So, what's next?'

I'd noticed that often when I asked questions such as this, ones that were beyond the practicalities of the task at hand, they were met with short, almost abrupt answers. It was clear that Felicity was not ready to open up, so I respected that and kept things on a simple level.

It was hard work, but by the end of that first day we had cleared the room. Felicity's sister had offered to take some photos to go on the rental listing. In preparation for this, we spent some time dressing the room so it would look its best in the pictures. I suggested we leave a couple of metronomes on the chest of drawers as a little nod to the history of the room. A fabulous Chinese silk kimono had been on a hook hidden behind the door, so we hung it on the wall as a decoration. And we collected up some beautiful glass paperweights and arranged them on the windowsill, where they caught the late afternoon light.

'As soon as the new bed arrives, it will be ready to let,' I said, as we stood back and admired our work. With the shift in energy, it felt like some flow was coming back into Felicity's life. I noticed a little smile that pointed to some greater positivity in her. And perhaps some softening in what I imagined was a powerful internal voice saying *I must be strong*, that may have been one factor holding her stuck in place.

As we walked downstairs, Felicity opened up to me a little about her feelings.

'Thank you, it's been great working with you today. I feel that I've been living alone so long. Not only in the house, but with my depression. As I may have said to you when we first met, I just got to a point where I felt I couldn't deal with it on my own.'

'You don't have to. I've had my own experiences with depression, and the way I look at it, depression ultimately wants one thing: to get you all to itself. It is like a jealous lover who keeps you from seeing your friends, from going out and trying new things. It can eat away at your self-belief until you start to believe that you can't do anything anymore. But it's important to remember that is a lie: you can. And you have started by getting in touch with me and making this commitment to yourself.'

We had reached the bottom of the stairs. I asked, 'Do you want to have a cup of tea and talk a little?'

'I'd like that, thank you. Shall we sit in the kitchen?'

We walked to the rear of the house and I sat down at the kitchen table.

'That negative voice is such a horrible thing to listen to in my head, day after day,' Felicity said. She filled the red stove-top kettle from a water filter that stood on the worksurface by the sink. 'Why do we do this to ourselves?' she asked with a sigh.

'It may be hard to believe, but I think in a way it's an aspect of the psyche that actually kicks in to protect us when we have experienced grief, loss or some kind of trauma. The over-zealous internal critic is, in fact, trying to stop us running any more risks and getting hurt again. To protect us from taking on activities or commitments that could under any circumstances fail. So, it keeps us safe, but after a while, that strategy can become counterproductive.'

'How so?'

'Let's face it, in life we usually fail more times than we succeed. That trial-and-error process is integral to learning, growth and change. I'm sure you know that from studying to perform new vocal parts.'

Felicity looked somewhat wistful and nodded in identification.

'It's not even necessarily what that voice is saying that's wrong; sometimes it's more the way that it says it. That critical tone can trigger a lot of shame and so, ironically, what it can end up "protecting" you from is living life and moving on from the trauma. I think that's why it's so important to seek help with it.'

'Right. That certainly chimes with my experience. So how do you stop that voice?'

'One thing that helped me was to enter into more of a dialogue with that inner critic, rather than allowing it to dictate,' I told her. 'To acknowledge and respect it, and to listen to what needs in me it was trying to meet, rather than trying to ignore or stop it. I think it's important to recognise that it is not you, and to notice when the strategies it employs to meet those needs are not helpful.'

Felicity thought for a while, digesting what I had said before she replied. 'That sounds like quite a challenge,' she said after a moment. 'As you say, whenever I notice that critical tone, I just want to ignore or get away from it.'

'It's not going to be easy to begin with, so just start with baby steps. Notice when the voice comes in and how you react. Then, rather than saying "I should do X," simply allow yourself the option of doing something different, of responding to it in a more nurturing way. There are more practical things that I found helped me as well. Do you exercise regularly?' I asked. 'I found exercise a good way to manage my depression.'

'No,' Felicity said. 'I used to go swimming. I quite enjoyed the little trips to the pool, but in the end, it didn't make me feel any better, so I don't bother anymore.'

'But Felicity!' I replied with a playful tone that our more established bond allowed.

'What?' she asked, in mock ignorance.

'Going swimming isn't about making yourself feel better. It is an act of self-care, of kindness to yourself and your body. If you change your intention, and say, my aim is to do a self-caring and self-supporting activity, then would you go swimming, even if you didn't feel better afterwards?'

'I guess so; I hadn't really thought about it in that way.'

So together, we came up with a plan to get her out into the world a little more. Hard to do, as depression and loneliness are bedfellows.

'Can you commit, maybe once a fortnight, to going for a swim and then having a coffee in a place in London you haven't been before? Just have a walk around and see if you like the vibe and how it feels. If you are feeling really up for it, you could even check out the house prices at a local estate agent. What do you think?'

'I don't know, that sounds a bit of a stretch.' Felicity fidgeted with her mug, tapping the rim with the back of her fingernails. 'I guess I can give it a go.'

For many, this would be an easy, enjoyable task with no pressure, but I knew it could seem a massive undertaking for someone with depression. I didn't say any more, but I hoped I'd sown a seed that might help with her low mood and also open up some options for a move, if that was what she wanted. My suggestion was also about giving her mind something new to attach to: a different thought process, one with a more positive energy that might replace or redirect the downward spiral of depression.

For our next session, we moved on to the living room. I knew Felicity's budget for my time was limited, and as this room was where she spent much of her time, it felt like a priority. We also needed to create space for the collection of musical scores that we were relocating from the new guest room. With a little research, I had sourced a set of outsized box files that were large enough to take the scores. We sorted them into categories that made sense for Felicity. My instinct had been to order them alphabetically, but she preferred to group them by period and genre. Felicity used a portable label-maker to neatly identify the contents of the files, so individual scores would be easy to find.

We decided to store them all in the old Chinese sideboard, which was of generous-enough proportions to take the large files. But to do that, we needed to clear the contents of the cabinet. This was something Felicity had confessed she was quite nervous about.

'Okay, are you ready for this?' I asked, putting down the last of the box files on an armchair and moving over to the side of the room where the cabinet stood.

'I guess so.' Felicity hooked her hands tightly together and drew a deep breath. 'I have to warn you, it's pretty packed in there,' she continued, looking somewhat shamefaced as I approached the cabinet.

'Don't worry, I've seen it all before. Let's take a look inside.' I unclicked the brass latch and swung open the doors. As I did so, out fell a large plastic carrier bag, crammed full of unopened letters. I could see that the shelves inside were filled with at least a dozen other such bags, each containing more mail and old paperwork.

Some aspects of decluttering, such as sorting out Felicity's old music room, can be done quite quickly. Others take longer. You open a drawer or box and find a whole little world inside. There's a different degree of complexity and detail. Not only in terms of the actual contents, but also when it comes to the emotional or psychological connection to what's inside. It's a bit like entering another level or dimension. I'm reminded of Dr Who's Tardis; small on the outside, but once you open the door and enter, time and space expand. Felicity's Chinese cabinet was just such a place: like a mythical labyrinth, where perhaps a secret treasure lies hidden – or maybe a sleeping monster.

One by one, we took out the bags and began to work our way methodically through them. It's common for people to find dealing with incoming mail quite challenging. It may be that they never acquired the habit growing up, or perhaps they learned a different and unhelpful way of acting around that area. For others, it may be due to an emotional issue that it is wise to address: some event in their life that has led them to make an unconscious decision to stop doing something that they previously did. Sometimes, in fact, it is almost a conscious decision, but over time the reason has become forgotten, lost or hidden. I suspected this was the case with Felicity. She had clearly once been a pretty prosperous and high-functioning person, with a successful career and a powerful calling. My guess was that something significant had happened to disrupt all that. As I have said, beneath every pile of clutter there is usually a story waiting to be told. What exactly this was in Felicity's case, I didn't know. But I sensed it was related to a deep and painful trauma.

Whatever was behind the block, it was apparent that Felicity was unable to process the old correspondence without my direct support. I upended the first carrier bag and emptied its contents on to the floor. There was a mixture of official-looking brown envelopes, shrink-wrapped circulars and takeaway menus. I guessed that for some considerable time, Felicity had just scooped up the piles from the front door-mat where they'd accumulated and deposited them straight into bags, without even a glance at what she'd picked up. Checking the postmarks on a few of the letters, I identified that most were nearly a decade old.

'To speed things up, why don't we separate out the personal correspondence and simply shred anything over five years old?' I suggested.

But Felicity was adamant that everything had to be looked at. 'No. I want to check them all. If I'm going to do this, I'm going to do it right,' she said, purposefully picking up a handful of brown envelopes.

And so we decided together that each and every letter would be opened and checked, and only then categorised and either filed or shredded. We agreed I would only directly throw anything away when it was obviously junk mail.

The thoroughness that Felicity insisted upon frustrated my

need to be efficient and optimise our time, and I wondered
initially if she felt she had to pay some sort of penance. But
I quickly realised it wasn't that, and it certainly wasn't actually about the practicalities of the letters' contents. It was
about facing her past. Felicity needed to do all the things
that had been left undone: or, at least, some symbolic por-
tion of them. There was something deeply courageous about
this. She was confronting, one letter at a time, the very fear
or pain that had caused her to avoid opening them over the
preceding years.

So, for hours, we sat together in her front room, literally
processing the past. The simple, intimate nature of this task
began to establish more of a connection between us. Perched
on a chair moved from the dining room, I would take a
letter and slice it open along the fold with the letter opener.
The empty envelope went into one of the pop-up laundry
baskets I use for sorting, lined with a recycling bag. I'd pile
up a little stack of maybe a dozen open letters, and then
pass this on to Felicity, who sat on the sofa going through
them. She put them in piles: Shred, Recycle, File. There was
also an 'Action' pile, as I usually suggest, but in this case
most of the letters were so old that the time for any action
had long passed.

'How come you never got disconnected, Felicity?' I asked,
after opening yet another final reminder from her gas supplier.

'That's a good question,' she replied, taking the pile of
bills from me and leafing through them. 'I imagine I just had
some sort of intuition about which were the critical letters
and opened them. Either that, or I waited for a phone call.'

After a pause, she added, 'You must think I'm terribly silly,
leaving all these letters to build up.'

'Not at all,' I replied. 'There's no judgement here, I know
there are reasons behind every piece of clutter.'

I never judge the condition of the homes of anyone I work with. I know there are always underlying factors that have led to the clutter and disorder. In fact, perhaps the term 'disorder' itself is misleading. There is always an order of some sort, it is simply often layered in such complexity that it is hard to ascertain. Every object is placed down as part of some process or narrative, be it practical, emotional or symbolic – or some combination of all three.

There was something meditative and healing in the rhythm of the sounds and movements as we opened, processed and piled the papers. As we quietly and steadily applied ourselves to the task together, my sense of a deepening unspoken bond continued to grow. I suggested we played some relaxing music while we worked, and Felicity chose some beautiful medieval choral songs. She had a wonderful hi-fi system, and the haunting sound of the harmonising voices filled the room.

Steadily, as the work proceeded, Felicity continued to open up and reveal a little more of herself and her life. She told me some tales of her sister's adventures, and how she had finally settled down with a family. We talked about Felicity's singing career, too, along with some of the exotic locations she had visited as part of her work.

To maintain momentum, we agreed it was best to tackle the paperwork one bag at a time and then move on to some other, less emotionally demanding work. This meant it was two sessions before we had completed emptying the cabinet. In one especially satisfying moment, I found and opened the missing issues of *Classical Music* from 2008, along with several letters prompting Felicity to renew her lapsed subscription. We reunited them with the other issues in the empty box files on the bookshelf. A little mystery solved, and an open loop closed.

When the emptying out of the cabinet was finally complete,

we pulled it away from the wall to vacuum behind it and remove the many years of dust that had accumulated.

'I find this helps to remove that sense of stagnant energy as well as dust,' I said to Felicity as we slid it back into position.

We both stood for a while and looked at the cabinet's empty shelves, which she'd wiped down with a damp cloth. Late afternoon sun filtered into the room through a partially drawn blind, and in its pristine, empty state, the shiny black interior and ornate lacquered doors seemed to shimmer with a different energy. There was a timeless quality to the moment. It felt like a combination of celebration and mourning, a marking of the passage of something.

'Let's just leave it empty for a while before we put the musical scores in there,' I suggested.

'Agreed,' said Felicity, with a little smile. 'We make a great team, don't we?'

That wasn't quite it with the paperwork, though. Every so often, another bagful would appear, one that had been stashed in another part of the house, and we would go through the same process again. Each time, as we sat and sifted through these papers, we talked some more. And as we talked, further stories were told. It felt like a kind of ancient circle, the way I imagined women used to sit together in sisterhood and work and talk to make sense of life.

Steadily, the bond of connection and trust between us deepened. And one day, as we sat together working through another bag of paperwork that had emerged from the back of the understairs cupboard, Felicity purposefully set down the pile of bank statements I had just passed her and turned to me. 'I want to tell you something.'

I stopped rooting through the bag of mail, sensing this was important and wanting to give my full attention to the moment.

'I haven't talked about this for years, and it would help me to tell you.' Felicity kept her face turned away and spoke with a steady and measured tone, as if she had rehearsed how to say the words many times. 'My son, my only child. He died.'

I'd suspected there was something deeply traumatic that Felicity had been holding in, but this in no way lessened the shock of hearing those words from her lips.

'Oh no, Felicity. I'm so sorry.'

What can one really say to a revelation such as that? We just sat together for what was probably only a minute or so, but the moment which seemed to expand into a deep silence, filled with emotion and meaning.

As I allowed the impact of what Felicity had shared with me to settle, I looked over at her with deep compassion. Something of the formality with which she had held herself seemed to have softened. It came to me that, of course, some of that had been her way of containing this profound loss. To hold at bay what I imagined must have been an overwhelming feeling of grief, one that no mother should have to bear.

From her eyes, I could see Felicity was lost in memory and pain, trying to find her way back to the present. There were no tears, but I could tell that it was taking a huge force of will for her to hold herself together and be with me in the moment. She inhaled deeply and turned her head slightly towards me for a second. I sensed that she needed to say more, and perhaps needed a little encouragement or reassurance that it was okay to continue.

'Do you want to tell me what happened?' I asked.

Some further moments of silence passed between us. I guessed Felicity was weighing up what to tell me, trying to choose the words to convey something that may have felt impossible to communicate. Eventually, with her eyes turned down towards her hands, she said, quietly, 'He took his own life.'

The shock of this further revelation reverberated through me and, again, I wasn't quite sure how to respond. So, once more, I sat in silence with my reaction, simply being with Felicity in her pain and grief a little longer. I'm not sure how much time passed, but I was stirred from the quiet and stillness by a soft flutter as the handful of letters she'd been holding slipped from her fingers and settled on the floor.

'That must have been so hard for you. I can't imagine how you felt. Did it come out of the blue?'

Felicity shook her head slowly. 'Not really. James had been unwell for quite a while.'

She bent forward and began to carefully gather up the papers that lay at her feet. 'He'd made several previous suicide attempts.'

Deliberately setting down the letters she'd collected on the coffee table, Felicity gently rested her hand on the pile for a while before turning to me and continuing. 'I don't think he ever got over the loss of his father – he died of a heart attack when James was ten. I tried everything I could to help him: medication, therapy, but nothing seemed to work. At times, he just seemed trapped in this impenetrable darkness; nothing seemed to reach him.' She paused for a moment and picked up the little pile of bank statements again, then, after a couple of seconds, dropped them back on to the table. 'Then one day, I hurried in from the garden to answer the door and opened it to find a policeman and woman standing there. As soon as I looked in their eyes, I knew that James was gone.'

Felicity took a deep breath and then exhaled slowly through pursed lips. 'August the twenty-third, 2008. It was such a glorious sunny day. I still remember it like it was yesterday.'

I couldn't imagine a worse or deeper blow for any mother. To discover that her son, her only child, whom she had brought up alone, had taken his own life. The tragic story evoked such sadness and empathy in me, and I expected tears and anguish from Felicity, but at that moment, there were none. She told me more details of her son's life in a calm and, at times, almost matter-of-fact way. This somehow made it even harder to hear. Then, slowly, as we continued to talk, she started to connect more to her emotions. There certainly wasn't a flood, but rather a gentle, steady flow of what she was able to release at that moment.

'James was such a shy, sensitive boy. He struggled to make friends growing up and it didn't get any easier for him as an adult.' I noticed her eyes start to fill with tears and the steady timbre of her voice faltered.

'It can't have been easy for you raising him alone,' I said.

'I tried my best, but I just couldn't give him whatever it was he needed.'

'Try not to blame yourself. It sounds as if you did everything you could to help him.'

'It's silly that I'm crying after all this time. I had a couple of grief-counselling sessions after his suicide, and thought I'd worked through all this.' She wiped her eyes, but the tears continued. 'There's clearly a lot still there.'

I fished through my bag and handed her a tissue from the small packet I found in there. 'Often this type of thing has to be processed in layers, and you need to return to it again and again. Maybe the time just hasn't been right up until now.'

'You're right. Perhaps I wasn't ready to face it. It's just easier to push it all down inside.'

We sat together for the remainder of the afternoon, and I just listened while Felicity continued to tell me about her son's life. As more of the story unfolded, I understood better that protective shell of hardness I had sensed when we first met. And the years of mail that had been left unopened began to make sense, reflecting a life that had been put on hold by an unbearable but repressed grief: part of her strategy for coping with a loss so crippling that I think I would want to withdraw from life for a while, too, to retract into solitude. But in that moment, she had me, and I offered what I could: the depth of my care, my support and, yes, my love. As therapists, we are sometimes told not to feel too deeply connected to our clients; to maintain a certain professional detachment. But, of course, when someone opens up to you as Felicity had, and you offer your care and compassion, there is love there.

As the words and the emotions flowed, I sensed Felicity was taking a vital step towards releasing something. It was as if she was able to set down, if only for a short while, something that she had been carrying alone.

'Thank you for trusting me with this, Felicity. I hope that in sharing what perhaps has felt like a closely and carefully guarded secret, there may be the seeds of a new stage of healing for you.'

She nodded. 'Perhaps I've held this all for long enough, yes.' She glanced up at the clock and realised the time. 'Oh, I'm so sorry, Helen, I've been talking for ages, and now we're behind on the schedule.'

'Don't be silly. We can finish off the understairs cupboard next time,' I said gently. 'We've been deep this afternoon. There's a lot for you to process emotionally without adding any more boxes to go through.'

I think I also needed some time and space to work through what Felicity had shared, as, when I left her place, the tragic story of the loss of her son stayed very present in my awareness. It's not uncommon for revelations such as this to have an impact that I carry with me, and part of my work is to hold and contain some of what my clients are processing during the course of our work together. But as I drove across town, I caught the end of the school run and became acutely aware of how many mothers there were walking with their children, unloading them from cars and carrying on with their lives. And as I noticed this, I imagined how sights such as these, ones that barely registered most of the time, must have affected Felicity in the days, months and years after her son's death. The passage of time can inevitably lessen the emotional impact of these reminders, but I wondered if, in her attempt to hold on to her connection with her son, Felicity had ever really allowed time to pass, and, with it, the pain and grief to fade.

The sense of lifelessness that had struck me when I first entered her house began to make more sense to me. It felt a bit like someone had died because, as I now knew, they had.

When I arrived home, I felt an impulse to call my mother, and we talked about our days. I didn't disclose anything of my work with Felicity, of course, but I did spend a little longer than usual on the phone, and our conversation took on a deeper emotional significance than usual.

A few weeks passed before our next session together. It was just after Easter, and with the longer, warmer days came green shoots and flowers. The lines of cherry trees on the street outside Felicity's house were profusely laden with bright pink blossom, and the magnolia tree in her front garden was in full bloom. When I arrived, Felicity seemed more animated than I had seen her before. She was excited to tell me she had found a lodger for the old music room we had cleared on our first day together. It was great that she had achieved that goal, and it also felt deeply significant that she would not be alone in the house. Perhaps, in a way, she had begun to let go of a little of the huge absence created by the death of her son. I can only imagine how hard it had been to deal with that loss. Who wouldn't want to try and find a way to hold on to someone who had meant so much to them and that life had cruelly snatched away?

We picked up our work on the understairs cupboard. It had been densely packed with boxes, but we'd cleared a lot of these during our previous session. I felt that we could see the light at the end of the tunnel, and I knew this was one of the last areas in the house we would tackle. Right at the back were quite a number of neatly stacked suitcases, which I pulled out and carried one by one into the living room, where Felicity sat, sorting through a small box of photographs.

'Oh yes, I thought those might be in there. I'd imagined they might never see the light of day again,' Felicity told me, her voice transmitting a sense of regret.

We unzipped the cases and, as I'd expected from their light weight, they were largely empty. Inside one, though, we found a small collection of programmes and books that I handed to Felicity to sort through.

'It's been years since I visited anywhere,' she said. 'I'd been getting fewer offers of overseas engagements for some time, and then after James died, I just stopped travelling altogether.'

'What, no holidays or anything?'

'No. At the time I think all I wanted to do was stay in the house, to remain connected to the familiar. There was a degree of comfort in the things around me, I suppose. The outside world simply seemed too much to bear for a while. I just wanted to keep it all sealed safely away. Then I guess it just became what I was used to.'

'What do you want to do with these cases?' I asked.

'That old grey one can go, I think; I never liked it much anyway. Let's keep the others, though. Maybe they'll get some use. As I mentioned when we first met, I feel a bit like I've become stuck here. So, I'm drawn to the idea of travelling or moving somewhere new. James loved to travel. He usually accompanied me on my work trips and acted as my PA when I went on tour.'

It was good that Felicity was connecting to some positive, happier memories of her son. It also showed me how integrated he had been into her life and her career, which perhaps explained why she had stepped away from her singing and teaching.

I was able to combine the different-sized cases by arranging them one inside the other, leaving us with just two large ones that contained all the rest.

'I suggest we put them here, to one side of the cupboard, rather than right at the back, so they're easier to get out when you need them. They'll take up a lot less space in there now.'

'That makes sense. I feel I can breathe a little easier now,' Felicity said as we stood and surveyed the largely emptied understairs area.

There was a little more to do in the house, but a week or two later, Felicity called me and explained that she felt she could complete the remaining work on her own. As we spoke, I felt a tinge of sadness. Although it had begun primarily as a professional relationship, the days we'd spent together had felt like more than just that. From her initial distance and formality, Felicity had really opened up and we had connected on a deeper level. However, I understood the financial constraints she was under, and also sensed that ending the work with me marked a further break from the past for her, from that period of transition that our time together had represented. I believe that as Felicity created space, sorted out the unresolved practical issues and organised the piles of papers into a filing system, we had brought her back to the present moment, the here and now. And from there, she was ready, I hoped, to move into her future.

I like to think our work together helped Felicity to get back in touch with her pain and grief: to allow herself to complete the natural cycle that had become stuck. Because we need to feel all our emotions, even the very painful ones. If we don't, we're not living life to the full. We can't supress one feeling without suppressing all feeling, and often going through our pain and distress enables us to experience joy. It is through the pain of loss that we know how deeply we loved and how much the person meant to us.

The way I see it, Felicity's pain had been held at bay by her stuck behaviour and patterns. Understandably, it had probably felt too much: too intense and overwhelming for her to feel or to process. Unconsciously, she had placed her life in a kind of suspended animation, perhaps as a way to try and dwell in the time before the terrible death of her son. This psychological strategy had steadily manifested in her home in the backlog of mail and the cluttered music room. Her grief had been stuck in much the same way that air becomes trapped in the matrix of ice crystals, until the thaw finally comes and it is released back into the atmosphere to rejoin the cycle of life.

Initially, Felicity kept in touch with little bits of news here and there. I was pleased to hear she had restarted bereavement counselling, and that she was getting on well with her new lodger. Then a year or so went by, and I stopped hearing from her. Nevertheless, those days sitting in her living room, chatting like sisters, sharing the burden of life, remained as alive in me as if they had been yesterday. Then, out of the blue, an email arrived. Felicity wrote that she had moved earlier that year. She was now living in rural France and, although it was a trial run, she was loving it and would probably stay. I was delighted. Felicity had often talked about moving, and I had encouraged her, as I felt it would be a massive step into a new life. Now she had done it. Not only that, she had moved not simply to another district of London, but to pastures completely new. More significant still in a way was the closing line of her email: 'I have to go now; I've recently joined the village choir and we have a rehearsal tonight.' Felicity was singing again. I knew that the loss of her beloved son would always be with her, but sensed that in leaving the house, she had been able to release something. An image came to me: of the clutter Felicity had accumulated, and eventually the home itself, as an almost physical manifestation of a mother's embrace. This had initially held her emotionally and provided a sense of some continued connection to her son, but it had ended up trapping her in the past, unable to either let him go or move on with her own life. I took her reconnection to music, which had been such a central and meaningful part of her personal expression, as deeply symbolic of a spirit set free.

*

In this chapter, I talked about categorising some clutter as a 'Gremlin'. I don't recommend doing this a lot, but every so often, it's the perfect solution. Consider, for example, if a relationship has recently ended and you know you need to deal with your ex's belongings, just not right now. Items like these, which are very emotionally loaded, are your Gremlins. This is the one occasion when I say it is okay to box and store clutter, as long as you give yourself a deadline and commit to a date to come back to them. Think about how much time you feel needs to pass before you'll be ready to face your Gremlin. Aim for no longer than a year and put a date on the box. Then put it somewhere you can't easily get to it, and add a reminder to your calendar for when you've committed to dealing with it by. This is called 'bracketing' in therapeutic terms, and is a great tool to use. Remember that this is done with the understanding that you will revisit the items once you've had some breathing space – don't just bury them away forever.

The Gremlin card is one of those that feature in my Home Declutter Kit, which encapsulates much of my process. If you find a lot of things are coming into the Gremlin category, it may be you'd benefit from some extra help in the form of a therapist or counsellor. There are details of places to find a good one in the Resources section at the end of the book (pages 281–285).

# The art of letting go

You may recall the story of Mike from earlier in this book, and how he decided not to work with me and instead to try and tackle his clutter alone. When I heard this news from our mutual friend who had asked me to help him, I was quite concerned. I felt that this man really needed to make a major shift and was unsure if he'd be able to do this without support. Thoughts about Mike popped into my head over the few weeks that followed, but I knew it had to be his decision to reach out for help, and, as I got involved in work with other clients, he slipped from my mind. So, it was something of a surprise when I got a call from him in the summer of the following year.

'Hello, Helen? It's Mike here.' He paused for a moment and then continued hesitantly. 'I don't know if you remember, but you came to see me last autumn about decluttering my place. I was quite resistant at the time, but I really need help to take this thing on now.'

'Hello, Mike. Yes, of course I remember you. Do you mind if I ask what has changed to get you to this point?'

'To be honest, I'm feeling really desperate now. I meant it when I said I was going to tackle things on my own. I really thought I could do it, but it's just been hopeless. I kept setting a date, but then I would forget about it. Or when I did manage to make a start, I'd get bogged down and simply give up. It seems like I set all these positive intentions and then keep procrastinating or undermining them in some way or another. I'm just at a loss about what to do.' He paused. 'I'm such a self-saboteur Helen, such a self-saboteur. You must think I'm a bit of a loser.'

I sensed that at his core, this man was quite vulnerable, and I realised how difficult it must have been for him to call me. As he seemed so quick to attack himself with negative self-talk, I sought to reassure him.

'Not at all, I hear this often, Mike. You haven't done anything wrong. I completely understand how hard it must have been. Dealing with accumulated possessions and all the emotions associated with them is not easy. That's why people like me exist – to lend a hand.'

He paused for a moment and then continued tentatively. 'I . . . I don't want to waste any more of your time, but do you still think you can work with me? I really want to reclaim the space upstairs so I can focus on getting my freelance work back on track. Are you available at all?'

'Yes, yes, of course. You're not wasting my time. Give me a second and let me check my diary for the next few weeks. I'm sure we can find some dates.'

His willingness to reach out for help, however hesitantly, told me that Mike had already taken a big step towards change. As we had spoken before at length and I'd seen the lie of the land in his home, all that was left was to briefly discuss some logistics, and then we set a date to get started a couple of weeks later.

Driving back to the east London suburb where Mike lived, I contemplated the work that lay ahead. I was cautiously optimistic, but, noting his fragile confidence, prepared myself

for obstacles. When I arrived again at Mike's street, I quickly
recognised his house by the dilapidated motorbike that was
still chained up outside, just as I'd remembered it.

Mike greeted me at the door. He looked relieved to see me,
and with a nervous smile ushered me in past the bike that
still hung in the hallway. The first task at hand was to plan
and prioritise, which we did at his kitchen table over a cup of
tea. Given Mike's history of procrastination and false starts, I
thought it would be good to tackle things head-on and build
some momentum. 'Which area do you think would have the
most impact if we cleared it?' I asked him. 'Maybe the place
you are most avoiding dealing with.'

Mike remained silent for a while, then took a couple of big
gulps from his mug. 'The attic . . . I suppose,' he replied appre-
hensively, half smiling, half grimacing. 'Dad's old studio.'

As he spoke, I noticed he had actually turned quite pale
and was beginning to sweat.

'I know it's a tough place to start,' I reassured him. 'But
I think you'll find that once we've got things shifted there,
it will make the rest of the process easier.' I drained the last
of my tea and picked up my decluttering bag. 'Shall we go?'

We made our way up to the first floor, along the landing,
and then continued via a narrow set of steps to the very top of
the house. Even though I'd been up there on my previous visit,
something about the tightness of the staircase left me feeling
as if I was about to enter into a secret realm. I wondered what
stories this room might have to reveal. As I turned the corner, I
passed a low shelf, on top of which stood a carefully arranged
collection of old wooden printer's letters. When we emerged
into the attic, the restrictiveness of the stairwell gave way to
a greater sense of space, despite all the clutter that greeted us.
The room was filled with bright, warm sunlight. It flooded
in from two large windows set into the roof and lay across

the furniture, casting strong shadows and bringing out the vibrant colour of the artwork that lay scattered everywhere. I could see why Mike's father had used it as a studio: natural light is vital for a painter. The underneath of the pitched roof was clad in yellowing pine with inset brass lights that lent the room a slightly nautical feel. At the far end of the room was an ancient-looking rocking chair beside a tiny fireplace, which was painted black. A small wooden mirror stood on the miniature mantelpiece. It was quite a contrast to the generous fireplace in the living room downstairs. I guessed that in years gone by, this would perhaps have been a maid's room. This thought conjured up a Dickensian image of a young girl sitting there on a winter evening, reading by candlelight and trying to warm herself in front of a small fire.

Below the farthest Velux window stood a large seaman's trunk, held secure with a sturdy cast-iron hasp and padlock. All around the room, large oil paintings leaned against the walls, along with a large easel and numerous rolls of canvas and paper. I noticed the distinctive odour of linseed oil, which artists use to thin their oil paints, and was instantly transported back to my days at art school. For a moment, I thought of the loft in my mother's house, where a number of my own paintings were stored. I paused briefly and noted that I needed to be watchful that I didn't bring any of my own history to bear when working with Mike. It would be easy for me to imagine that he'd have the same sense of regret that this space would quite possibly arouse in me, when, of course, his feelings might be completely different. *I must check for my assumptions*, I told myself.

Scanning the room again, I saw that one side of the eaves was screened off with a pair of old roller blinds made from split bamboo that hung from the joists.

'What's behind there?' I asked, remembering that when I'd

looked round before, Mike had hurried me out of the room, indicating that perhaps he hadn't wanted me to explore it too thoroughly.

'Ah, yes. The beast.' Mike smiled.

We pulled up the blinds, revealing an enormous wooden plan chest: the type of chest that printers use to store large sheets of paper and prints, with drawers that were shallow, but very wide and deep. A cross between a set of drawers and a workbench, it was a functional, you might say industrial, piece of furniture. The top bore the signs of activities that had been done on it over the years. Its laminated surface was criss-crossed with cut marks, paint and ink stains, strips of masking tape and various measurements scribbled in pencil.

'My father used to work at it all the time,' Mike said pensively as he slowly traced his fingers across the top.

'It certainly bears a rich history of his time up here,' I said as I examined the traces of many years of focused work. I gently lifted the loose edge of a strip of wooden laminate and a large piece came away quite easily. 'It has perhaps seen better days, though, hasn't it?'

'I know what you mean, but I don't think we'll be able to get it out,' Mike replied, resting his hand on the chest. 'I remember carrying it up with Dad. I seem to recall that it came in two pieces; that was the only way to get it up the stairs. Even then it was a tight fit. Some time after that, Dad modified the stairway to box in some pipework, so I doubt it will even come out in pieces now.'

Here was the first sign of resistance. It would take some work, for sure, but it would certainly be possible to remove the plan chest. Contemplating this seemed to be painful for Mike. Perhaps difficult memories had been stirred at the thought of removing this piece of furniture, which clearly had very strong associations with his father.

'Let's take a look,' I said. I slid out one of the top drawers. It only ran half the width of the unit, but was still big: around two by three and a half feet. Looking back once more to my art-school days, I recalled the old imperial name for that size was 'Double Elephant'. It was certainly an appropriate phrase for this monster. Inside the drawer were piles of paper, mostly covered in drawings and watercolour sketches, along with bound notepads and sketchbooks, stacks of photographs, worn pencils and numerous other artist's implements. I quickly opened and looked through the rest of the drawers to get a good picture of what each of them contained. They were all similarly filled with loose drawings, books and art supplies. Upon closer inspection, however, although there were many wonderful and finished pieces of work, some of the drawings were quite rough, while others were torn and crumpled, and there was also a lot of blank paper. Plenty to let go.

'How do you feel about all this work?' I asked Mike. 'Do you have a sense of what proportion you want to hold on to?'

He picked up a piece of artwork from the open drawer. 'I know we can't keep everything, but look at this; it's stunning.' He handed the painting to me, holding it gently by the edges. It was indeed an exquisite watercolour, depicting a broken and twisted mature oak tree set in a freshly ploughed field.

'You're right, it's lovely. Your father was clearly a very talented man.'

I carefully handed the watercolour back to Mike.

'I did speak to Dad about it all before he died. You know, it was a bit horrible talking to him about it because he just said, "Chuck it all away!" As if his work didn't matter at all. He could do that, my dad. Although he was committed and brilliant, he could be quite dismissive about the value of what he created.'

'I can imagine that was very upsetting for you to hear.'

'It was. I imagine it was probably a bit of a defence mechanism – I can be the same way with my own work. But I also know that he actively undermined his career at times. I remember several opportunities he had for exhibitions that he never followed up on, and I expect there were many more I never heard of.'

'It's a real shame more people didn't get to see this work.'

'I agree, it is. So, despite what he said, I can't just throw it all away. There is so much of him in this work, and so many beautiful pieces. I want to give his work more respect than it sometimes seemed he did himself.'

As I listened to Mike, I could see some parallels beginning to emerge between his own behaviour and that of his father. This further reinforced my expectation that our work in the attic was going to be about much more than the practicalities. I sought to reassure Mike that I understood this.

'I get that completely. And I'm absolutely not here to tell you to throw everything out. This process is about carefully looking at what is here, and connecting to what has meaning and value for you now. At the moment, it feels like all of this is just one big category called "Dad's work". And, naturally, it's also all wrapped up with your feelings about him as a man, as a father, along with your relationship with him and your own place in the world. My strong sense, though, is that you need to start to fully process all that, however painful and challenging it is, in order to move forward. It might also help you recognise some of the unhelpful behaviour that you may have picked up from him. It sounds as if he might have had a tendency to self-sabotage as well.'

I know that many men have a difficult relationship with their fathers. They find it difficult to free themselves from their subtle and not-so-subtle expectations. Often, these expectations come to reside in their own self-judgement, and can be projected on to other authority figures or even their personal notions of God. For this reason, some men might feel a sense of liberation when their father dies. While quite normal and natural, this can, of course, bring with it feelings of guilt and shame. All of this can also be true for daughters, and in relation to mothers, too, but there is something specific to the father–son relationship that can be particularly challenging. I knew it would be important to bear all this in mind with Mike while I also focused on the practical aspects of the process.

As we were at the very start of our work together, and mindful of Mike's tendency to make false starts and lose focus, I felt it would be helpful to establish some physical momentum.

'Here's what I suggest. Let's start by emptying one of the drawers and using it for the work you definitely want to keep. I think the chest itself probably has to go if you want to reclaim the space, but the drawers will be a good way to keep the artwork organised and safe until we source something more permanent. All the blank and scrap paper can be recycled, along with any damaged drawings, unless they have deep personal significance. It's entirely your call, but I'd ask you to consider that it could be okay to let go of some of the drafts and preparatory sketches that led to the beautiful pieces. You can dispose of the things that aren't quite pristine and finished, while really valuing the things that you do choose to keep. In fact, you are respecting these *more* fully, by letting go of the ones of less value.'

With care, Mike placed the watercolour, which he had been holding throughout our conversation, back in the open drawer. 'That makes sense,' he said. 'I can photograph the ones I'd like to have a record of and keep them in that way.'

'That sounds like a great idea. I'll put all the tubes of paint, pens and pencils, and other art materials into these big plastic boxes and sort through them later. Obviously, we'll bin any dried-up or empty ones. How does that all sound?'

I'd given Mike quite a lot to take in, but it seemed to have the desired effect, and he nodded in agreement. 'Okay. Let's do it.'

So, I set up my cards and containers at one end of the room by the little fireplace, with a chair at the centre of the semi-circle. With Mike established there, I began emptying out the contents of the first drawer, passing him a small pile at a time so he could make his decisions.

'I'm amazed there's so much,' Mike said as I handed him the latest batch of drawings. 'I remember Dad disappearing up here to work, and then bringing down the finished, framed paintings, but I never got a sense of all the preparatory sketches.' He opened up another sketchbook. I could see that this one was more of a journal, densely filled with handwriting that he started to read. 'I'd forgotten that Dad wrote these.'

'They could be a nice way to connect with him. A way to get more of a sense of who he was outside being a father,' I said gently. 'But I suggest you start a "Read it later" pile for them, or you'll lose focus on what we're doing. It might have more meaning to read them when you have time to give his thoughts your full attention.'

This is something I always suggest to my clients, and my intuition was that, as Mike's emotions were probably pretty stirred up, this was particularly important. Reading his father's private thoughts was definitely best left to another time.

Clearing the plan chest was a major task, but by the end of the day we had emptied all the drawers and categorised most of the contents. Two drawers were carefully filled with the best artwork, a rich and varied collection of watercolours, oil sketches and pencil drawings. There were several bags of paper for recycling and another large drawer stacked with work that Mike would photograph later. I often suggest that clients photograph things with their mobiles as we go along, but his father's artwork deserved more careful documenting. As a professional photographer, Mike obviously had high standards in that regard. Along with emptying the plan chest, we were also able to go through all the framed paintings and collect them neatly in one corner.

We stood admiring our work and the new sense of space in the room before making our way downstairs. I congratulated Mike on completing what must have been a challenging task. 'You've done a great job. Next will come the challenge of how to get that monster out of the loft.' I laughed, gesturing at the empty plan chest. 'But let's leave that for another day.'

'Don't worry,' said Mike. 'I'll get rid of it before the next session.'

'We need to open up that seaman's trunk as well,' I said, aware that we'd been working around it most of the day.

Mike didn't respond to the suggestion and changed the subject. I guessed there was something significant about the chest or its contents, but now wasn't the time to go into that.

'Next time we meet, I'd like to focus on clearing my bedroom,' he said. 'I'd really like to get all my work gear out of there. Now the loft room is largely clear, I want to start consolidating my workspace up here. It will be nice to have the bedroom just as a bedroom as well.'

'Okay. That's going to be a big job, so I suggest we set aside the whole day to complete it. My advice is that it's really important to do this work thoroughly. I find it can undermine people if they leave little pockets of clutter, areas they haven't addressed. It's a bit like leaving a few roots or areas of brambles when you're weeding a garden; things can grow back faster than you think.'

It wasn't ideal that there were still things undone in the loft, but I respected Mike's decision. I left him with some 'homework' to do. We agreed he would clear some of the larger items out of his bedroom so we could get in there and start working. He also committed to collecting all his photographs and notebooks into one place, as they were currently scattered around the house.

It was quite frustrating when I arrived the following week, fired up and ready to go, only to discover that the bedroom was still inaccessible due to boxes that were piled up behind the door. I also noticed that, although there was a pile of photos and notebooks in the hallway, there were still many more in various locations around the house. I tried to contain my frustration, as I knew that if Mike was easily able to tackle this sort of task, he wouldn't have needed my support. But I guess that some of my irritation may have been apparent, because Mike was quieter than usual, and appeared a little shamefaced and apologetic.

'Okay. I see you haven't been able to move any of these boxes,' I said, moving into the room and pushing the wedged door back. 'Let's get them shifted now, shall we?'

Mike followed me into the room a little sheepishly. 'I'm sorry, I don't know what's wrong with me,' he said, slumping down on the edge of the unmade bed. 'I'm just so useless when it comes to getting things done around the house. I start with good intentions but always seem to find ways to sabotage myself.'

I slowed down and took a breath to get centred. I also took

a moment to remind myself of the importance of retaining boundaries between my own issues and those of my client. 'It's okay, I know it's not easy for you,' I said putting down the box I had picked up and paying more direct attention to Mike, who was still sitting on the bed. 'Is this a repeating pattern in other areas of your life?' I asked.

'I guess so. It's the same with my personal photography projects. I'm fine when it comes to contracts or when I'm working for other people, but when it's for me, it often gets stuck and forgotten.'

'That's not the first time you've mentioned self-sabotage. It sounds like it could be a real issue for you.'

Mike nodded.

'If you're willing, there's a little exercise I sometimes do with clients that I think might help you understand this pattern better,' I said.

'What did you have in mind?' Mike replied, looking a little nervous.

'There's nothing to worry about, it's not too heavy, but most people find it helps them get greater clarity about what underlies some of their behaviour. What we do is set up a grid and capture some of the behaviours and beliefs that contribute to the pattern, and then brainstorm some alternatives that might be more helpful.'

'Okay, that sounds intriguing. Let's give it a go.'

'Great. Let's take a pause from what we're doing and set up what you'll need. Can you find a couple of sheets of paper and some tape or pins in the studio? I've got a set of coloured pens in my bag that we can use.'

'I'm sure there's plenty of paper upstairs, I'll take a look.' Mike stood up and headed off to the studio.

I delved into my bag to retrieve the pens, eventually finding them buried at the bottom. A moment later, Mike returned carrying a large sheet of drawing paper and a roll of masking tape.

'That's perfect,' I said. 'Why don't you tape it to the back of the door?'

Using one of my large markers, I divided the sheet into four segments.

'Would you agree that self-sabotaging is the overriding issue we need to examine?' I asked.

Mike nodded, so I wrote 'SABOTAGE' at the top of the first box.

'Okay, in the first box, I'd like you to start by listing some of your unhelpful behaviours,' I said. 'Things you do that undermine your work towards goals you've set yourself.'

'Right. We might need a bigger sheet of paper,' he joked. Picking up a green pen, he wrote 'Avoidance'. He thought for a moment. Then more words and phrases began to come to him quite quickly, and he added them to the list:

Not following up opportunities.
Procrastination.
Not asking for help.
Missing deadlines and targets.

'Right, that's probably enough for now,' I said, conscious that he was doing a great job of identifying some unhelpful behaviours, but not wanting to over-encourage any negativity. 'Now, let's work on your beliefs,' I continued, writing 'BELIEFS' in the square below. 'What are some views you hold about yourself and life that might be behind these behaviours?'

Mike paused, perhaps carrying out some emotional introspection, his hand still holding the pen to the partially completed sheet of paper. Then, steadily, the beliefs came, and he noted them down in his neat handwriting:

It'll go wrong.

I need to stay small to keep safe.

I don't deserve success.

I have to do it all alone.

I'm not good enough.

'That's great. You're starting to build up a good picture of what might be contributing to what you describe as self-sabotaging.'

As I said this, I sensed that Mike was becoming less present and starting to look a little down, perhaps because he had gone into some negative self-talk.

'But please don't use this awareness to beat yourself up,' I continued. 'It might be more helpful if you try to exercise some greater compassion for yourself. Think about how you might react if a friend was saying these things about themself.'

Hearing this, Mike seemed to regain a little more focus. I felt his attention returning to me and what was taking place in the room, so I continued to explain some more of how I saw things might be for him.

'It's hardly surprising, given those beliefs, that you'd want to stop yourself doing these things, is it? You feel anxious that things will go wrong. You have this sense that you don't deserve success, whereas of course anyone who works hard on something deserves success. You feel isolated and that you have to do everything alone. So, if these feelings come up every time you try to make a change, it's no wonder part of you tries to hold yourself back. It's a way of keeping safe, avoiding what you believe the negative consequences will be. We can come back to these themes another time if you want to, as they sound painful, but for now, are you happy to continue with the exercise?'

Mike nodded. 'Yes, let's keep going.'

'The next step is to think about what you could change in order to overcome some of these barriers that stop you achieving more of what you want. Let's start with those behaviours. What could you do differently or put in place to counter those unhelpful tendencies? Let's begin with "Missing deadlines or targets".'

Mike gave it some thought. Eventually, he said: 'Okay. I can use timed reminders on my phone. I can stick to goals.'

'That's good, but a little general, perhaps. What can you do to help you stick to goals? One thing that helps a lot of people is to write them down and be very precise about what you are doing and when you will do it by.'

'Okay.'

'You could also find someone to work with as an accountability buddy. You tell them what your goals are and check in with them regularly to keep an eye on progress.'

'Right; I suppose I could ask my friend Charlotte to do that with me.'

He wrote 'Accountability buddy' on the sheet.

'I can focus on completion?' he said timidly.

'Again, what specifically could you do to be more focused on getting things done? What I find really helpful is to get clear on what exactly the very next action is for each project.'

Mike nodded and carefully wrote 'Define next actions' on the sheet.

'Great,' I said. 'You could also give yourself little rewards for completing each stage of a goal.'

He wrote that down too.

'Right, so let's move on to procrastination,' I said. 'That's a big issue for many people. It might be helpful to look at what feelings are usually behind this behaviour for you. In my experience, it's often boredom or fear. People often put things off because they're afraid that the outcomes won't be what they want. Alternatively, they may know that the act of doing the thing itself could be unpleasant in some way: perhaps either dull or painful.

'I've been reading this fascinating book called *The Procrastination Equation*,' I continued. 'It takes a quite scientific approach, examining lots of research into the phenomenon. Let me see if I can remember how it goes. The author says that the factors on the top of the procrastination equation are expectation and value. These things multiply together. The bigger the pay-off and the more you believe you will get it, the greater the motivation for you to do something. For example, if I told you that somewhere in this room, there was a letter you needed in order to claim a £1,000 tax refund, you'd be very motivated to look for it. But if I said it *might* be in here, the expectation of finding it would be lower, and so would your motivation to look.'

I looked at Mike to check he was with me. 'That makes sense,' he said.

I continued, 'If it was only a £20 tax refund, you'd be far less motivated, and if it was a letter for a £20 tax refund that *might* be here, you'd probably have zero motivation.

'Then on the bottom of the equation are delay and impulsiveness,' I went on. 'So, the higher the consequences of delay, again, the bigger the motivation. If that tax refund had to be claimed before 3 p.m. today, you'd be searching for it right now. But if you had until next year, you'd be far more likely to put off searching. And this is multiplied by impulsiveness. Basically, this is a measure of how likely you are to be distracted away from a task.'

'I see. So if I was a very steady, sensible person, I'd be much more likely to look for the letter?'

'Exactly. But even if you were extremely impulsive, it would have to be a very powerful distraction to pull you away from the search if that refund had to be claimed within the next hour.

Let's apply this to the example of moving the boxes upstairs – that's what prompted this exercise, after all. I'm guessing you value having your boxes upstairs, and you had a high expectation that moving the boxes would give you that outcome. Meaning the motivation on the top of the equation would be quite high. But, like many creative people, you are probably quite impulsive, and there was no real time constraint.'

'Yes – and actually, this morning, when I realised you were about to arrive, I carried a couple of them up.'

'Right, so a week ago, there was a long delay until you'd experience the consequence of not doing it, so the motivation to overcome those distractions would have been very low. I suggest you read the book to get a little more information. What I take from it is that one way to reduce procrastination is to get really clear about the value of tasks you are taking on: why they matter to you. So, while you probably don't value carrying boxes upstairs very highly, you do value having all your things together in a dedicated space.'

I was aware that we'd spent a lot of time talking about procrastination, but this seemed quite a key issue for Mike that he had mentioned a few times. I looked back at the chart on the wall.

'Okay, I think we've taken a good look at the behaviours; let's move on to the beliefs. For each one, can you think of some alternative beliefs that could serve you better? Firstly, what about "It'll go wrong"?'

'I'll be okay?' said Mike.

He seemed unsure, so I asked him to consider it a little more deeply. 'Do you think you will be okay?'

He thought for a moment. 'You know what, I guess I will. I mean, I'll probably make some mistakes, but it won't be the end of the world, will it? What doesn't kill you makes you stronger, as they say.'

'Great, so write something of that sort opposite "It'll go wrong" in a different colour.'

Mike picked up a bright orange pen and wrote: 'I might make mistakes, but I'll be okay.'

'Before we move on, can I just ask about when you say: "It'll go wrong"? I'm wondering what you imagine might happen. It sounds as if you are talking about a bit more than a few mistakes.'

'I'm not exactly sure. There's just this sense that something big might happen.' Mike closed his eyes and paused for a moment before continuing. 'I remember growing up, I used to have this recurring dream. It's dark and I am making my way through this endless area of rubbish and weeds, a bit like a wasteland or a war zone. Eventually, the path opens up, straightens and transforms into a broad, well-paved street heading up a hill into a gleaming city. Everything is clean and bright, and there are tall, glass buildings on either side of me shining like crystals. I slow down a little and walk on, enjoying the view and this sense of having made it, having finally arrived after all these struggles.'

I listened, transfixed, as Mike recounted the dream to me.

'One time I was at this part of the dream, when all the buildings started to collapse around me. I remember I was desperately trying to hold them up. The next thing I knew, I was half-awake and pushing against the wall beside my bed. I was dripping in sweat and my dad was there. He told me I'd been shouting "No, no!" and had woken him up.'

'Wow, that's a powerful dream.'

'As I said, I had this dream regularly, and I began to think it was some sort of prophecy.'

'Right. I can see how that might feed into this idea of it all going wrong, of a catastrophic failure. But dreams aren't really prophecies; they are much more likely to be a reflection of past events or things that are very present in your life at the time.'

I suggested to Mike that he gave the dream some more thought and reflected on what was going on at that stage of his life.

'It might be worth adding to the sheet that some things might go wrong, but that you have built solid foundations. That there are robust structures around you that can withstand setbacks. You own this house, for example, and you have a solid background of experience and skills.'

Mike took the lid off the orange pen and added: 'I HAVE THE ABILITY TO WITHSTAND SETBACKS.'

I noticed he had switched to writing in capital letters, which indicated to me he was connecting to a greater sense of self-belief and confidence.

'That sounds quite powerful now. What about the next belief: "I need to stay small to feel safe"?'

'How about: "It's okay to stand up, stand out and take some risks"?' Mike said, appearing quite engaged with the process now.

'I'm guessing you may have been practising this tactic of staying small for many years, and probably picked up this belief that it was a way to stay safe in childhood,' I said.

Again, Mike nodded, this time with a little more conviction.

'It *is* good to step up and take more space,' I told him. 'But it's probably unrealistic to expect yourself to shift overnight into an ultra-confident risk-taker. Be gentle with yourself and start with small steps, build up your confidence steadily. Is there something you can do that will put you out there in the world that you'd feel reasonably confident with? It's good to move towards what feels like your edge without going completely beyond your comfort zone.'

'I really want to create an online portfolio of my work,' Mike replied. 'A new website to promote what I do. That's part of my motivation for reclaiming the space upstairs.'

'That sounds great. That sort of action, one that feels like a stretch without being unbalancing, is ideal.'

We worked carefully through the rest of the limiting beliefs on the list.

For 'I have to do it all alone', Mike came up with: 'IT'S OKAY TO ASK FOR HELP' and 'I CAN LEARN FROM OTHERS'.

'I don't deserve success' was countered by: 'I'VE WORKED HARD', 'I ADD A LOT OF VALUE FOR MY CLIENTS' and 'I'M GOOD AT WHAT I DO'.

The whole process took maybe an hour. During this period, I began to see more and more of the confident, professional man I'd caught glimpses of previously. At times, it was almost like a different person was in the room with me.

Mike stood back from the big sheet of statements and took a deep, steady breath. 'That's really helpful, thank you,' he said with a measured tone, setting down the pens precisely on the window ledge by the door and carefully lining them up.

'You are very welcome. I suggest we leave it there for now. You might find it useful to stick this sheet somewhere you will see it. You can read it each morning and when you notice you are getting stuck. This sort of process can be highly valuable, but the real power lies in repetition and embedding new habits. You've probably had these beliefs and employed similar behaviours for a long time, possibly since you were very young. In a sense, it's like having to retrain the brain. Listen out for those unhelpful thoughts, and every time you hear yourself saying them, see if you can repeat one of these different thoughts you've identified.'

Mike was carefully removing the tape and taking down the sheet of paper. 'I'll put this in the kitchen, where I'll see it during the day.'

'That's a good idea – and remember, it's there to help you. It's not a reminder to beat yourself up for doing those things. When you picked these tendencies up, probably at a very formative age, they were adopted to help you feel safe. And it's likely they did a good job at the time. But like those boxes of old pens that we threw out last time, they simply aren't serving you anymore.'

'I can see that – thank you,' Mike said.

We got back to work, and with Mike's new-found energy, we made great progress in his room. In the remainder of the afternoon, there wasn't time to move everything he'd chosen to keep up into the attic studio. However, as we had booked in two consecutive days, we piled his work and equipment on the landing, ready to go up the following morning.

At the start of the next session, we ascended the narrow staircase to the attic room, carefully carrying a couple more of his father's paintings, along with a batch of Mike's framed photographs. As I'd half expected, the giant plan chest was still there, standing in the middle of the room.

'Right,' I said to Mike. 'Don't you think now's the time to tackle the remaining art materials and get that plan chest out of here?'

'Absolutely,' he replied with some energy. 'I'll go and get my tools.'

While Mike was gone, I set down the items I'd carried up and opened the window to let in a little fresh air. I have a dust allergy – not great in my chosen career – so I like to keep a good flow of air as I work. I noticed with curiosity that the old seaman's trunk had been moved from where it had previously been positioned under the window. Scanning the room, I saw it now stood half hidden behind the plan chest, covered by an old blanket.

Just then, Mike returned, carrying a toolbox. As he had remembered, once a couple of stubborn screws had been undone, the top half of the chest came loose, and together we were able to lift it off. Minus the heavy drawers and top, what remained weighed less than we'd expected, but we measured it and the pieces were still too large to carry down the narrow stairway.

'Why don't you focus on taking it apart further while I finish organising the paints and pastels?' I suggested.

In order to break down the detached top section, Mike began by unfastening a pair of diagonal wooden cross-braces. With these removed, the heavily scored worksurface lifted off, and he was left with the shell. At this point, the deconstruction process stalled. The ancient screws that held the wooden panels together must have been rusted in place, because despite the application of some loosening oil and Mike's increasingly vocal and frustrated efforts, they remained stubbornly fixed.

'Bloody things won't budge,' he muttered under his breath. 'Let's try it another way.'

He stood the shell on its end to try and get a better purchase on the screws. As he leaned on it, the whole thing shifted out of square and emitted a slight creak.

'Aha! Maybe there's an easier way,' Mike said, setting down his screwdriver. Leveraging its weight, with barely any effort Mike pressed the shell over into a parallelogram and then, with a splintering sound, it flattened all the way out. Straightening it up again and skewing it back the other way, the whole thing just broke into pieces with a loud crack, leaving the stubborn rusted screws protruding from the timber.

Mike stood for a moment, surveying the wreckage, then he turned to me. 'It seemed so solid, had such presence. But emptied out and with the bracing removed, it's really quite insubstantial – fragile, even.'

I could see he was welling up.

'A bit like your father?'

'Exactly,' he said, forcing a half-smile. 'Growing up, I remember him as such a big, powerful man, not only phys- ically, but also in terms of his personality. But towards the end, he lost so much weight. He just seemed to be shrinking away.'

I sat down next to Mike, who had deposited himself on the rocking chair. 'Had he been very ill?' I asked.

'Not really. He had a minor heart condition, but when my mum passed on, he lost some sort of spark and started eating less.'

I could tell that these were deep and perhaps buried emo- tions for Mike that he might need to talk about. 'This is clearly a painful memory for you, Mike. Why don't we go downstairs for a break and a cuppa?'

We made our way quietly down the narrow staircase, along the first-floor landing and down again into the kitchen. As we sat waiting for the kettle to boil, Mike continued to tell me about his father.

'A year or so after Mum's death, although his physical decline continued, he regained some enthusiasm for his art. He began spending more time up in the studio and started painting again. He had an exhibition of his work lined up with an old art-school friend that he was working towards.' He looked out of the window for a few moments, took a deep swig of his tea, and then continued his story. 'Then one day, this man came to the door, saying he was there to check the gas. It's a bit of a cliché, really. Anyway, after he left Dad had an intuition, checked his jacket pocket and realised the guy had swiped his wallet.'

'Oh no.'

'Like many people of that generation, Dad preferred to use cash, and had drawn out a few hundred quid to pay for the framing of his paintings. It was a big shock, plus I guess he felt really ashamed for being taken in. This all came out later, of course. The first thing I knew was when I got a call from the hospital telling me he'd had a minor heart attack.'

I could tell it was taking some effort for Mike to keep a lid on his emotions as he revealed more of the story.

'That's so sad. It must have been really difficult for you,' I said.

Mike nodded, then drew in a deep breath and exhaled before continuing. 'In the hospital, all Dad could talk about was how stupid he'd been. How he wouldn't be able to get his work framed for the exhibition now. I said I'd pay for the framing, naturally, but it wasn't really about the money. The exhibition never happened, and few weeks later, he was gone.' Mike wiped away a tear.

'I'm so sorry. That's awful, and so unfair.'

'It's years ago. Silly to still be crying over it, really.'

'Not at all. It must have been a horrible time for you. I can see how hard it must be, reawakening those memories as we go through his studio.'

Mike sniffed. 'There's something about the fact that he never got to finish that show that makes it all worse. That may seem odd to say, but if you knew how much his work meant to him, you'd understand.'

'Of course. I do understand; I was an artist myself.'

I really did empathise with Mike and felt his pain and loss. His story was especially poignant to me because my own father had died a few months earlier. Part of me wanted to share this with Mike, but I didn't. I think I wasn't certain how I'd cope with the feelings, and I was aware that I was there in a professional capacity to support my client. Was this the right thing? I don't know. What I do know is that when we see someone in pain, our first impulse can be to want to do or say something to take that pain away or alleviate it somehow. But often what they need is to feel the feelings and allow the natural grief cycle to continue to run its course. This can be particularly true when someone has become stuck in avoidance and denial, which I thought might have been the case with Mike. So, instead of offering any further words of consolation, I simply sat with him at the kitchen table, and also sat with my own feelings of grief. I'm not sure how long we remained there in that extended moment, but after a while the boiler on the wall fired up, pulling us back into the flow of time. We exchanged a glance of recognition at the significance of this and had a little laugh.

I glanced up at the clock on the wall. 'It's getting on. I suggest we leave it for today,' I said, guessing that now wasn't the time to be stirring up any more emotions.

I went back upstairs to collect my things. When I returned a few minutes later, Mike was still sitting there, gazing out of the window, but looking a little more collected.

'I suggest you take it easy this evening, there's been a lot to process,' I said as he showed me out.

There was a two-week gap until our next session, and I checked in with Mike via email and a short call to see how he was. I was concerned that reopening the grief about his father might tip him back into depression, but I needn't have worried, because when I arrived the following week, he seemed to be doing well. I was impressed to see that he had followed through on the commitments he'd made. All the larger items he had decided no longer served him had gone, along with the charity donations and the broken pieces of the plan chest. He'd also cleared and reorganised the kitchen shelves, which hadn't even been within the scope of our project.

That day, we cracked on with great energy and finished the weeding stage of the decluttering, both keen to move on to reorganising the spaces in a way that best supported Mike in his work and life. I made some suggestions about the new layout of the attic studio and his bedroom, and we discussed a few items of furniture that he might buy. There was a huge sense of progress, not only in the space, but also in Mike himself. I was under no illusions that it would all be sunshine and roses from here on; I knew from my own experience that grief and depression can be a rollercoaster ride. But I certainly felt that Mike had turned a corner.

As I surveyed the room before I left that evening, somehow the room felt lighter, as if something was missing. Of course, we had removed a lot of things, including the huge presence of the old plan chest, but there was something else that I couldn't quite put my finger on. Then I realised: the old seaman's trunk was no longer there.

During our final session, we completed moving the last of Mike's photographs and equipment into the attic studio and arranging things logically. Most of his work was now digital, so he required far less physical storage than his father had, although we still needed a pair of new drawer units to contain his prints. We had bought a new desk, setting it up where his father's old plan chest had sat. The one Mike had chosen was custom-made from extra-thick plywood with a matt white surface.

'Easier to keep clean and free of dust,' Mike told me. 'Dust is the photographer's enemy; it can really mess with lenses and delicate equipment.'

On the wall by the staircase, opposite the fireplace, we hung Mike's favourite of his father's paintings: a bold, multi-coloured abstract derived from cloudscapes. Positioned there, you could enjoy it when you were leaving the room, but it didn't dominate the space.

To one side of the room, placed discreetly under the eaves, were all his father's paintings and several large, lidded containers holding his sketchbooks and drawings. They were safe and secure in there, and Mike could easily access them for the archiving process that he had committed to.

'I'm going to photograph everything carefully and publish it all on a website, along with a personal history and some of Dad's writing,' he told me. 'I don't know if anyone will visit the site, but I'm doing it for Dad and for me. His work deserves to be seen.'

I had a real sense that sorting through his father's work and relocating his own workspace had created a space for Mike's spirit to grow. My hope was that the archiving project would also help him build some momentum in his own work and that he'd be able to avoid the self-sabotage that had so dogged him. So, I was delighted six months later to get an email from Mike with a link to the website of his father's work, along with an invitation to an exhibition of his own photographs.

His father's uncompleted project and Mike's struggle to find closure around his death were clearly strongly linked. And leaving the unkempt studio as it had been during his father's life was, of course, a way of holding on to him. But instead of doing something with the work, it had all just lain around waiting. To review, inventory and clear his father's work from his old studio, which he had now taken ownership of, seemed symbolic of Mike stepping out of the parental shadow.

To look closely at our past can sometimes be so hard and

painful because it feels like letting go of it. In fact, often what we are actually struggling to let go of are our resentments, our very holding-on itself. Often, it is a person or relationship that we can't release, and what we are holding on to, of course, is some *idea* of the person: usually one that is a restricted or distorted image, warped in some way by something unresolved within us. By letting go of that false image, we can begin to better connect to the reality of who they were, their life and the fullness of what they mean to us.

I never did discover what was in that seaman's trunk. I wondered if it had been more of his father's possessions or perhaps something from his childhood. Whatever it had contained, Mike had parted ways with it.

*

Do you have a tendency to sabotage your own efforts to create more space and order in your home? Perhaps the behaviours that cause clutter to build up are actually a way of unconsciously sabotaging some other aspect of your life. Maybe this stems from a belief that you were born an untidy and disorganised person and will always be one, or that you don't deserve to live in a more nurturing environment. That's simply not true. I believe everyone has the right to a beautifully organised home that supports them in living their best life.

Many of us fall prey to the idea that our beliefs are fixed and unchangeable, but that's not the case. In my experience, we can choose beliefs that serve us better. Instead of holding on to attitudes and behaviours you have inherited from your family, viewpoints you were taught at school, in church or at the workplace, you can instead shift your focus to your values. It may serve you better to consider what and how you want to be, and to look for beliefs and behaviours that will support you best in realising that vision.

Try the grid exercise I did with Mike for yourself by downloading a free template at helensanderson.com/secret.

# The lost key

One beautiful autumn day, I'd just finished raking up some leaves in my garden when the phone rang. It was an elderly man called Alistair. He started talking the moment I answered the call, his voice so full of emotion he could barely make himself understood.

'Please help me,' he said, 'I've lost the key – I just can't find it anywhere. I put it where I always put it, I know I did. I know it was there, it's always there, that's where we always keep it – and now it isn't there.'

'I'm really sorry to hear that,' I said. 'How can I help?'

But Alistair wasn't listening. 'My dear Mary would have known where it was,' he continued. 'This sort of thing never happened when my Mary was around, but now she's gone, and the key is gone as well.'

And so he continued at great pace for several minutes, until I felt I had no choice but to interrupt him and suggest he took a deep breath. There was a pause for a few moments, after which he seemed to have calmed down a little.

'I hear you're very distressed and need some help, Alistair,' I said. 'Are you willing to tell me a little about what's happened to disturb you?'

'I'm sorry I got so upset; I don't know what the matter is

with me. I shouldn't be so emotional. But you see . . . my wife, Mary, she passed away two months ago . . .'

There was a silence, during which I could tell he was trying to collect himself again.

'And, and since the funeral and everything, I just keep losing things,' he went on. 'It's just not like me. And now I've lost this key. I really need to find it, and it's just not there where it should be. I don't understand it, I really don't . . .'

I could sense his distress rising again as his speech accelerated.

'I've always been such an organised person, you see,' he continued. 'I ran a successful business for many years and was something of a pillar of the community. Not like this. What is wrong with me? I'm so stupid . . .'

'You're not stupid, Alistair,' I said gently. 'You've just had a serious bereavement. That would be difficult for anyone to cope with. It's very normal to be overwhelmed and confused.'

'Maybe. But I need to find that key, you see.'

I felt a deep empathy as I listened to Alistair's distress, and found myself wondering how I could best help. I considered whether I should refer him to a grief counsellor, but it seemed a little presumptuous – Alistair wasn't asking for a counsellor. He had called me. Since I'm a professional organiser, I imagined he thought the key was lost amidst clutter and that he would like me to help him find it. And perhaps he also wanted me to clear some of it, help him get organised and create some order – that was my job, after all. But I was aware, too, that people often call me when it's their emotions that feel overwhelming, not just their clutter. This is often the case when someone's going through a significant life change, such as a divorce, or when their children are flying the nest, or – as in this case – after the death of a loved one. Objects and places that are intimately connected in our imagination to a person who is leaving or has left can carry a powerful emotional charge. From an apparently simple thing, such as throwing away an old toothbrush, to the greater complexities of sorting through their personal papers, the feelings that come up can be very powerful. Visiting a counsellor can seem a step too far – too intimate and too challenging – while talking to a nice lady who is helping you organise your home can feel much less scary.

'Are you hoping I can work with you to help you get on top of things and to maybe find the key?' I asked Alistair. But he couldn't quite give me a clear answer. I decided the first and best thing to do with Alistair in that moment was simply to let him know his distress was being heard; if nothing else, I could give this dear person some support, kindness and compassion after such a life-shattering loss.

'Life must feel very topsy-turvy for you right now,' I continued. 'I remember when my father died, how life seemed to have been turned upside down. I felt like an astronaut, hanging there in limbo without the gravity of that significant relationship to hold me in place. It was all very surreal for a period of time.'

'I certainly feel quite odd and confused. Perhaps a fresh pair of eyes would help. Although I'm not exactly sure how you propose to find something I've been looking for in my own home for days.'

I noticed the touch of irritability and guessed it wasn't easy for him to admit this problem had him stumped. 'I'm sure you know your home far better than me, Alistair, but as an outsider, I might be able to bring a bit of objectivity and help you see the picture more clearly.'

'That's what my daughter said,' Alistair replied, pausing for a few moments. 'Maybe it would be useful if you could come over, if that wouldn't be too much trouble.'

'I'd love to meet you in person and have a longer chat,' I replied. 'I can't promise anything about the key, but perhaps I can help you create some order out of the confusion you're in right now. Let's see what comes to light.'

Alistair might not have known quite what he wanted from me, and so I wasn't entirely clear about the brief, but yes, I would definitely visit this man.

Three days later, I duly arrived at Alistair's home. I sat for a moment in my car at the end of a long gravel driveway and took in the scene. In front of me stood a large, timber-framed house set in several acres of Suffolk countryside. This was the heart of Constable Country, and it struck me as very beautiful.

Happy to stretch my legs after a long drive, I got out of the car and walked up to the entry phone, mounted on a substantial red-brick gatepost. The name 'Hill House' was beautifully carved into a piece of slate just above it. Admiring the typography, I pressed the buzzer. There was no reply. Checking my phone to make sure I had the right time, I took a moment to breathe the crisp, late October air and take in the stunning views over rolling fields and autumnal woodland. My reveries were interrupted by the entry phone buzzing, and a slight creaking as the automated gates slowly opened.

Feeling a few nerves, as I often do when I first meet a new client, I drove down the driveway, stones crunching under my tyres, past numerous bird tables to either side. As I drew up in front of the house, I saw Alistair waiting to greet me at the open door. He was a tall, upright man with a shock of white hair and a friendly smile. I imagined he had been a strong and somewhat imposing presence in his day, before time and the stresses of life had taken their toll on his health. But although his physical frailty was clear, there was little sign of the distressed man I had spoken to on the phone. Over the years of doing this work, I have become accustomed to the many facets of a personality that people present. I recognised that Alistair was showing me his outwardly successful and coping persona, as my clients often do when we meet in person for the first time. Their vulnerability, which often lies just beneath the surface, is only revealed as our work progresses and they become more comfortable and willing to trust me.

'You must be Helen; nice to meet you,' Alistair said, offering me a slightly brusque handshake. 'Come in, please.' He ushered me briskly through the door. Despite some mild concern at his manner, once I entered the house I felt immediately energised. Although the exterior of the house was traditional, the rooms inside were modern and light, and, at first glance, seemed to be pretty ordered. There were very few signs of the disarray I often encounter when I first visit my clients' homes. In the entrance hall stood a tall lady with long dark hair and a big, generous smile, who Alistair introduced as his daughter Kate. 'Thank you so much for coming, Helen,' she said. 'I'm just here to give Dad a little moral support.'

'Don't fuss, Kate. I told you I'll be fine.' Alistair offered to take my jacket and hung it on a classic Thonet-style bentwood coat stand just inside the hallway. 'I'm rather afraid we may be wasting your time with this business, Helen. I know you're supposed to be some sort of expert, but frankly I think this is a lost cause.'

Together they guided me towards the open-plan kitchen. Kate put her hand on my arm. 'Don't worry about Dad, he'll come around,' she reassured me in a hushed tone. 'I'll put the kettle on, Dad,' she called out to Alistair. Her elderly – but evidently still spritely – father headed determinedly into the kitchen, gesturing for me to follow, and sat down at a large marble-topped table facing the window.

I looked around the pristine space. It didn't look like my decluttering or interior design skills were needed here. *How on earth can I help?* I thought to myself. It isn't unusual to find myself experiencing a little doubt when I first meet a client; it's something I've learned to acknowledge in myself and then just carry on. I reminded myself that my work was rarely about the surface issues alone, but nearly always something much deeper, unseen and emotional.

I've come to understand that what I'm initially presented with rarely tells the whole story. It's once the decluttering process gets underway in earnest that the reason I'm really there comes fully to light. I haven't come unstuck once, so it is easier to trust that now.

'It's a beautiful house,' I said. 'Have you been here long?'

Alistair smiled a little and looked around the kitchen with a look of pride on his face. 'Oh, thank you. We've ... I mean I've, lived here for over thirty years now. There have been some changes over the years, I can tell you, but there are memories still alive in every corner. That makes the house so special to me, and it's why I would never want to leave or change it.'

With some pride, Alistair proceeded to describe a little of the history of the house. 'The original building dates back to around 1760, but most of what you see now is much more recent. We had to completely renovate the old house and build around it. It would have been far easier to start from scratch on another site, but Mary just fell in love with the view.'

It certainly was a stunning vista, and I took a moment to gaze at it through the full-height French doors and windows that flanked one side of the room. From the back of the house, the land sloped gently down towards a small lake, and then rose again into diverse and ancient woods.

'I can see why. It's very beautiful,' I said. 'You must love to watch the colours change at this time of year.'

Alistair smiled slightly and nodded, a faraway look in his eye. I was reminded that here was a man still coming to terms with a profound loss.

After a few moments of silence, Kate returned, carrying a laden tea tray. 'Have you told Helen about how the key went missing, Dad?'

'I haven't had a chance, we've been talking about the house,' he said brusquely, pushing aside his pen and a copy of *The Times* that was folded open at the sudoku page. 'Put that down here, won't you?'

Carefully setting down the tray, Kate removed a hand-knitted tea cosy to reveal an ornate teapot decorated with a hunting scene. She poured our tea into elegant bone-china cups and offered me a generous plate of assorted biscuits. Over the cup of tea, and several delicious biscuits, the story of how they'd come to call on me gradually unfolded.

'There were so many comings and goings leading up to the funeral that I decided to lock Mary's rings away, to keep them safe,' Alistair said. 'I couldn't face the thought of losing them, so I put them in my father's bureau. It's a lovely eighteenth-century piece, beautifully lacquered and gilded. Venetian, I think. It's all I have left from him. I keep all my important papers in that bureau, and I always keep the key hidden in a special place in the understairs cupboard. Kate's the only person who knows where the hiding place is. You helped me put the rings away one afternoon just before the funeral, didn't you?'

Kate put her hand on his. 'I remember that much, but to be honest, Dad, that whole period after Mum passed is a bit of a blur . . .'

Alistair leaned forward, rather abruptly, I thought. 'I just want to see Mary's rings,' he said. 'To hold them again. Especially her wedding ring. I saw it on her hand every day for fifty years.' He stood up and began to pace. 'Do you think you can help, Helen? Because if you can't help, I'm going to have to take drastic measures and get the locksmiths out. There's also some important papers in there that I need to put her affairs to rest.'

I could sense his growing anxiety, revealing itself in a little bit of impatience – and this was familiar to me, too. A client suddenly unsure if this was a good idea, even before we'd got started. I smiled at him. 'Getting the locksmiths in wouldn't be so bad, would it?'

There was a pause. Alistair seemed to be lost in thought. I could tell there was something running through his head, but I wasn't sure what.

'The thing is, Helen, they told me on the phone they might have to damage the bureau, my father's bureau,' he said, eventually. 'I just couldn't face that right now.'

I could see why this would distress him – and not just because his beautiful, much-loved bureau could get damaged. A forcing open would be traumatic. This was a moment for gentle unlocking – a teasing open of its own accord. Slowly, it was beginning to make sense to me why I had been called to this house.

Alistair's eyes had filled with tears. He excused himself and left the room. Kate leaned forward. 'Dad is so distressed and I just don't seem to be able to help, so I did a bit of searching and found you online,' she said quietly. 'I liked what you said about our spaces and our mindsets being closely linked, and how you talked about working with the whole person, not just the clutter. Usually, Dad's very reluctant to ask for help, but I just had a feeling that you might be able to get to the root of the problem.'

We sipped tea for a moment in contemplative silence until Alistair returned. I offered some words of reassurance to him, while thinking about the best way to help. Clearly, there was a lot more going on than just the simple loss of the key. It seemed to me that Alistair's fretting over the key's loss was a way to express, in a more manageable way, something of the bigger loss he was coming to terms with. It was only a few short months since his wife had passed, after all. His desire to get the key back was perhaps a reflection of his desire for her to return. And there was another interpretation that could simultaneously be true. Losing the key and refusing the locksmiths could be Alistair's way of making sure he didn't see the rings again. And perhaps by not finding them, Alistair could, in some unconscious way, keep the symbolic hope of his wife's return somehow alive.

As with all interpretations there was an element of speculation here. One thing was certain, though: this was clearly very distressing for Alistair. His agitation started to surface each time the bureau, rings or key were mentioned, and with it, I felt the pressure mounting. I was beginning to wonder if he really did think I could wave a magic wand and that the key would appear and all his sadness would be resolved. It wouldn't be the first time I found myself wishing for that magic wand, or a Mary Poppins bag. If only I could sort out all the mess in the world with just a whistle and a click of my fingers. In reality, however, some doubt was definitely kicking in – not because I questioned my skills, but because this was a pretty well-ordered home, and I couldn't entirely see where, on a practical level, I could help.

I could sense this would be one of those cases where the listening, support and empathy would be more important than the physical decluttering. But I did have to do what I said on the tin. What on earth could I declutter or reorganise here?

However, when Alistair took me on a tour around the house, I saw that the understairs cupboard – which he was initially reluctant to show me – was bursting at the seams. So, this was where the clutter was. That's often the way – some people are able to keep their unwanted, unused or sentimental things contained in one room or area of the house while the rest of their home remains in good order. Given that this was where he said he usually kept the key, I was curious about Alistair's reluctance to show me the cupboard. Again, I found myself wondering if there was more to his not finding the key than appeared on the surface. Perhaps there were aspects of his relationship with his wife that he was avoiding taking a closer look at, and which might be revealed if we delved deeper. Either way, the cupboard was certainly in serious need of a good sort-out and I was relieved that I had found a practical way that I could be of assistance. This was the place to start work with Alistair.

I told him that all I could promise was that the cupboard would be clearer and better organised. Maybe the key would turn up there, maybe not. Alistair said he had already searched the house – and the cupboard – a hundred times, so it seemed unlikely we would find anything. But I knew from years of experience that this work could bring extraordinary and surprising – dare I say 'magical' – results. I decided to keep the faith.

The understairs cupboard was large enough to walk into – it was more of a little side room, really. It was lined with shelves on three of the walls, which were tightly stacked with probably a lifetime's worth of accumulated objects. My first priority was to get the adjacent room set up with the tried-and-tested system I use in my work.

Kate picked up a small enamelled box from a shelf near the entrance to the cupboard and looked at it pensively for a moment. 'I have some things to do at home, Helen, so I think I'll leave you to it if that's okay,' she said. There was something in her tone that suggested to me that maybe sorting through things that were likely to remind her of her mother wouldn't be easy for her. This might have been a further reason why she had encouraged Alistair to contact me. Although I liked Kate, I was pleased that I'd be able to work with Alistair one-on-one. Experience has taught me that when people are decluttering in part at the request of a family member, things don't always go smoothly. Relationship dynamics can add a complicating factor to what is already a challenging process. Further resistance from the already cynical Alistair was the last thing we wanted right now.

'Okay, it's down to the two of us then, Alistair,' I said, taking out my decluttering kit and some pens and sticky notes from my bag.

As with all my clients, I explained to him my gardening metaphor for decluttering, and that we'd be going through the phases of weeding, planting and maintenance.

I have found from years of experience that this structured, layered approach really works. People often try to clear and reorganise things at the same time, and that rarely works out well. Once you start putting things away, it's easy to get distracted and not make good progress on letting things go.

I arranged my decluttering cards in a large circle on the dining room table, with Alistair sitting down in what I jokingly call 'the hot seat' or 'the naughty chair'. This often brings a smile and helps break the tension some people feel when there is a stranger in the house going through their precious stuff. It was essential that he had space to focus on all the items I would be bringing out of the cupboard, so he could make decisions and find it easy to pile things into different categories. I have honed this method over the years, developing my system carefully to help tackle people's sense of overwhelm and inspire decision-making. I know people are anxious at this first stage, so I sat Alistair down facing the window, with a nice view of the garden. I knew he wouldn't have much time to look at the scenery, but I wanted him to feel comfortable. This meant he would have his back to me as I went in and out of the cupboard, but it seemed the best way to keep him calm. Then I explained slowly and clearly what he had to do. I would be carrying out piles from the cupboard for him to sort through. His job was simply to allocate things to each pile and tell me what he was happy to let go of.

'I won't get rid of any photos or children's storybooks,' Alistair said firmly.

I nodded at him. 'That's absolutely fine,' I said. 'You're in charge, and of course you don't have to throw away anything you don't want to.'

But Alistair's fears were not to be so easily assuaged. The first thing I pulled out of the cupboard was a shoe box packed with various birdwatching books and a rather battered pair of green military-style binoculars.

'I am sure the key hasn't fallen into a binocular case!' he said immediately, scowling at me quite ferociously.

'Probably not,' I replied. 'And I can't promise anything. But let's just see what happens.'

It seemed impossible to explain to Alistair, but I knew that extraordinary things can happen when energy shifts – and decluttering shifts energy like nothing else. I was hoping that this process would support Alistair in changing his consciousness, helping to create some physical and psychological space.

It felt significant that, even though he had a large and spacious house, the understairs cupboard was jammed full. I suspected it might have reflected a part of his psyche that was also jammed or overloaded. As we worked to clear it out, I found myself wondering if this might relate to aspects of his marriage or family history that he had a more painful relationship with, now that it reminded him of loss as well as happiness. Maybe this would become clearer through our work, and perhaps some sort of resolution could be reached. I could not guarantee anything beyond a clear, beautifully organised cupboard, but I remained full of hope.

We set to work. Out of the cupboard came various books, including some early editions of *The Tales of Beatrix Potter*, whose peeled and faded covers conveyed just how well-read and loved they were. Alistair caressed them with tears in his eyes. 'I will give these to my granddaughter,' he said and placed them in the 'Action' pile. A little collection of Kate's report cards and schoolbooks followed, which Alistair assigned to a memory box. Next were two more sets of old binoculars.

'Mary loved her birds,' said Alistair, firmly adding them to the memory box pile.

I had to weigh up whether challenging him on keeping three pairs of binoculars was worth a battle at this delicate stage, and I held off because I wanted to keep intact the trust I was building up. I told myself to stop worrying that Alistair would want to keep everything as I pulled out antiquated camera and video equipment, VHS tapes and audio cassettes. There were piles and piles of them.

'It's a bit of a museum in there,' I joked as I piled them on to the table. Out came more and more dusty pieces of technology, all of them obsolete. Alistair, thank goodness, agreed to let them go. Behind them were out-of-date manuals and periodicals – always a quick and easy win for the recycling bin, unless they are collectables, which, thank goodness, these weren't. Instant shelf-space cleared.

I noticed that Alistair looked a little overwhelmed, so we

took a short tea break, after which I ventured deeper into the cupboard. It was a veritable cornucopia. Rolls of colourful wrapping paper and reels of ribbons, a little pile of gifts that had never been given – once-scented candles, unread books and novelty knick-knacks, many still in their original packaging, all completely forgotten about. Alistair looked blankly at them: 'Presents were very much Mary's domain.' As I bagged them up for the charity shop, I reflected on our findings so far. I was getting a real sense of Alistair's dear departed wife: a mother and grandmother, organised and busy, always thinking of others, while keeping some parts of herself squirrelled away in places like this cupboard.

We continued on methodically – and as Alistair got more relaxed with the process, something seemed to be shifting. He seemed happier, brighter, more willing to let things go. Then, in the far corner on the top shelf, I came across an old hat box. I handed it to Alistair and his face lit up as he lifted the lid. 'Valentine's cards! I don't believe she kept all of these, and for all that time!' Tears welled up in his eyes. In the box were dozens of cards, tied into bundles with red ribbon. There must have been one for every year of their relationship, each in its original envelope. I peered discreetly over his shoulder and saw 'My Dearest Mary' on some envelopes, written in Alistair's spidery hand. Others were formally addressed, with colourful stamps from all around the globe. I imagined long business trips away, Alistair in his hotel room writing out his own address to send his love home. What a gift for him. I could sense that he would look through the box of cards carefully later and deeply connect to his memories of his wife.

I sat down beside him. 'Definitely a keeper,' I said.

When I emerged from the cupboard with the next load, I noticed that Alistair was still looking at some of the cards, and his mood had changed quite suddenly. He pushed a pile of papers I had handed to him to the floor and stood up abruptly.

'Why are we doing this?' he said. 'I didn't want to clear out a cupboard! I wanted to find my key! I've just lost my wife and now we are going through my dirty laundry.' He took a step forward and glared at me. 'I can assure you there are no skeletons in that closet.'

'I understand completely,' I said calmly. 'Let's take a break. And then we can see if you want to go on.'

Alistair was far from alone in finding it painful to unpack and look at things that we've half-forgotten. There's a reason they become hidden away in the first place. And it isn't unusual for resistance to follow a moving moment. Alistair had been very touched by the discovery of the Valentine's cards, but awakening his feelings of tenderness towards his wife had, of course, also awoken his pain and anger at her loss. It was time to stop, rest and reflect on the progress.

After more tea and a slice of Victoria sponge, served on the beautiful tea set, Alistair looked a little better. 'How are you now?' I asked, and Alistair leaned forward in his chair.

'Okay,' he said. 'Let's do a little more.'

And so we proceeded, an hour at a time, with plenty of breaks for sustenance and recuperation. At around half past three, Kate returned, and we sat back and surveyed our handiwork.

'Wow! I can't believe how much you got done,' she said. 'Well done, Dad.'

In total, it had indeed been a grand day's work. All the unwanted items were bagged for charity, boxes of photos and books had been sorted through and neatly put back, and memories had been lovingly organised and boxed up. My body felt tired, and yet I was buzzing. I suspected Alistair felt the same – we had created some order and it was easy for him to put his hands on the things he wanted and needed – except for one thing. I felt my buzz recede. There was no key anywhere to be seen.

I looked at Alistair anxiously, but he didn't seem concerned – far from it. In fact, he looked completely relaxed, and he seemed to be riding a new wave of motivation. All of a sudden, he was full of beans. He took me by the arm and told me there were a couple more things on his mind that he wanted help with around the house. Could I help move his wife's old chaise longue to a new position? 'It's just too distressing to see it without her sitting on it.' Could I help him get rid of an old, threadbare sofa? Of course I could. With Kate's help, we moved the chaise longue to a far less visible place in the room, and I arranged for a local charity to come later that week and collect the sofa. To my surprise, Alistair leaned forward and confided that he'd always hated that sofa, but that Mary would not let it go. It was the first hint of a disagreement between them – and I took this as a healthy sign he was expressing his independence. As the saying goes, death can make saints of us all. Alistair was perhaps beginning to let go of the rose-tinted glasses that come with grief and loss, and was remembering the realities of life with his wife. This might be a small step towards letting go of the wish that she would magically return and that life would somehow go back to how it had been.

I decided I'd better check down the back of the cushions before the sofa was collected. My fingertips touched a small metallic object, just out of reach. A moment of excitement – and then, an old two-pence piece. Still no key.

We shared a final cup of tea, plus a few more stories from Alistair's life, before I hit the road. I felt, as I often do, that I had been granted a window into someone's life, that I was a voyeur by invitation, but I also knew this was more than that. In the irascible but charming Alistair, I had made a new friend.

As I said goodbye to him at the front door, Alistair remembered the key. 'I don't know if I'll ever find it,' he said as we parted, 'but I certainly feel a bit more like I can breathe since we moved those things around.'

I was delighted to hear it, partly because I simply wanted Alistair to feel better, but also because I recognised that feeling able to breathe more easily can be a sign that the first intense stages of grief are beginning to ease. Going through the cupboard, deciding what he wanted to keep and what he could let go of, had provided Alistair with an important opportunity to process his feelings by proxy and to feel in control again. And I also knew that Alistair, like many of my clients, was likely to need a period of space and calm now. Once we have shifted things around in the home, we often need that respite to let some things settle and others to rise to the surface.

'Just let things rest for a few days,' I said. 'Don't be too hasty with the locksmith and let me know if anything changes.' I deliberately let my words be vague – whatever happened next would be interesting, and I wanted to hear about it.

A week later, running to my car to get to a meeting, I picked up the phone to hear Alistair's excited voice. 'I found it, Helen! I found the key!' I could hear a marked change in Alistair: his tone was deeper and more measured, the sentences clearer. 'I can't believe it!' he was saying. 'It's such a relief.'

'How wonderful!' I replied. 'Where did you find it?'

'I don't know why, but I decided to look in the drawer of the console that sits in the hall near my spare room. I don't really go to that area of the house much, but I was walking past it this morning ... Helen, I know this sounds odd, but since we cleared that cupboard, I've somehow been walking about the house more freely. After a restless night, I woke up today with the key on my mind. You know how when you've lost something, you keep picturing it in all sorts of places that you're convinced it might be, despite the fact that you've already checked there? Well, that's how it was for me. I was sitting at the breakfast table, trying to focus on the sudoku puzzle. It was a devilish one today, by the way. I'd given the key some time to reveal itself as you suggested, but had pretty much resigned myself to getting the locksmiths in. I hadn't fixed a date, though, as I still had this feeling that the key was waiting to be found somewhere. Anyway, I headed over to the spare room to pick up a book I'd promised to lend my brother, and as I passed the console, an image popped into my head of the key sitting inside. I knew I had searched in that console drawer a number of times – and very thoroughly. "Don't be daft, Alistair, you already looked in there," I said to myself, but something drew me to open it again. And there it was! The key, just lying underneath some old photographs, as plain as day. How I'd not seen it before I don't know!'

'Amazing.' I grinned, imagining the warmth of my smile conveying itself through the phone. Despite the doubts I'd had at the start of our work, I had that familiar – but always joyful – feeling I have when my work with clients brings about the results they'd sought.

I love this story of Alistair and his lost key. It expresses something fundamental about how we can become blocked, and how we can unblock ourselves. Like Jung, I think of the psyche as a house – and for me, the house is also like our psyche. To me, Alistair's predicament was so much about being emotionally full and showed how creating space, both practically and symbolically, in our homes can make room for something to come in, whether that's something new or something we are trying to reconnect with. In this case, Alistair was full of grief and loss – he could not move forward. And he created the perfect metaphor for this in his actual loss of a key – a key that was needed to unlock his sadness and enable him to move forwards. The humanistic psychotherapist Carl Rogers argues that each person has an innate desire to move towards self-actualisation, to grow towards becoming the best we can be, and I believe that people find many and varied ways to grope through the darkness towards what they need. It seemed to me that Alistair needed to work through his grief, and that he began that process by looking through the possessions that he and Mary had accumulated together. It was painful for him, and there were times when he wanted to stop – times, perhaps, when he wanted to go back into the dark, blocked stage of grief as a way of holding on to his sense of love for Mary. But he chose to go on. By working with and despite his grief, he literally and metaphorically created space that allowed him to 'roam more freely'.

Like his understairs cupboard, a part of Alistair's mind was full, and some letting go and shifting around needed to happen. I strongly believe, in the light of many experiences with clients, that dealing with the practical aspects of someone's space and belongings alongside the psychological factors that might be blocking them can really bring about change that doesn't always happen through talk alone. Maybe the physical moving around and letting go of old things that Alistair and I had done that day had precipitated a shift in his inner world. And into the space we'd created had popped the still, small voice that guided him back to the key, and back to the things of value that he had hidden from himself in his time of grief.

\*

In mindfulness there is the idea that consciousness can be usefully seen as the space within which sights, sounds, feelings and thoughts appear. I believe that by creating more physical and mental space, we are making room to be more present. The physical and mental clutter can be what gets in the way of us perceiving our homes and possessions, ourselves, others and life more clearly.

I'm sure you're familiar with that 'tip of the tongue' experience, when you can't quite recall a name, date or place. The harder you try to remember, the more elusive what you are after appears to become. The trick is actually to stop trying to recall what you're searching for. In fact, if you give your conscious brain something else to work on, it can help your unconscious to work its magic in the background. It can be much the same in our homes, where we can often fail to see what is right in front of us. So, instead of searching for the specific thing you've lost, focus on clearing your clutter. By creating space in your home, you are freeing your mind – and what you are looking for will probably turn up.

Are there objects in your home that hold some deep resonance with people who, for whatever reason, are no longer with you? It can, of course, be valuable and meaningful to keep possessions that act as vessels for precious memories of significant people and relationships from your past, but it is also true that holding on too hard, or to too much, may prevent you from moving on.

It can be useful to consider that grieving has a natural cycle: we tend to move through different stages. These are denial, anger, bargaining, depression, acceptance and then finding meaning. This is rarely a simple, linear process, and many people find they move backwards and forwards between these stages. It is also not uncommon for people to get stuck in a particular phase. Usually this is because they have not been able to fully work through one or more of the preceding stages. If this does happen, the 'stuckness' can often become expressed in the home, as happened with Alistair.

If you feel you or a loved one might be stuck somewhere in the grief cycle, I recommend some sources of support and further reading around the grieving process in the Resources section at the end of this book (pages 281–285).

# Closing thoughts: Making room for your future

As you've read the stories I've shared, you might have noticed yourself looking at your home in a different way. Perhaps you have begun to understand more about how aspects of your psychology and your past are showing up in how you organise and relate to your home. And maybe you've started to learn why you might be holding on to certain things, and are moving towards a place of greater understanding and compassion for yourself. If so, I feel this book has fulfilled the intention I set when I started to write it.

I hope I've been able to do justice to what each client taught me about our homes and about life, and that I've taken you on a similar journey of discovery. You have heard how telling the story that their home had been holding for them led my clients to significant and often life-changing shifts in their understanding, and how this psychological shift enabled them to define a more empowering relationship with their homes and their possessions. This allowed them to move beyond the impasse that their clutter represented, and so to move into a new phase in their lives. I hope that you have been inspired to make a similar change.

When I began my work, I very much trusted my intuition,

along with what I had learned through workshops, study and my experience in previous jobs. Over the years, I both honed my intuition and undertook a lot of further study to delve deeper into how our minds work. As a result, I have evolved a methodology that helped me create my Home Declutter Kit and develop my workshops and programmes. I have also defined and adopted a set of tenets that underpin and inform what I do. I have established these in the evolution of my work. Some of them have been discovered in my workshops or studies, but they are always tempered in the forge of hands-on work with clients.

In his book *Getting Things Done*, David Allen says that our minds are for having ideas, not holding them. This is why he encourages people to build habits of getting things out of their heads and into systems and structures that free the mind. I'd say something similar for space: it is there for us to live full, creative, joyful lives, not to hold our clutter. Which leads me to my first tenet:

## Clutter is decisions that haven't been made

How many things end up in a pile, container or drawer because that seems easier than deciding where to put them or what to do with them right there and then? 'I'll deal with that later,' you tell yourself, and you probably mean it. But years later, it is still there, buried beneath countless subsequent things that you've not processed in just the same way. All those open loops stack up – literally. The key to dealing with them is encapsulated in my next tenet:

## A cluttered home is like an overgrown garden

As I've shown, there are three stages to clearing a cluttered home: weeding, planting and maintaining. Weeding is making all those unmade decisions: keep, let go, action. Planting means creating beauty, harmony and optimally organising what you choose to keep: a place for everything and everything in its place. And maintaining is about building new habits with compassionate self-discipline, so your home supports you in living with greater ease.

## Living with clutter is like living with debt

It takes a lot of time and energy to be constantly stressing about or dealing with unfinished business from the past. And, like debt, clutter charges interest: the extra cost of the mental load you carry by keeping stuff beyond its natural lifespan. Once you have cleared the physical and mental clutter, you can instead invest your time and energy in your future, and focus on living in and enjoying the now.

## The less you have, the less you have to manage

Nothing in your home comes 'rent free': it all requires effort and attention to maintain. So remember, everything you choose to keep – either consciously or by default through postponing the decision – will cost you time and energy to clean, maintain and repair. Life can be a little easier with a little less to manage.

## Your home is your flight deck

Have you ever been in the cockpit of a plane and seen all those dials, switches and display panels? Imagine if they were all buried under the pilot's old bank statements, utility bills and laundry. Would you want to take to the air? Your home is the place from which you manage your life, and that of your family. So get it clear and organised, allowing you to clearly see what's happening and have easy access to the levers you need to pull to stay in control of your life.

## Beneath every pile of clutter is a story to be told

I hope you have seen from this book that addressing clutter is about much more than the practical. That's not to say that the solution is just to think it out: you need to get into action while at the same time listening to what your home has been holding for you. Clutter has a tale to tell, and once you have discovered the meaning, it can help to set you free.

## Clutter often buries a trauma, an unrealised dream or an abandoned creative project

In a way, clutter is the unconscious of the house. It is the place where the unprocessed and repressed accumulate. Often, these things will find a way to be expressed or come to the surface, but at other times they may stay submerged until you go digging. When you are taking on a decluttering project, be mindful that you may uncover some pain, but never forget that on the other side of that is freedom.

## Decluttering is about connecting to what you have and what it means to you, as much as it is about letting things go

You may have good reasons for burying what may be difficult or painful, but things of value, things that can enrich and bring joy to your life, inevitably also get buried in the process. As well as considering what you will gain from getting rid of a lot of that clutter, know that you will probably also find lost and long-forgotten treasures that may have great meaning. Over the years, my clients have rediscovered invaluable and unexpected things, from uncashed cheques and unique family heirlooms to the contact details of long-lost friends.

## Treat yourself with compassion and empathy

Whatever you discover in your home and about yourself, remember that when you took the actions that led to where you are now, you were doing your best. You made your choices on the basis of what you knew at that time and with good intentions. Don't beat yourself up. Instead, treat yourself with the same love and empathy you would give to a child learning to make their way in the world.

## Complete, complete, complete

If there is one thing that leads to clutter it is the act of not completing. Instead of leaving things undone and letting them build up, ask yourself, 'What is the next action?' and then take it. Put the laundry away after folding, unpack the shopping, finish the tasks on your to-do list and then complete the action by recycling the scrap of paper that it was written on. This is the way to a calmer state of mind.

## Shifting things around makes room for your future

Do you want to stay stuck in the past, as represented by the clutter you have accumulated? Or will you instead choose to embrace change, the one constant in the universe? Life and nature abhor a vacuum, so by creating space in your home, you are making room for new experiences and opportunities to enter your life. Extraordinary things happen when energy shifts.

I hope this book has given you some insight into the secret life of clutter, the hidden psychological factors that may be at play in your home. More importantly than that, I hope reading of the shifts my clients were able to make inspires you to take action. I believe that with the right insights, you too can create a home that truly reflects who you are and what matters most to you: a home that is clear, calm, beautifully organised, easy to maintain and empowers you to live your best life.

At the end of this book I've given a few suggestions for further reading if you want to dive deeper into some of its themes. I've also signposted some sources of support that might be helpful, depending on your individual circumstances. Finally, I've offered you a gift of some free bonus materials that I hope will be of help if you choose to work through some of my process and experience for yourself the magic of letting stuff go.

Every one of the people I met on my hectic travels around London town and further afield touched me in some way. I've had the honour of being invited into the homes, hearts and souls of some very special people who trusted me to be their 'clutter doula': the one who helped them give birth to something new. Together we took action and made room; you can too.

# Resources

## Further Reading

### Personal development

*Nonviolent Communication – A Language of Life*
by Marshall B. Rosenberg
A beautiful and practical way to bring empathy, honesty, strength and compassion into your personal and professional relationships, and how you relate to yourself.

*Feel the Fear and Do It Anyway: Dynamic Techniques for Turning Fear, Indecision, and Anger into Power, Action, and Love* by Susan Jeffers PhD
Whatever your fears, this classic guide will give you concrete tools and insights to improve your ability to handle any situation life throws at you.

*The Highly Sensitive Person: How to Survive and Thrive When the World Overwhelms You* by Elaine N. Aron
Highly sensitive people find they are quickly overwhelmed by sensory input; this book helps them understand themselves and how best to cope in various situations.

## Grief

*How to Go on Living When Someone You Love Dies*
by Dr Therese Rando
This seminal guide to grief gently walks you through essential and often overlooked aspects of the grieving process and is inclusive of all types of loss.

*The Other Side of Sadness: What the New Science of Bereavement Tells Us About Life After Loss*
by George Bonanno
An alternative to the conventional 'Five Stages of Grief' model, with fascinating insights into the bereavement process and ways to find positive meaning in loss.

## Psychotherapy

*On Jung* by Anthony Stevens
A great overview of Jung's personal and professional development, his life and his ideas.

*Knowledge in a Nutshell: Carl Jung* by Gary Bobroff
Introduces Jung's ideas in an engaging and easy-to-understand format.

*Man and His Symbols* by Carl Jung
Jung explains to the layperson his enormously influential theory of symbolism as revealed in dreams.

*Memories, Dreams and Reflections* by Carl Jung
Includes his dream about the storeys of his house relating to his psyche.

## The psychology of home

*At Home in the World* by John Hill
A philosophical and psychological exploration of the meaning of home, including examining the understanding of home as a metaphor for the process of self-realisation and discovery.

*The Poetics of Space* by Gaston Bachelard
An exploration of the various kinds of space that attract and concentrate the poetic imagination, asking us to go beyond our everyday experience of space.

## Habits and productivity

*Atomic Habits* by James Clear
A wonderfully useful book that presents the latest findings about forming habits, and gives a comprehensive guide on how to change your habits so they better serve you.

*Getting Things Done* by David Allen
Sets out a simple, practical and structured approach to productivity that focuses on creating headspace so you can both get more done and focus more on what matters most to you.

*The Procrastination Equation: How to Stop Putting Things Off and Start Getting Stuff Done* by Piers Steel
The latest science on the causes of procrastination and how best to overcome it.

## Sources of Support

### Clutter and hoarding

Association of Professional Declutterers & Organisers (APDO)
www.apdo.co.uk
Represents the UK decluttering and organising industry.
Founded in 2004, it is now a thriving professional community
with over 400 verified experts across the UK.

If your clutter is at the extreme end of the spectrum, it
may be characterised as hoarding. These two organisations
are focused on supporting people impacted by hoarding
behaviour.

Help for Hoarders
www.helpforhoarders.co.uk

Hoarding UK
www.hoardinguk.org
info@hoardinguk.org
020 3239 1600

### Addiction

Search 'Twelve-Step support groups' for help around issues
with alcohol or other drugs, overeating or other addictive
behaviours.

## Therapy and counselling

These are the UK's three leading bodies for professionally trained and qualified counsellors and therapists. Each of them has a searchable database of members and helplines, allowing you to find one local to you and specialising in your area of need. Their members abide by codes of practice and standards set by the organisations.

British Association for Counselling and Psychotherapy (BACP)
www.bacp.co.uk
bacp@bacp.co.uk
01455 883300

UK Council for Psychotherapy (UKCP)
www.psychotherapy.org.uk
020 7014 9955

British Psychoanalytic Council
www.bpc.org.uk
hello@bpc.org.uk
020 7561 9240

# Bonus materials

## Free resources

If you are inspired by the stories that you've read and wish to learn more about my processes and perhaps take on some of the exercises I describe, I've created a set of free resources. These include:

- 'The best way to get support and clear your clutter' – assessment and clutter score
- 'Uncovering the secret life of your home' – guided meditation
- 'Getting clear about your future home' – a visioning process
- 'Stop procrastinating, start clearing' – worksheet and process
- 'Letting go' – an honouring ritual
- 'Your House Charter' – worksheet and process
- 'The keys to managing your paperwork' – worksheet and process

You can download these at helensanderson.com/secret.

## Make room for your future with the Home Declutter Kit

The Home Declutter Kit offers a simple, easy way to detox your living space and clear clutter from your life – fast! It features over 30 beautifully illustrated action cards and a book that guides you through a clear, easy-to-follow method for doing a declutter or tidy up. If you're into healthy living you'll be familiar with the idea of regularly detoxing or purging the body. This handy tool will help you do the same on the home front. Because now's the time to make room for the future you deserve.

You'll be amazed at the changes that happen when you declutter your home. A new energy will emerge from beneath the clutter. Most people feel a surge of energy and very often significant things start to shift. As you get rid of the old and make room for the new, you may find family relationships improve, and new possibilities open up at work and in other areas of your life.

You can learn more and order a copy at homedeclutterkit.com